FEELING LEFT BEHIND

Permission to Grieve

Praise for *Feeling Left Behind*

Kim Murdock profoundly describes her anguish of having been left alone by the death of her young and vibrate husband, who was her best friend. This is a must read for widows and widowers, and is helpful for family and friends of the deceased. This work sheds light on the difficulties that are aced by the ones left behind.

A galaxy of feelings collide within one's heart like falling stars, but not the starry night that once brought hearts together. No one has the right to take an eraser to one's heart, for Love is forever. Grief is emotional pain, and the experience of it is like walking through Jell-O.

The author shares her experience in the hopes that it will give you a sounding board for expression of feelings. It will give you, the reader, permission to remember, never forget, and to slowly live from the place of heart again.

—Patty L. Luckenbach, MA, DD, associate minister and author of *The Land of Tears Is A Secret Place*, *The Kingdom of Heart*, and *I Only Walk On Water When It Rains*

Kim's words, ripped from her diary, are raw, painting a picture of the excruciating anguish that so many left behind by the physical departing of a loved one express. Over time, our hope for the widow or widower is to find that a part of his or her soul, as well as all of their love, remain; but while grieving, the ache of loss cannot be consoled. What we each need to do is to reach out, be present, hold a hand, mute your desire to advise, just listen, and be lovingly patient.

—Duck White-Petteruti, Founder, Domus Pacis Family Respite

Kim Murdock's brave expression of her intimate and moving experience of grief is a must read for any widow who has no idea what to do, whom to talk to, or how to manage the multitude of complex emotions that might emerge at any moment or time, for as long as it takes. Thank you, Kim, for this healing elixir and loving proof that we are never, ever alone.

—Patti Ashley, PhD, psychotherapist and author of the books *Living in the Shadow of the Too-Good Mother Archetype* and *Letters to Freedom*

FEELING LEFT BEHIND

Permission to Grieve

KIM MURDOCK

This one's for Reg!

CONTENTS

Preface

If you are reading this book, I assume your spouse/partner or someone dear to you has passed away. If so, let me first say I'm very sorry for your loss. I wrote this book because I know how hard it is to lose someone you love. I also wrote it because I want to show you you're not alone and your emotions and feelings are normal. When you lose a spouse/partner, you join a club that no one wants to join. I'm sorry you're now part of this club.

Maybe you're a friend or family member close to someone who has lost a spouse. If so, kudos to you for reading this book and trying to understand the feelings and experiences your friend/family member may be having. I hope by reading about my experiences, you'll have more understanding and possibly compassion.

So, what's my story? I lost my husband and best friend, Reg, after a grueling journey with cancer that began two and a half years before his death. This cancer journey started with a lump on his thyroid. When it appeared, our doctor suggested a biopsy. The biopsy showed lots of fluid but no cancer. The person who performed the biopsy drained the lump, and the doctor said we should consider having the thyroid removed. I was insistent we shouldn't have his thyroid removed if there was no cancer. After all, our bodies have a thyroid for a reason. A few months later, the lump returned, and a biopsy again showed only fluid and no cancer. Once again, the lump was drained; once again, the doctor told us to consider removing the thyroid just as a precaution. A few months later, the lump returned yet again. So, my husband had surgery to remove the lump and part of the thyroid. Unfortunately, the surgeon discovered cancer and had to remove the entire thyroid. It was an extremely rare, aggressive form of cancer. I was 39 years old; Reg was 45.

I wasn't concerned when I found out Reg had cancer. After all, thyroid cancer is almost always curable. It never, ever occurred to me it would kill him.

He immediately started weekly chemotherapy and daily radiation for six weeks. The radiation temporarily made him unable to swallow, so he had to get a feeding tube. He also couldn't talk for a few months, though he could whisper. But no more tumors showed up, and we hoped we were in the clear. Periodic PET scans showed no tumors, and we felt on top of the world. We figured many months without tumors meant victory! Woohoo! Life had never been better!

But roughly ten months later, his oncologist became worried about a spot on his lung. So Reg had part of his lung removed, which showed the same cancer had returned. He once again started brutal chemotherapy, including one nicknamed the Red Devil. His cancer was so rare that there were no protocols. In some ways, he was an experiment. His oncologist discussed his case with doctors across the country who also specialized in head and neck cancers.

Unfortunately, by the following spring—six months after his lung surgery—tumors showed up on his spine. He had the tumors and multiple vertebrae removed from his spine, and the surgeon inserted a cage to replace the vertebrae. We hoped that was it. Unfortunately, he then got blood clots in both legs and had three more surgeries to fix those. In all, he had six surgeries in six weeks (a total of nine surgeries throughout the whole cancer experience). But it wasn't enough. A few weeks later, a tumor once again returned to his spine. It pressed on a nerve that paralyzed him. So my husband, who previously spent his spare time hiking, snowboarding, walking, and riding 70-mile bike rides, was confined to a wheelchair. Once again, we started yet another aggressive chemotherapy and radiation.

But, as time went by, Reg continued to lose weight, and three months later we entered home hospice. I wasn't afraid to enter hospice, as I still thought he would recover. His hospice doctor and I agreed that if we continued with natural treatments, such as intravenous vitamin C treatments and cancer-fighting supplements, while taking away the burden on his body from chemotherapy, he stood a good chance of surviving. So, I felt relieved to enter hospice.

I was in denial. Despite the extensive research I had done on surviving cancer and implementing many of the treatments, a month later, my beloved husband and best friend left this world. I held his hand, stroked his forehead, and told him our deceased animals were waiting for him on the other side. He stared into my eyes without blinking until he closed his eyes for the last time and took his final breath. And at that point, my life changed. I shrieked in pain, like nothing I even knew was possible.

Days before he died, I told him it was okay to let go; I would be okay. But when I told him that, I had no idea how difficult his death would be. I had no idea how much it would shatter my world. My sister died when she was 38 years old, and I was 31. Her death had been challenging, but I had survived. I thought I knew what death would do to me and how it felt. I never anticipated the excruciating pain—sometimes unbearable—that would come from losing my husband.

A couple of weeks after Reg passed away, one of his coworkers contacted me. While Reg had worked on a project with her, her husband had died of a brain tumor. She was my same age, and though we had never met, she knew my pain. Her husband had died 355 days before Reg. She took me to lunch and brought me a packet of tissues, knowing I would cry. I asked her, "How did you get through this?" She said she didn't know. I remember feeling I could breathe for the first time. Someone understood how I felt! I knew I didn't have to figure out how to survive.

That night, I felt like eating dinner for the first time since Reg had died. I actually had a second helping of chili, which was almost shocking to me. Before that, I couldn't even eat a single serving of anything. But, I was so relieved to know someone understood.

In addition to Reg's coworker, I also received tremendous support from Reg's sister, who had lost her husband five years before Reg died. Unfortunately, she and Reg were not close. But she and I became close after he died, and she listened to me and empathized with my feelings. She helped me feel normal because she had felt the same as me. I was so incredibly grateful to her for understanding and for helping me realize my feelings—including the deep sadness—were not wrong; they were normal.

Because of these two women, I decided to pay it forward. They had helped me so much that I wanted to help other widows and widowers as much as I could. I also realized I felt best when I interacted with other grieving spouses. While I was grieving the loss of Reg, my closest friends were chasing around after their toddlers, worried about career stresses, making vacation plans with their husbands, and living the life I used to live (minus the kids). Now, I couldn't relate to them. I could, however, relate to other mourning spouses.

A few days after Reg died, I went to a class at my church called Surviving the Holidays After a Loss. It was too soon to get anything out of it. But I reconnected with an old colleague, Laurence. I had known his wife died almost a month before Reg, but I hadn't seen him. We ended up in a small group together and decided to get together periodically. The first time we met, I felt a little lighter. I didn't feel happy, but I felt lighter. I felt normal. Again, I felt relieved to know someone understood. I know, too, that hanging out with me was tremendously helpful to him, as I could listen to him without judgment and understand his deep pain. So we became good friends. Throughout this book, you'll see many references to him, and I will share his experiences as well as mine.

Five months after Reg died, I joined a young widows group with eight participants, all under the age of 50. It was so nice to be in a group who understood and shared the same feelings, such as despair, anger, and hopelessness. Today, two of the women are still close friends. Around seven months after Reg died, I went for a walk with one of them. I told her my feelings, and she said, "That's why I like being with you. You tell the truth. We all feel the same way but don't want to admit it." That's when I knew I had to write a book for widows and widowers. Someone had to tell the truth and help grieving spouses know they are not alone.

My grief counselor asked me to contact a couple of her widowed clients because she agreed that relating to another widow was extremely helpful. This is especially true as time goes by, and the rest of the world thinks it's time to move on with life. Similarly, my mom had an acquaintance, Brad, who lost his wife and felt tremendous pressure to move forward with his life and to be happy. He, meanwhile, felt sorrow and pain. She asked me to contact him, so I could help to normalize his feelings.

I've become friends with all of these widowed people. In total, since Reg died, I've become friends or interacted with twelve widows/widowers. The youngest was 23 when her fiancé passed, and the oldest was 72 when her husband died. Some lost their spouses unexpectedly; some lost them after a long illness. Some had kids in grammar school, some had teenagers, some had grown kids, and some (like me) had no kids. I've discovered that regardless of our age, gender, child status, or the circumstances of the deaths, we've all felt many of the same feelings, such as deep and unexpected sadness, anger, bitterness, and many more, which I will detail throughout this book.

When I searched for grief books after Reg died, so many of them talked about how to get through the experience. They discussed how to survive and what you needed to do to take care of yourself. They talked about how you can feel happy again, and how you can thrive. I didn't want to be told that—at least not that early in my grief journey. I didn't see any books that would just help me feel normal, that would just say my feelings were acceptable. I knew I would survive. What other choice did I have? I didn't need anyone to tell me how to do that.

Reg's death changed the trajectory of my life, and I needed someone to tell me that no matter what I was feeling, it was fine. My grief counselor and my widowed friends did that. I figured there are so many widows and widowers out there who either don't know any other widows/widowers or who aren't comfortable sharing their grief and experiences. I wanted to give you, my readers, permission to grieve fully and not move through the process quickly (unless you choose to). I wanted to give you permission to feel your feelings. Hence, I wrote this book.

In this book, I share my feelings and experiences. Some of them may make me sound harsh, uncaring, or ungrateful, which I am not under normal circumstances. But during my grief, especially in the earliest stages, sometimes these emotions took over. To give you permission to allow your feelings and to not judge yourself, I committed to tell the truth regardless of whether I would be judged or look bad, even in chapters where I cuss like crazy. I committed to tell the truth even though some of my non-grieving friends may become insulted or angry with me.

This book also includes stories from widowed friends who gave me permission to include their experiences and feelings. These friends are Gina, Dakota, Desiree, Jennifer, Jessica, Rachel,

Tara, Dawn, Laurence, Brad, Angela, and Bill. Except for Laurence, I've not disclosed any other names and instead have given my friends fake names to protect their privacy.

I've also included information about England's Queen Victoria, who lost her husband, Prince Albert, in 1861. For the remainder of her life—40 years—she wore only black. She even got the moniker "the widow of Windsor." Through her daily journaling, we gain insight into her widowhood journey. I was lucky to see a museum exhibit on Queen Victoria that provided intimate details about her grieving process, illustrating her life before and after Albert's death. I also found the book *A Magnificent Obsession: Victoria, Albert, and the Death That Changed the British Monarchy* by Helen Rappaport to be helpful in researching Victoria's widowhood. You'll find many references from Rappaport's book throughout my book.

Again, I'm sorry for the loss you've experienced that has led you to pick up this book, which I hope will serve you. I've made each chapter short, because I know reading and concentrating can feel overwhelming in the depths of grief.

I wish you peace and blessings.

Summarizing the Loss

Throughout this book, I will detail the different struggles, thoughts, and feelings I've experienced since Reg died. But in this chapter, I'll just summarize these through my eyes and through the eyes of my widow and widower friends.

When Reg died, I felt as if my world shattered into many pieces. I felt pain like nothing I'd ever experienced or even thought was possible to experience. The day after his death, I sat on my couch with my mom. I sobbed uncontrollably and told her, "I can't do this." Then I realized that, of course, I could do this (meaning go through his death) because I had no choice, and I'm tough. However, I didn't want to do this. I repeatedly said, "I don't want to do this." The grief felt so unbearable. Since that day, I've felt as if his death broke my world into "before" and "after." In many ways, it feels as if his death broke me.

A woman in my widows' group read a book where the author said that with grief, every event is tainted. I feel the same way. It's as if the thought of Reg and my grief sit on top of my head all day long. No matter what I do, they are constantly there. When I attend events or go places we had visited together, it saddens me to remember our past and to know we will never have those experiences again. New experiences are challenging for me because he can't be a part of them, he isn't there to talk to me about them, and he can't support me through them. Even though he is dead, he's woven into every fabric of my life. Every event, place, or experience is tainted, and it's tainted with sadness or bitterness.

My widow friend Jessica says she believes the best thing you could ever do for your spouse is to outlive him/her. It's just too painful to be the spouse left behind. I agree. My widower friend Laurence, on the other hand, said he loved his wife enough that he was glad she died first. That way, she didn't have to experience this pain.

As Prince Albert was dying on December 14, 1861, Queen Victoria declared, "Why must I suffer this? . . . It is like tearing the flesh from my bones."[i] After he died, she declared, "How I, who leant on him for all and everything—without whom I did nothing, moved not a finger, arranged not a print or photograph, didn't put on a gown or bonnet if he didn't approve it shall go on, to live, to move, to help myself in difficult moments?" The British prime minister at the time of Albert's death affirmed that Victoria had "sustained one of the greatest of human misfortunes."[ii]

A few months after Albert died, Queen Victoria wrote to the King of Prussia that, "For me life came to an end on December 14." Like Queen Victoria, my widow friend Gina has repeatedly said she feels her life is over. I know my life is not over, but it feels as if my truly happy life came to an end. My age of innocence and naivety certainly came to an end. I, along with my widow and widower friends, am now forced to make a new life that I don't want. I often say I just want my old life back. Queen Victoria never recovered. We will see if I do.

Everyone Reacts Differently

After meeting other widows/widowers and discussing their feelings and situations that upset them, I realized that interacting with grieving people is similar to walking through a minefield. Despite attempting to walk carefully through a mine-field, people can still unexpectedly set off hidden explosives. With widowed individuals, even when people try to be careful and say the right thing (and many don't try), it seems that any given comment can set off a bomb inside of us and upset us. Plus, what comforts one of us might upset another. So at some level, I have compassion for our friends, our families, and anyone dealing with us.

Let me give you a few examples. As I explain in another chapter, my widow friend Jessica kept her husband's name on the caller ID for her home phone. One day, she called a friend of hers. Her friend told Jessica that she needed to get her husband's name off caller ID, because it was too hard for the friend to see Jessica's husband's name. Jessica became offended by this. How dare that woman tell her to take her husband's name off the phone! On the other hand, while her friend's comment upset Jessica, it would have comforted me. It would have shown me that some-one cared that Reg is gone and found it painful to be reminded of that reality. After he died, it felt to me as if everyone—his friends, his coworkers, our families, and my friends—went back to their lives and didn't care that he was dead. Therefore, if one of them told me it was too heartbreaking to see Reg's name and be reminded that he was gone, it would mean his death hurt someone else and not just me; it would mean I wasn't so alone.

Laurence became irritated when people asked him how he was doing. He wanted to say, "My wife just died. How do you think I'm doing?" That question wouldn't have aggravated me. To me, it would have shown again that people cared. That question would have meant they realized I wasn't okay. So while this question angered him, it wouldn't have affected me. Or, I may even have found it comforting.

On the other hand, I get angry when people tell me to move on or to date again. However, that approach doesn't bother some of my widowed friends.

As I said, everyone reacts differently. I share this chapter with you because I think it's helpful to remember we all enter widowhood with diverse backgrounds, beliefs, sensitivities, and annoyances. Even people who know me well make comments they think are caring or comforting but that upset me. I can't tell you the number of times I've had to tell my mom that her comments upset me. She thinks she's being supportive. She knows those same comments would help her. Instead, they've made me angry or upset.

Yes, I believe dealing with widowed people is like walking through a minefield. You never know what will help one and hurt another. In some ways, we're all the same. However, we all get triggered and react in diverse ways.

Similarly, each person grieves differently. Each person takes a different amount of time. There is no "right" way to grieve. My widower friend Brad thought he was grieving incorrectly because his friends told him he should move on and be okay, while he still felt pain and tremendous grief. When I met him and told him he gets to grieve however he needs to grieve, he felt so relieved. I hope to give you the same permission.

You, Reader, may read this book and relate to all of it. You may be just like me and feel the same emotions, find the same experiences distressing, and have the same fears. Or, you may read this book and not be able to relate to a lot of it. That's okay. I'm guessing there are at least a few chapters that you can relate to and that I hope will bring you comfort in knowing you're not alone.

It All Seems Surreal

According to the Merriam-Webster dictionary, the definition of surreal is: *"Marked by the intense irrational reality of a dream"*

I think "surreal" perfectly sums up the entire experience of becoming a widow/widower. It's truly hard to believe that this has happened, at least for me. I cannot tell you the number of times I've asked, "Wait, is he really gone? Is this really happening?" It seems so surreal; it seems impossible. This is not what I planned for my life. When I think back to myself as a teenager or in my early twenties mapping out my life, it didn't include becoming a widow at 42. This can't be happening! I think even for people who lose their spouses in their 80s or 90s, this surreal feeling is just as prevalent.

This experience first felt surreal when I had a meeting with the hospice social worker to pick out a mortuary for Reg. My mom, his mom, his stepdad, and I discussed where to take his body, and I was tasked with making the final decision. While part of me went on autopilot, there was also a part of me that thought this couldn't be real. We also discussed having some of his shirts and important possessions, such as his snowboard, at the reception for his memorial service. I remember thinking it was impossible that we were having this conversation.

Later that night, my menstrual cycle started. I so distinctly remember thinking, "How can I be young enough to still get my period while I'm picking out a mortuary for my husband?" My brain couldn't understand how this was possible.

When Reg died, it felt extremely surreal as I watched the people from the mortuary wheel the stretcher with Reg's body down my sidewalk to the waiting van. The chaplain played a peaceful song on a wooden flute as he followed the stretcher to the vehicle. As I sobbed uncontrollably, I kept thinking this couldn't be happening. I will never see him again! How could this possibly be real?

The next day, I had to go to the crematorium to fill out the paperwork for his death certificate and to release his body. I went for a walk in the park first and kept thinking, "How can I be at the park taking a walk like any other day, and Reg is gone?" Then, I put on Reg's jeans, sweatshirt, and Disney hat. My mom picked me up, and I hugged Reg's pillow throughout the entire drive.

As I filled out the paperwork for his death certificate, I just kept thinking this couldn't be real. The form asked for his mother's maiden name, but I couldn't remember how to spell it. I remember pondering why his death certificate needed to know his occupation. The woman at the mortuary was an older woman who was socially awkward. I remember thinking she seemed perfect to work at a mortuary because the whole experience was a nightmare, so why not throw in a tongue-tied worker? But more than any other thought, I just kept wondering how I could be filling out this paperwork while my friends were meeting their kids at the bus stop or sitting in their offices at work.

That night, I curled up in the spot in our bed where he died. The mortuary people had placed a red rose in his spot. I slept next to it and transported it to the living room when I awoke. Then I moved it back to the bedroom when it was time to sleep again, as if I was bringing Reg back to bed with me.

When I got Reg's ashes back, I received a green gift bag like you get for a birthday present. Inside, there was a Ziploc bag with his ashes. How could my athletic husband—my hero and best friend—now fit in a Ziploc bag? How could that possibly be him? This is the man who took care of me, who made me laugh, who listened to me, who danced with me, who made love with me, who did everything with and for me, and now he was in a Ziploc bag. How could that be? I waited a couple of months to have an urn made for him, so he just sat in the gift bag by the fireplace until that time.

One of Reg's best friends traveled from Wisconsin to attend the memorial service. He asked me where Reg was and when I pointed to the green gift bag, he stared at it in shock. He couldn't fathom that the man he had shared so many memories with was now on the floor sealed in a Ziploc. Although not much else made him cry, knowing his friend was in that bag brought him to tears.

I held Reg's memorial service at my church. I remember getting out of the car and seeing the sign that had his name on it. It had an arrow directing people to the sanctuary where the service was held. Of course, I immediately burst into tears. I thought, "How can his name be on that sign? How is this possible? This can't be real!" It felt like a cruel joke. That sign will forever be implanted in my brain. I had arrived early, and when I walked into the sanctuary alone, I walked toward the stage. By the podium, I saw a poster of Reg with my mom's dog. On either side of it, there were Green Bay Packers pompoms, and the background stage lighting was Packers green and yellow (Reg was a huge Packers fan). I had given the church those pompoms and poster, but seeing them rocked me to my core. I was nearly brought to my knees seeing the poster because that meant this was real. This memorial service was really for Reg. I wanted to scream, "No! This can't be happening!"

Before Reg died, I was reading a book called *Pope Joan*. It was incomprehensible to me that I was reading the same book before and after he died. There was no plot change from page 100, the page I was reading the day before he died, to page 101, the page I read the day after he died. But the entire plot of my life had shifted and in an excruciating way. Similarly, I went to the gym within that first week. I saw the same people and did the same workout. How could the gym be exactly the same while Reg was gone? My brain truly couldn't understand it.

For a long time, I would constantly shake my head. Somehow, if I shook my head, it wouldn't be true. I especially did this in the car. I'm frankly surprised that I didn't give myself whiplash or crash my car, because I literally shook my head hard and constantly. The whole thing was so wrong to me that I had to physically shake my head to try to vehemently deny it.

Other examples of how this whole widowhood experience dumbfounded me occurred while watching television. For instance, a couple of months after Reg passed away, I watched a TV drama that we'd watched together. The plot included a backstory, which we didn't like, about a serial killer. Finally, the show revealed the identity of the serial killer. I remember thinking that it seemed crazy to me that the storyline lasted longer than Reg! Similarly, Reg had some websites, and I discovered that he had renewed his domain names on GoDaddy for four years past his death date. How could his domain names expire after he did? It made me so sad that he had renewed them, thinking (or hoping) he would still be alive. How could they live longer than he did?

In our neighborhood, the city sweeps the streets once per month. On our designated day, we cannot park in front of our house. The ticket is pretty pricey, so Reg put a note in our shared, online calendar to prompt us not to park on our side of the street. Once per month, those reminders still pop up to alert me that street sweeping occurs the next day. How can I get those reminders when he is gone? They lasted longer than Reg did!

Another unreal feeling to me is that I now own our house by myself. Reg purchased this house, and I moved into it. I remember the first time he invited me to the house for dinner. It never, ever occurred to me that someday he'd be gone, and I would own the house by myself. Seven months after he passed away, I discussed whether the neighbor could install a fence between our properties. I told the neighbor I didn't care so long as it was on his property and didn't take up space from *my property*. It felt so baffling to me that it's now *mine*. How could this happen? It felt so surreal.

After Reg died, I repeatedly thought about how 12 years earlier, I had innocently gone on a first date. I wasn't looking to get married; I just wanted to have fun. In my mind's eye, I could see him greet me and how I naively had no idea it would end so devastatingly. I kept thinking, "All I did was show up for a date. How could I be his widow 12 years later? I just showed up for a date like any other date." I didn't meet him in a dangerous neighborhood where pain and loss could happen. How could this have happened? Why didn't anyone warn me? It feels too surreal to me.

Reg obviously didn't know he wouldn't survive either. I found old videotapes and watched them after he died. In one of them, he and his friends were at a New Year's Eve party. Reg was in his twenties and had the camera. They started to discuss having a 30-year reunion. When I heard that discussion, I felt dumbfounded that Reg hadn't lived long enough to make that reunion. One of them asked if Reg would ever watch the videos again. I thought, "No. But his wife will after he dies. Bet none of you would ever anticipate that!" Again, my brain could not wrap around how he could possibly be gone before he even got to this 30-year reunion.

One way my brain tried to comprehend the death was to alter reality in my dreams when sleeping. I frequently dreamt that I was trying to save him. If I tried hard enough, maybe I could succeed. I also dreamt that he was just away on a business trip or consulting somewhere. My brain couldn't grasp that he was gone; instead, I made him travel or commute in my dreams, which would explain why he wasn't at home. I always felt so sad and disappointed when I woke up and realized he was truly gone. Then the pain would set in again.

I cannot begin to tell you the number of times I've said, "Come home, Reg. It's time for you to come home!" Sometimes, I get so frustrated that he doesn't seem to hear me or cooperate with my desires that I bang my hand or my head on the chair. Or, I stomp my foot to emphasize my point. I'm not normally a person to have a tantrum, but I get so frustrated that he hasn't come home that a tantrum feels necessary. Surely, if I say it more emphatically or loudly, he'll hear me and come home, right? Or, I've often pondered whether he could just find a new body. Though his body became invaded by cancer and could no longer function, surely he could find another body and come back to me.

His death seems so surreal that it definitely feels as if Reg could walk through the door at any minute. A friend told me that it wouldn't surprise her if he walked through the door, as it's just too incomprehensible to believe he's gone. Frankly, if he walked through the door right now, I wouldn't even be mad at him for being gone so long and for putting me through this. I would just be so happy that he's home and by my side once again.

My widow friend Jessica has tried to bargain with God, so her husband can come home. She has promised that she will not tell anyone and just keep her husband in the house if only he can return. She saw his body in his casket, watched as his casket was lowered into the ground, and subsequently moved him to a new location. But, she has still tried to bargain with God.

My widow friend Gina has sat staring at the door, trying to will her husband to walk through it. She frequently tells him that it's time for him to come home. She watched the funeral director shove her husband's ashes into an urn that was too small as she desperately wanted to scream, "That is my husband!" Yet, even though she witnessed his ashes being rammed into the urn, she still frequently tells her husband it's time to come home. It's just too surreal to believe he's gone.

Sometimes, it feels like maybe Reg never existed. How could he be so real and then be dead? Was our love real? I almost can't remember, as if I read it in a book or something. Did I imagine it? I see his photos and have such a deep sadness in my heart, so I know he must have existed. But sometimes it feels as if maybe I made up that part of my life. I guess it's so unfathomable to me that he's dead that I conclude he must not have ever existed. Maybe I just dreamt the whole thing.

Perhaps you feel the same way; perhaps you can't comprehend that your spouse is gone and never coming home again. If so, I understand. For me, it defies logic.

Freezing Time

After Reg passed away, I wished that I could just freeze time. I wanted nothing to change, which seems a pretty typical response for many widows/widowers. Queen Victoria was a perfect example of this. After her husband, Prince Albert, died, she kept his room, where he had died, unaltered for the rest of her life. After he died, she had the royal photographer take a photograph of the room. That way, the staff could clean and preserve every item, including his many books and lists, and put them back exactly as they had been when Albert died. By doing this, she could freeze the room in time, as if he had stepped away and would be home soon.

She had fresh flowers delivered to his room every day, and the glass from which he took his last sip remained on his bedside table. She had a plaster cast made of his ear, so she could pretend she was talking to him at night; she had a plaster cast of his hand, so it was the first thing she touched each morning, just like in life. She kissed his pillow whenever she entered his room and kneeled and prayed by his bed before going to bed at night. The royal staff filled his shaving mug with hot water every morning to prepare for his morning shave. The staff laid out his clothes and fresh linens for him each day. Victoria also hung a photograph of Albert above his side of the bed at their homes in Windsor, Balmoral, and Osborne.

While Victoria's actions may seem extreme, I completely

understand. Last year, I was fortunate to see an exhibit on Queen Victoria. The museum guard who told me about the hand, ear, and unaltered room clearly felt disdain for Queen Victoria's mourning. His tone and words were judgmental and dismissive, and his condemnation stopped just short of his rolling his eyes. I wanted to tell the man that he'd clearly never lost anyone important to him; otherwise, he wouldn't be so judgmental. I feared I would burst into tears, though, so I remained quiet and just listened to him. But, I understood. Perhaps if I had the resources, I, too, would require the people around me to pretend Reg was still alive.

Like Victoria, I desired to freeze time. The hospice nurse had set up a bed and a reclining chair in our living room. Even though the medical equipment represented a small time in our lives and a pretty awful time, I felt sad when the hospice staff removed the bed and chair. It felt as if Reg was being erased. They had other patients to attend to and were not leaving us behind. But that's how it felt. His time in hospice was not a good time for us, but I still wanted to freeze my house exactly as it had been when he was alive. It also felt as if taking that equipment away meant Reg wasn't coming home; knowing that was too much for me to process or handle. As they carried the bed, chair, oxygen tanks, and other equipment out of my house, I stood there feeling a pit in my stomach and cried. I wanted to beg them to leave the room as it had been—to freeze time—but I couldn't.

Similarly, I didn't change the sheets on our bed for almost five months. While I'm sure that seems quite gross, I knew once I replaced those sheets, I would never sleep on sheets that he had slept on again. He had passed away on those sheets, so I felt that sleeping in his spot brought me closer to him. Once I switched the sheets, I felt sad every time I walked into the bedroom. Even once I changed the sheets, I still kept the pillowcase on the pillow that he had used.

Once I changed the sheets, the only thing remaining from when he was alive was some food in the refrigerator and pantry. I couldn't bear to get rid of his food, and I felt he couldn't be dead that long if I still had his food in the refrigerator and pantry. However, when I left town for a couple of days, the friend watching my cats cleaned out the refrigerator and threw away Reg's food. Even though the food had mold on it, I was devastated. If Reg's food were still in the refrigerator, he couldn't possibly be gone, right?

About a month later, that same friend once again watched my cats for the night. He ate the last can of beans that Reg had purchased. I distinctly remember when Reg and I purchased those beans because we were in a new vegan grocery store. We ate a plant-based diet, so we felt excited that we could eat every single item in the store, which hadn't happened previously. We were like kids in a candy store, so those beans represented another happy memory.

I still have one box of cereal that belonged to Reg. It sits exactly where it had been when he was alive. Also, we had separate cupboards in the kitchen. I've kept his cabinet mostly intact. Because Reg liked to cook, we stored the spices and baking items in his cabinet. On the rare occasion when I now cook, I open the cabinet and am comforted that it still looks mostly the same.

I've also kept Reg's razor, comb, deodorant, and other grooming items in the bathroom. I no longer keep them on the actual sink; instead, I put them in the medicine cabinet above the sink. In that way, I guess I haven't frozen time exactly, but I can't bear the thought of not having them there and having that become solely my bathroom. I've joked that the bathroom remains ready for him to come home.

My widow friend Tara has also kept her husband's shaving gear sitting in the bathroom. She has saved his favorite aftershave hoping that smelling it will help her feel better. However, she moved the towel that matches hers—his towel—out of the linen closet and now just has her towel. She said that was extremely difficult. People who haven't experienced a deep loss like this cannot imagine how agonizing it is just to remove a towel. I still have all of Reg's towels on the bathroom shelves.

I've kept Reg's cell phone number. For a while, I just suspended the number, so I didn't have to pay for it. Then, I converted it to an internet phone. I couldn't stand the idea of someone else using that number. If someone calls it, it forwards to my phone. On the few occasions when someone has called him, it has been a jolt. I had a ringtone specifically for him, and I hear that ringtone. It surprises me every time but also makes me smile. Gina has also kept her husband's cell number. In fact, she paid for cell service for a couple of years after her husband died and only recently converted it to an internet phone. Dawn gave up her husband's number right away. But about a year after his death, she texted the number to say how much she missed him. She received a text back saying, "Who is this?" That is heartbreaking.

For a while after Reg passed away, when I had purchases shipped from Amazon, I shipped them to his name. I liked the idea of his receiving packages at our house. Also, if anyone saw the packages, they would think a man lived here, which made me feel safer. I haven't told the post office he is gone and like getting mail for him. In fact, one day my mail included a slip of paper from the post office asking me to list the names of anyone allowed to receive mail at my house. I included Reg's name.

I didn't tell his college that he had passed away. That way, he still receives the alumni magazine and the calls for donations, just like when he was alive. I never once read the alumni magazine when he was alive, but now I read it cover to cover. When the fundraisers call, I rarely answer the phone. If I do, I say he's not available. I know at least two of my widow friends also haven't told people calling that their husbands have passed.

Reg was a software developer and ran a small side business selling software. Most of the programs on his computer are ones that I don't understand. In some ways, his computer is very symbolic of him and his life's work. Therefore, while I knew the password and could access the computer anytime, his computer was mostly off limits. For this reason, I kept the computer the same even after he died. For a while, I didn't even make Windows updates to it. He arranged it so that the taskbar appears when the mouse touches the top of the screen, which I find annoying. But, I haven't changed it.

About five months after he passed away, his computer's hard drive needed to be replaced. Reg had built his own computer, and I had no idea how to replace the hard drive. Thankfully, one of his friends did and was kind enough to help me. However, when the friend replaced the hard drive, he added software. Of course, he thought nothing of it, but it upset me. I didn't want to change the computer. It felt as if his friend was messing everything up and disrespecting Reg's computer (and therefore Reg). Ultimately, he uninstalled the software and I had nothing to fear, but it made me anxious as it was happening.

I'm sure it will not surprise you to know I've kept the decor in the house mostly the same. Of course, I was never someone to change the decor even before he died. Some people like to rearrange furniture and decorations to have newness in their homes. I've never been one of those people. If one of his family members or friends visited who hadn't visited since before his death, the house would probably look the same. I like it that way. I was happy in this house once, and if I had it my way, I would have frozen time. Since I couldn't do that, I can at least keep my house the same. That way, it feels as if he could just be in the other room.

My widow friend Dakota told me she had thought about switching her dining room and living room. She liked the idea until she realized that switch would change the house from how it had been with her husband. Her family members encouraged—almost nagged—her to make the change. But she told them it would no longer be her husband's house if she did that. Her family didn't understand. I do!

It's not just the inside of the house that I've needed to preserve. I hired my neighbor to paint the exterior because the wood was becoming exposed. My neighbor has worked in construction most of his life and has good taste and high standards, so I trust him. He wanted to add tan stripes to one window. When he asked me, I burst into tears and said, "No, that wouldn't be the same house where Reg had lived." My neighbor also asked to change the garage colors from white to tan. I resisted and said it would be a different garage than the one where Reg had parked his car. My neighbor told me the garage would look much better and that he had a lot of tan paint; therefore, I wouldn't have to purchase more paint. I finally let practicality win out and, after tears, I let my neighbor change the colors. In my mind, I pretended that Reg would want the new garage colors. I wasn't in the space to feel as if I could make decisions without Reg. I only could make decisions with him and for him.

I tried to explain to my neighbor that each change I make to the house brings me further and further away from *our* house, from the house where Reg and I had lived our life. Each change makes it more *my* house, so I hate that. I've tried to preserve our life together, so I'm constantly torn between preserving our life and improving the house. When I tried to explain that to my neighbor, he pointed to his heart and said, "You know he is here, and the house doesn't matter." I know in theory he is right but emotionally, it's painful for me. I feel as if I remember Reg more when I see the house and surroundings as they were. Then, it's as if he's still here. All the changes make the absence stronger and make the house mine. I don't want the house to be mine and mine alone.

Similarly, I hung two of my grandmother's paintings in the home office. While the paintings look great, they weren't there while Reg was alive. Hence, the paintings remind me that it's now *my* house and not *our* house. I realized at one point that when I referred to the house, I often was more likely to say "*my* house" than "*our* house." That made me sad.

I know I'm not the only widow/widower to feel this way. Laurence told me he did nothing to his house for a year. It was as if the house was suspended in time. Ultimately, he decided it felt too painful to live in that house without his wife. But for a long time, he kept it exactly the same.

Besides keeping the physical things—like the house—the same, I've also tried to maintain the same lifestyle. For example, I decided to garden because that is what we had done. Yet, the first time I went to the store to buy seeds, I burst into tears looking at them because Reg and I had always done that together. I picked the same seeds we had grown before, which in all honesty were mostly the crops I wanted. My desire was to do exactly what we did together. I couldn't—and still can't—even think of a new life. I just want our old life together, and if I can't have that, then I try to re-create our life or come as close as possible to it.

Sometimes when I make decisions, I wonder what would work for him rather than realizing I'm all alone, and decisions—such as hanging my grandmother's paintings—only affect me now. I don't want to disappoint him, and I'm still operating or want to operate as if decisions matter to him and affect him, as if we still have a life together. I get upset when anyone mentions changing my life or my house, or selling my house. This is where we had our happy life together.

Of course, I recognize that not every widow and widower has

this desire to freeze time and life. Some—perhaps you—have an easier time closing this chapter of their lives and don't feel the deep desire to suspend time. Some are not sentimental and are more practical. Some have the same belief as my neighbor (that the memories reside in the heart) and don't need to keep everything the same. For example, my mom's friend sold her house soon after her husband passed away. The Denver housing market was skyrocketing, and she wanted to make money. I understand and respect that. For me, however, all the money in the world couldn't make me change, let alone sell, this house. If I had it my way, I would have just frozen time, so I could still feel Reg and always be able to remember our life together.

Perhaps trying to freeze time stops life from moving forward; maybe that's why the guard at the Queen Victoria exhibit criticized Victoria. I recognize that we can't stop time from marching on and stop change from happening. But if you're like me and have wanted to freeze time, I think that's a normal and loving response, even if society disapproves.

The World Goes On

As I explained in the last chapter, I would freeze life if I could. But I can't. One of the things I've found most difficult is that the world moves on. While I've just wanted to stop time or go back in time to when Reg was alive, the world has continued to move forward. Things have changed.

A few months after Reg passed away, I drove to Boulder (about thirty-five minutes from my house in Denver) to hike with a friend. As I was driving, I saw that the highway was under construction. Buildings were being constructed where there had previously just been open land. I became so distressed about this. Changing the highway and the surrounding area made it a different highway from the one Reg and I had driven together. I wanted to scream for someone to stop the construction! As I looked with dismay at the scene, all I could think was that the world was changing. It was moving on without him, and that felt so distressing for me.

In 2012, Reg and I had the opportunity to attend a soft opening for a new vegan restaurant, Native Foods, a chain from California. A soft opening is a way for new restaurants to quietly launch and get practice before opening to the public. Because we were basically guinea pigs, we received a free, tasty dinner (appetizer, entrée, and dessert). We loved the restaurant, so we visited it periodically and got on the list for other soft openings. A few weeks before he died, another location opened, so we went there for his last birthday. Within one year of his death, the chain opened three more restaurants in Denver; I got invited to the soft opening for all three. Though I felt glad the restaurant had new locations (and I always enjoy free food), I felt sad that I had now eaten at more locations without Reg than with him. It felt so symbolic of the world moving forward without him.

Television shows also highlight how the world is moving on without Reg. I know that programs—even popular ones—end, and new shows always begin. I hadn't felt this before, but now the end brings pain. For some reason, many shows that Reg and I watched together for years ended right after he passed away. It made me so upset—and still makes me upset—every time a show ends, as it takes me further and further away from him. I now watch shows that he and I had never seen together. I hate that!

At the same time, when the new season started, I had difficulty watching shows we had always enjoyed. For example, Reg and I watched *The Big Bang Theory*. Just like always, when spring rolled around, the season ended. In the fall (the first fall after Reg died), when the show's new season began, I had a hard time watching it. How could it be a new season without Reg? He had watched it with me the previous season, so how could I see it now? Ultimately, I watched *The Big Bang Theory*—along with other shows we'd seen together—in their new seasons. However, I didn't watch them for a while, and it was difficult the first few times.

Technology moves rapidly and is another example of the world moving forward without him. Reg had a Samsung smart phone, and one day I saw a commercial for the next generation Samsung phone. I burst into tears. How could enough time have gone by that it was now time for a new Samsung? It felt like another example of the world pressing forward without him.

Even more distressing than shows and technology moving

forward is feeling as if his friends, his coworkers, my friends, and our families are going on without him. For example, his company hired someone to replace him after he passed away. I know that his company had to do this and couldn't hold the position open for him. But, it still pains me to think someone else has replaced Reg; someone else sits in his cubicle. After he died, one of Reg's coworkers showed me a video of the office's Halloween party. The video panned by Reg's cubicle, and I could see someone else's belongings at his desk. I lost it!

Further, I hate to think the systems he built will soon become obsolete and replaced (Reg was a software developer). Given the nature of technology, this is a possibility. I saw one of his coworkers at a restaurant almost ten months after Reg died. The coworker mentioned that he'd been working with two systems Reg had helped build. I became distraught that they could be changing the systems. Things need to stay the way Reg left them! I went into the bathroom and sobbed for a while.

The rational part of my brain understands that his coworkers and former company have to move forward without him. But, it's still distressing for me. Even worse, I hate hearing that his friends have gone about their lives. Do they even miss him? Have they all moved forward even though he's gone? I think they have, and that breaks my heart.

Having grown up forty-five minutes from Green Bay, Wisconsin, Reg was a huge Green Bay Packers fan. Every year, Reg traveled to a different city with his buddies to watch a Green Bay Packers football game. They had traveled to Charlotte, Phoenix, Washington DC, Seattle, San Diego, New Orleans, San Francisco, Atlanta, Dallas, and Houston. After Reg passed away, I received a text from his friend saying he had traveled to Miami to watch the Packers play the Dolphins. I felt devastated to hear he had traveled to see the Packers without Reg. I knew he would eventually, but I felt absolutely tormented that it happened so soon. When I asked him how the trip was, he said it was "great." That was so hurtful to me. He didn't say he missed Reg or that it wasn't the same without Reg. He said the trip was great, and that brought me deep sorrow. How could he move forward and travel without Reg? I realize that life doesn't stop for others the way it stops for the widow/widower. But, I still felt devastated knowing his friend could travel without him, do what they used to do, and still have a "great" time.

Again, I realize the world doesn't stop, and it's normal to want to move forward with life. Perhaps you've wanted to move on quickly. If so, that's perfectly acceptable and even normal. That just hasn't been my experience; but, as I stated at the start of the book, we all grieve differently and in our own time.

Of course, the majority of the world doesn't even care that Reg died. They never knew him, and their lives haven't changed with his absence. It's so hard to believe people can be out enjoying life and feeling happy when he is dead. When I did the Turkey Trot 4-mile race on Thanksgiving (nine days after Reg died), people were so gleeful at the race. It was unfathomable to me how people could be happy and laughing when my universe had just turned upside down. I remember after my sister died, I went to fill my car with gas. I felt shocked to see people at the gas station laughing and having fun. How could that be? The same thing happened when Reg died.

Similarly, I went to a Colin Hay concert two years after Reg passed away. For some reason, Reg had compiled a funeral playlist on his computer when he was healthy and long before he received a cancer diagnosis. (I often wonder if deep down, his soul knew he would die at an early age, because there was no rational reason for him to create a music playlist for his funeral). Colin Hay had a few songs on Reg's playlist. Coincidentally, Colin played Denver's Botanic Gardens, so I attended with one of Reg's friends. When Colin sang the songs on Reg's playlist, I sobbed with grief. Meanwhile, the couples surrounding us (yes, it was mostly couples at this venue) laughed, chatted, and had a nice summer evening. It felt so heart-wrenching and unfathomable to see these couples having fun and not caring that these songs played at Reg's memorial service.

While I felt as if the world didn't care that Reg had died, Queen Victoria had the sympathy of much of the world. After Prince Albert died, most of England went into mourning. People wore black, and even the poorest people (those who couldn't afford to purchase new black clothing) wore a black armband. In fact, much of the economy thrived because people purchased black garments, mourning jewelry, and mementos commemorating Albert, such as small busts and medallions. Public places, law courts, museums, and art galleries closed. Theaters and concert halls canceled performances. Parties and the "London Season" were canceled. Queen Victoria's staff had to be in mourning and wear black. The whole country went into mourning and came together in grief. For many years (or maybe even for the rest of her life), if someone wanted Queen Victoria to sign a document, the document had to be on mourning paper with the proper amount of black around the edges. Otherwise, she wouldn't sign the document.

Other countries also grieved. For example, Emperor Napoleon III of France ordered three weeks of court mourning; the King and Crown Prince of Prussia had the court go into mourning for a month. Because Victoria was queen of a vast empire, throughout the world people grieved.

Unlike Queen Victoria, for most of us, the world around us doesn't care about our spouses. No one declares periods of mourning, and nothing closes. The world moves forward without our spouses whether we want it to move forward or not. The fact that the world doesn't care about Reg's death and continues to march forward is tremendously upsetting to me. I recognize, however, that many grieving people don't feel panicked that the world and life are moving on. I realize that for many—maybe even most and maybe you—it's more normal to move on quickly. I'm more similar to Queen Victoria but understand why others are not.

The "Firsts"

When Reg received the cancer diagnosis, I remember thinking if he died I would move far away, because there is nowhere I could go in Denver that wouldn't remind me of him. Interestingly, I had absolutely no desire to move when he passed away. In fact, I rarely wanted to leave my house. My house is where he had been, and I wanted to be near him. His energy was still in our house; his footprint was everywhere. Moving away would have meant starting a new life without him and leaving him behind; there was absolutely no way I could bear to do that. I wanted to preserve my life with him, so that meant staying in my house. But, not moving away meant that I had to go to places where we had gone together, and the first time going to these places—restaurants, stores, friends' houses, or any other place where I had gone with him—brought pain and sorrow.

Experts say the first year after a loss can be the most challenging, largely because you have all these experiences for the first time. It's the first time you have to face the locations and experiences without your spouse. Also, the first holidays, birthdays, and other events can bring intense pain. Below, I've tried to describe various "firsts" that I experienced.

First Thanksgiving

Reg passed away nine days before Thanksgiving, so my first Thanksgiving was absolute hell. In the past, we often held Thanksgiving at our house. We would invite my family and friends who had nowhere else to go. Reg loved to cook and was an amazing chef, so he cooked the meal.

In the morning, I would run a Turkey Trot 4-mile race to benefit the United Way in the park near our house. Reg wasn't a fan of big crowds, and this race always has thousands of participants. So, he only ran it once. Instead, he would usually sleep in and then sit on the couch watching football. I would walk in the front door from the race, and he would ask, "How did it go, girl?" He always, always asked me how I did.

On the first Thanksgiving after he passed away, I had already registered for the race, not knowing he would be dead. So, I participated anyway. I remember thinking I had nothing else to do, so I might as well run. It was a warm day, so there were many people there, and they all seemed happy. The Green Bay Packers were playing football that day, so there were many people wearing Green Bay jerseys, hats, and T-shirts. Reg was a huge Packers fan, so seeing the Green Bay gear on all of these joyful people was absolute torment for me. In fact, being around people in high spirits—whether or not they were Packers fans—felt agonizing. Seeing the reminders of my old life—a happy life—was nearly debilitating.

I remember arriving home from the race and walking through the front door. He wasn't there to ask me how the race went. I remember just bursting into wrenching tears. It was so incredibly painful. Thankfully, my cats greeted me at the door, so I at least felt some love. It was, of course, not the same.

My brother and his wife had a Thanksgiving lunch and had invited my mom and me to join them. We had never gone to their house for Thanksgiving before, but since I had nowhere else to go, I thought it might be a good idea. My sister-in-law's family members had met Reg but, of course, his death didn't affect them. I walked into my brother's house, and they were celebrating. They had just finished eating (we had not planned or wanted to eat there), and they were happy. I burst into tears, hid in the bathroom, and sobbed for a while. I thought, "This was a huge mistake!" It was absolute hell! I couldn't understand how they could celebrate when Reg was gone.

Unfortunately, someone had to use the bathroom and kept trying to open the door while I was in there sobbing. This forced me to come out. When I came out of the bathroom, my brother's dogs greeted me with the love only a dog can give. I sat on the floor with them sobbing. I felt so thankful to them. Then, my brother came over to check on me. He told me that at the start of the meal, he said how they were missing an important person and that the person (Reg) was at God's table now. That made me cry, but it also made me feel better because it meant my brother at least acknowledged Reg was gone (rather than only celebrating).

I had dressed in Reg's clothing—his shirt, jeans, and parka—and in my coat pocket (or his coat pocket), I had Minnie and Mickey Mouse salt-and-pepper shakers. We had bought these shakers the last time we'd gone to Disney World. They were decorated in pilgrim hats and pilgrim costumes, and we loved the idea of having them on our Thanksgiving table. Our first Thanksgiving after we purchased them, Reg was going through chemotherapy, so he was too tired to cook and have Thanksgiving dinner at our house. We went to my mom's house instead, so we hadn't used the Mickey and Minnie salt-and-pepper shakers. We said we would use them the following year, but he died before we had the chance. I was distraught that these salt-and-pepper shakers had never made it out of the packaging. Therefore, I put

them in my pockets and held on to them all afternoon and evening. They were like anchors for me—something to keep me
connected to Reg.

My mom and I ended up going to a restaurant for
Thanksgiving dinner. We'd eaten at the restaurant before but
never for Thanksgiving. It was a vegan restaurant attached to the
Hare Krishna Temple. It was the perfect place for us to go. I felt
as if it was the place for misfits, for people who had nowhere
else to go. They didn't play celebratory music. They just played
mellow, spiritual music. I remember seeing a man with his laptop
sitting by himself. There was one family, but the other tables had
groups of friends. I saw no couples, which was a huge relief to
me. It was such a relief to be in a place that wasn't a traditional
Thanksgiving venue, such as a home with happy couples, celebratory families, and traditional Thanksgiving food. I set the
Mickey and Minnie Mouse salt-and-pepper shakers on the table.
Truly, I can't explain how relieved I was to be in a space that felt
like a place for misfits and that wasn't traditional. I'm not sure I
would have survived Thanksgiving otherwise.

First Christmas

My widow friend Jessica told me she read a book by a man who
lost his dad when he was young. In his book, he said Christmas is
its own special hell for those who've lost someone, because their
absence is so obvious then. Boy is that true!

In my past, I was that person who *loved* Christmas. The song
"It's the Most Wonderful Time of the Year" was true for me. I
spent the holiday season doing all the traditional festivities and
enjoying every minute of it. My husband and I would go to the
Christmas parade and sit in the grandstand seats, and I would
squeal with joy when Santa and the floats cruised by me. We decorated the house with many Christmas decorations, including a

Dickens village and a fresh, beautiful Christmas tree every year. Twice, we even went to the mountains to cut down our own Christmas tree. We had a Santa with reindeer on the lawn, a Santa by the front door, lights on the bushes, giant candy canes hanging from the tree, and toy soldiers leading up to the door. We used only dishes decorated with Christmas themes. We had Christmas sheets, a Christmas bath mat, and Christmas hand towels.

At night, we watched Christmas movies on the Hallmark and Lifetime channels (yes, my husband was a good enough sport to watch them with me even though they were always corny, and he didn't like them). I listened only to Christmas music and couldn't understand why people didn't want to hear Christmas music. How could stores not have Christmas songs playing? Didn't they know people want to hear the music, and it makes people happy? Those were the thoughts I used to have. I used to read only Christmas books during the holiday season rather than my normal murder mystery and crime books. Yes, I loved Christmas!

I also believed in the idea of Santa Claus, a loving, giving presence who brought joy to children and adults. I believed in the magic that Santa could bring and the sense of wonder and happiness. Every year, we went to dinner at my mom's house on Christmas Eve. While we were there, I had friends bring presents into my house and stuff Reg's stocking. Sometimes, I hired the pet sitter to bring the presents, so Reg would arrive home and know Santa had been there for him. Reg enjoyed spending time by himself on Christmas, so I would open presents with my mom and family at her house on Christmas day. When I arrived back at my house, my stocking would be full (from Santa of course). A few times, Santa even hung mini candy canes on our tree. I was so delighted to see what Santa had done and loved that Reg would "help" Santa, giving me this surprise and the joy of knowing Santa had come for me. Our pets also got new toys for Christmas, and we loved watching them play with their new toys on Christmas night.

Not only did I believe in Santa, but he also became a reality for us when Reg dressed up and pretended to be Santa. Many years ago, our local costume shop went out of business, and we thought we would just go in there to browse. Sure enough, the store had a Santa Claus outfit. Reg picked it up and said, "Everyone needs a Santa outfit." So he bought it. There was even a Mrs. Claus outfit. I only got the chance to wear the Mrs. Claus outfit one time before he passed away. But, he played Santa on at least three or four different occasions, bringing joy to my young nephew and even the adults in my family. Christmas was a magical time at our house!

Then Reg died. After that, I didn't like to hear Christmas songs. It felt as if those songs were just there to torment me and rub in my face that my husband was gone; magic no longer existed. I dreaded them. The song "I'll be Home for Christmas" was especially tortuous, because he'll never come home again. I felt relieved when I went into a store, and it wasn't playing Christmas music. For the first time, I understood why all radio stations don't just play Christmas music.

I stopped watching Christmas movies or even shows I normally watched that had a Christmas episode. I couldn't stand seeing happy families and people celebrating even though the shows were fictitious. The commercials were particularly tormenting. Jewelry stores love to show blissful couples with jewelry and engagement rings during the holiday season. Car companies also like to show happy couples receiving their new car. I'm not suggesting that I want jewelry or a car for Christmas. I just wanted the happiness and love, and seeing the commercials was torment. In my past, I didn't want the season to end. However, after Reg died, I just wanted to get through the Christmas season and couldn't wait for it to be over.

And let's talk about Christmas cards that people send. My first Christmas without Reg was just five weeks after he passed away. People sent me their Christmas cards with their joyful family photos. It was absolute anguish for me to receive those cards. I wanted to scream at people, "Do you really think I want to see photos of you and your spouse having an exciting vacation together, loving each other, and looking happy with one another? Do you need to rub it in my face that you have your spouse and I don't?" My brother and his wife even sent out a card with family photos on it that said it had been a great year. I felt completely crushed by it. The only cards I didn't mind receiving were the ones from Reg's family. Those cards made me feel as if I was still connected to his family and hadn't been thrown out of the family when he died.

Even after eight years, I know Jessica still doesn't open the Christmas cards she receives because she doesn't want the pain of seeing other people's intact, happy families. I know that often those photos are staged, and people aren't necessarily content. They may have even bickered before they took the picture. People share the cheery stuff in their Christmas letters rather than the bad things that have happened over the year. But in my mind, they still get their spouses, and I don't! I didn't—and still don't—want to see their happiness when I will never be able to spend Christmas with my husband again or send a holiday photo or holiday card from the two of us.

As I said, my first Christmas without Reg was just five weeks after his death. I remember wishing I could just skip right past Christmas. I wondered if I could go somewhere tropical where maybe there would be no indication of Christmas. The rest of my family, however, still wanted Christmas, so I had to face it. I didn't have a single present for anyone except my brother. I only had a present for him because I went to the mall with my mom (who had a present to buy), and I saw a booth selling Green Bay Packers barbecue grill items. Because Reg was a loyal Packers fan, I got my brother a spatula with the Green Bay logo. That way, he would be forced to think of Reg. Other than that, I had no presents.

The following Christmas, my second without Reg and just a little over a year after he passed away, I had a dentist appointment a week or so before Christmas. My dentist exclaimed, "Have a Merry Christmas." I wanted to say, "You're kidding right?" That same year, I talked to a man at the gym who had two young children. We talked about whether his kids still believed in Santa Claus, and he said something about how even adults believe in Santa. I think he said something like, "Do you believe in Santa Claus?" I thought, "Not anymore." It broke my heart to realize that I had always believed in Santa and believed in the magic of Christmas, but I no longer believed in Santa or magic. My husband's death had taken those from me as well.

Yes, Christmas is its own special hell. It's supposed to be a time with your loved one and family. It's supposed to be a merry and enchanting time. But, when you've lost your spouse, it's a time that highlights yet again that the person you love is gone. Dakota said that on the first Christmas without her husband, she just wanted to stay in bed until it was all over. She didn't want to go on with life and wanted to crawl under a rock and die. Even now (two and a half years later), she said she wouldn't celebrate the holidays if she didn't have children and grandchildren. She feels as if she is just going through the motions and forces herself to purchase gifts (for their birthdays too).

I will not pretend to tell you how to get through Christmas without your loved one. Unfortunately, though, I know you cannot just go to sleep until the holiday season passes. I can only tell you what I did that helped me, especially the first Christmas.

At first, I did not plan to decorate my house at all. How could I do that? But I decided to get a small tree and decorate it in honor of my husband. The only ornaments I put on the tree were ones we had purchased together when we got engaged, as well as his favorite ornaments that in the past, I had relegated to the back of the tree. It was the Reg tree, and I loved that little tree. I felt as if it brought me closer to him.

Every year, he would give my mom a new Christmas ornament on Christmas Eve, and he loved the TV show *A Charlie Brown Christmas*. Therefore, that first year, she got a perfect Charlie Brown tree. It was a pathetic little thing, and she decorated it only with the ornaments he had given her. It was a tree in his honor. I loved and appreciated that.

At the first Christmas Eve dinner, I put a votive candle in front of each place as a memory to honor him. During subsequent Christmas Eve dinners without him, I have set a place for him at the table and put a gold candle on his plate along with a photo of him. I have put a Green Bay Packers stuffed animal bear in his seat. Those have all helped me feel just a little bit better and as if I am sharing Christmas with him. Also, he loved the movie *A Christmas Story*, so I watch the movie just like he would do. One year, I went to a candlelight ceremony and lit a candle in his honor. No, these things don't make up for the fact that he is gone. But, by honoring him and going through some of his Christmas rituals, they help me live with Christmas and to feel a little bit better.

First New Year's Eve

New Year's Eve was another particularly difficult time for me after Reg passed away. New Year's Eve wasn't a day or night we celebrated. In 2002, we had gone to a party on New Year's Eve to celebrate. When we returned home, there were messages from my mom, and I found out that my sister had passed away that day. Also, as we got older, it was no longer important to go out and party or celebrate on that evening. Usually, I would run the Resolution Run 5K (3.1 miles) race in the late afternoon, and we would get dinner and just hang out on the couch watching TV for the night. I usually fell asleep before midnight; Reg would wake me up, so I would witness New Year's Eve. We would wish each other happy New Year's Eve, give a brief kiss, and then I would immediately fall back asleep. It wasn't necessarily an exciting evening.

However, although this was never an important day in our lives, my first New Year's without him felt brutal. Like always, I raced in the Resolution Run. At the start line, hundreds of people surrounded me who were excited for the new year. I distinctly remember turning around and seeing a couple wearing huge glasses in the shape of 2014 with red flashing lights on the 2014. I burst into tears and started sobbing. Unlike those around me, I didn't want to go into 2014. Reg had never lived in that year! How could I move forward into a new year without him? I didn't want to go forward; I only wanted to go back. People felt excited for a new year, new changes, and maybe a new life. All I wanted was my old life. All I wanted was to go back. Therefore, seeing those glasses absolutely traumatized me and brought overwhelming grief.

After the race, my friend and I got takeout food from Reg's favorite Chinese restaurant. We went back to her house and played cards. I was so upset, and I remember she said, "Kim, all you're doing is moving from one day to the next. All you're doing is moving from Tuesday to Wednesday. It is no different from moving into any other new day." That helped me tremendously, as I couldn't get over the idea of moving into a new year without Reg.

The following year, I wasn't as traumatized, as I had

experienced moving into a new year without him. But it still felt uncomfortable, as it made me feel as if I was getting further and further away from him. Also, it's one thing to do nothing and sit on the couch when you're a couple. It's an entirely different thing when you're a widow, single, sitting home alone.

First 4th of July

Reg's mom decided to have a memorial celebration for him on July 5. So for my first Fourth of July without him, I traveled to his hometown in Wisconsin. We had never traveled to Wisconsin for the Fourth of July, but he had told me what he did as a child. Therefore, his sister and I, along with her kids, went to the lake where they had watched fireworks as children. In many ways, it was nice because I was with his family and because my brother-in-law had passed away many years before, Reg's sister understood my pain. We watched the fireworks over the lake, and I tried to imagine what Reg was like as a little boy.

After watching the fireworks, we went back to Reg's parents' house. I remember sitting on Reg's childhood bed and sobbing uncontrollably. Feeling completely alone, I almost hyperventilated because I was crying so hard. I called my mom and finally calmed down when I crawled into Reg's bed. Although it had probably been 25 years since he had slept in that bed, I felt comforted knowing I was in his bed. I felt safer and protected, as if young Reg were there.

My next Fourth of July without him, the first one I experienced in Denver, felt incredibly difficult as well. For many years, Reg and I had watched a wonderful fireworks display in a nearby section of Denver. We would pack a picnic dinner and lounge chairs, and we would stake out our spot relatively early in the evening. I loved those evenings and watching fireworks with him. After he died, I didn't want to go back to that same location, as I figured it would be unbearable. (In fact, just driving by that spot at other times of the year brought me to tears.) But, I didn't want to spend the Fourth of July alone. I reached out to numerous people to see if they had plans or wanted to do something. They either didn't respond or already had plans.

I ran a 5K Liberty Race in the morning and got a massage in the afternoon. Otherwise, I was entirely alone on the Fourth of July for the first time in my entire life. I had sobbed for days before the Fourth of July holiday, knowing this would happen. The Fourth of July is a time to be with families, and my friends all have spouses and families. So, everyone was busy. After reaching out to the fourth person who had plans or just didn't respond to me, I finally got tired of trying. I realize people's lives were busy, and they weren't consciously excluding or abandoning me. But, I felt completely rejected and distraught. My friend Meg (who is not a widow) texted me to see if I was okay; everyone else was busy and didn't even check to make sure I was surviving, which made me feel so sad.

That Fourth of July fell on a Saturday. After feeling so much pain and shedding so many tears, I finally decided to treat it like any other Saturday night, which I usually spent alone. I decided there was no reason to expect to be happy or okay that day. I decided older widows probably stay home alone on the Fourth of July. I generally think people my age are supposed to be out having fun with others. But, I decided to just be like an old widow: content being alone.

Once I told myself I would be alone and that I shouldn't expect to be happy, I felt okay. Many years ago, I had an outdoor cat enclosure built for my cats, which is a large cage with a doggie door to let the cats into the space. I decided to sit in the cat enclosure with my cats, who didn't know it was a holiday, and read. To them it was just another day, so I tried to imitate them and treat the day like any other. They were thrilled to have me in the enclosure with them, and I felt so thankful to them. While everyone else had rejected me, they still loved me and were happy to have me home with them. I finally settled down. I read my book outside all day and night. It was pretty relaxing, and I felt content. I felt sad when I had to hear fireworks throughout the city for about two hours. But otherwise, I was all right.

At one point, it poured rain. I felt happy about that, as I figured other people's plans were getting ruined for at least an hour. I imagined they had to get soaked or run for shelter and abandon their barbecues, picnics, and gatherings, at least for an hour. I know that doesn't make me sound like a nice person, but the rain made me feel better.

While I felt awful that I was all alone on the Fourth of July, Dakota had the exact opposite experience. She had always spent the Fourth of July with her family. After her husband passed away, she didn't want to be around any of them. Although they missed her husband, they were happy and celebrating, and she understandably didn't want to be near them. Therefore, she just stayed home by herself and felt miserable.

My First Birthday

I dreaded my first birthday without Reg. My birthday is in the summer, and I always like to hike on that day. Reg was usually my companion for those hikes and often took a vacation day from work, so he could be with me. On one birthday, he surprised me with a trip to Aspen and on another birthday, he surprised me with a trip to Telluride. One year, I had my 40th birthday the day after he started chemotherapy, so he didn't have the energy to hike. But, we went to the mountains anyway and stayed at a friend's condominium. Two friends met me in the mountains, and we hiked. When I returned to the condominium, Reg had decorated it with happy birthday banners. I was so thrilled! He had gone to the local market and picked up a yummy birthday dinner and even vegan birthday cake, which was so surprising. I never thought anywhere in this mountain town would sell vegan cake! He sang "Happy Birthday" to me and lit candles on the cake. Even when he didn't feel well, he still made my birthday a big deal.

Knowing my first birthday without him would likely be challenging, I tried to arrange to have the day set. I asked my widower friend Laurence to hike with me. I had spent the day with him on his first birthday without his wife, so I figured he'd understand how challenging that first birthday was. Laurence agreed to hike with me, so I assumed he would schedule the entire day. I assumed he would know that a hike is an all-day experience. In retrospect, I realize I should have communicated to Laurence that a hike meant an all-day experience. I learned later that Laurence often overcommitted to people and had difficulty managing his time. However, at the time I didn't know that.

The night before my birthday, when we discussed where we would hike, he told me he'd only set aside two hours to hike with me. That is not a hike. That isn't even enough time to drive to hiking trails from Denver. I felt absolutely devastated that he bailed out on me. I realize now that he didn't mean to abandon me on my birthday. But at the time, I was distraught and heartbroken. It made me miss Reg even more. Reg made me the center of his attention on that day. If I wanted to hike, he took the day off to hike. He didn't squeeze me into his schedule.

Now, however, I was being squeezed into someone's (Laurence's) schedule. I was no longer the center of attention on that day. I felt absolutely devastated. My mom had injured her knee, so she could barely walk, let alone hike. Thankfully, an acquaintance didn't have plans that day, so at the last minute, she agreed to go with me. I was so thankful to her. Of course, I hated that I had to be thankful to her. Reg should have been there!

On my birthday morning, I tried to put water into my pack and couldn't get the water container open. I thought I didn't have the strength, but it turns out I was trying to open it incorrectly. While I had opened the container numerous times, my grief made me unable to figure out how to open it this time. I sobbed, just wishing so much that Reg were there to help me put water in my pack. It felt truly too much for me to handle. There happened to be a man walking by my house, so I went outside and asked for his help.

That night, I celebrated dinner at the restaurant where Reg and I often celebrated birthdays. Many years ago, Reg had purchased a tiara for me to wear on my birthday, as I was his princess. On this first birthday without him, I showered with his shampoo, conditioner, and soap, and I wore my tiara to dinner. That made me feel as if I was getting as close to him as I could. I figured he would want me to wear my tiara. Laurence came to dinner with my mom and me. It ended up being a nice dinner. I was sad to return home, though, and be alone on my birthday for the first time in my life.

Dakota said her first birthday without her husband was truly awful. She felt as if she couldn't breathe. She called her grief counselor and cried and screamed. She said she felt so lost without her husband.

First Super Bowl

Watching my first Super Bowl without Reg was excruciating. For probably at least five years, we had gone to my friend's house. But the Denver Broncos played in the first Super Bowl after Reg passed away. My friend had never gone to the Super Bowl, but as a diehard Broncos fan, she wanted the chance to see them in the Super Bowl. Therefore, she went to New York City (the Super Bowl's location) and didn't have her normal gathering.

I was absolutely devastated she would not be home. I couldn't handle the fact that Reg wasn't there, and having to move locations was almost unbearable. I had asked friends what they planned to do for the game and if they wanted to come to my house. They all had other plans and didn't even ask if I had plans or would be okay. I felt extremely hurt by this. It was as if everyone had gone back to their lives already.

Ultimately, I decided I had to go to my friend's house. Thankfully, she loved Reg and because her mom had passed away the year before, she understood the pain of loss. So, she let me watch the game at her house even though she wasn't there. My mom and I went over and hung out alone with my friend's dogs during the game.

During the Super Bowl, a commercial aired for one of the car companies. It showed a couple holding hands and had a sad song playing in the background. It turns out it was a commercial to celebrate cancer survivors. I became absolutely distraught viewing that commercial. I also became irate because I wanted to shout that we should honor my husband as well! He fought incredibly hard to live. Yet, this commercial honored the people who survive and not him. I was literally depressed for days after seeing that commercial.

The Denver Broncos lost that Super Bowl. In fact, the Seattle Seahawks dominated the game (the final score was 43 to 8). While I'd always been a Broncos fan and under normal circumstances would have wanted them to win, I felt glad they lost. Before the Super Bowl, it felt as if the whole city of Denver was happy, whereas I was miserable. When the Broncos lost, I felt that for at least a day or a week, other people would feel sad as well. I remember driving home and feeling glad I would not be forced to face joyful people. Everyone was sad that night. I loved that because I wasn't alone in my depression and for the first time since Reg died, I could travel in Denver without having to face happiness everywhere I went.

First Valentine's Day

Surprisingly, my first Valentine's Day without Reg was fine. Valentine's Day was on a Friday, and his sister had decided to visit over that weekend. She had never visited Denver or seen our house. For days leading up to Valentine's Day, I focused on cleaning the house and getting ready for her visit. When she arrived, we talked and laughed all day about him. We then went to a restaurant that Reg and I enjoyed. It never had many customers but this night, it was full. We finally realized that it was Valentine's Day. Until that point, we had forgotten.

I did feel sad when I realized it was Valentine's Day and looked around the restaurant to see the couples. I remember seeing two couples in a booth together and thinking I will never have that experience again. Reg and I will never be a couple sitting in a booth laughing while eating dinner with another couple. Reg and I had never eaten dinner in a restaurant on Valentine's Day, as he thought restaurants overcharged, served inferior food, and were just too crowded on Valentine's Day. However, I still felt jealous watching the couples at the restaurant knowing he and I will never eat dinner in a restaurant together again. But all in all, my first Valentine's Day wasn't that awful because my sister-in-law distracted me. Generally, I didn't try to distract myself from grief and instead faced it head on; but in this situation, the distraction helped Valentine's Day become a pleasant day.

My widow friend Dakota, on the other hand, had a lot of difficulty on her first and even her second Valentine's Day. She took flowers and a picture of her and her husband to put on his grave. She then tried to act as if it were any other day. But, she had to see happy couples and women around her, including her daughter, receiving gifts from their husbands. While she felt glad for her daughter, she felt tremendous jealousy because she will no longer celebrate that day with her husband.

Valentine's Day was also sorrowful for my friend Jessica. The six-month anniversary of her husband's death fell on Valentine's Day. After her husband passed away, every Thursday (the day of the week that he died) and every 14th were traumatic for her. Thankfully, her first Valentine's Day fell on a Saturday, but the 14th was still traumatic for her, let alone it being Valentine's Day. Her sons had basketball games that night, so she was forced to face the world. When people asked her, "How are you," she responded by telling them it was the six-month anniversary and Valentine's Day. She wanted people to understand her pain, even though obviously they could never understand it unless they had also been widowed, which none of them had. But she talked and talked and shared her pain anyway.

Valentine's Day is a day I don't think matters when you have your spouse. But, it definitely takes on a whole different meaning when your loved one is gone. Then, seeing all the commercials on TV, hearing them on the radio, and seeing all the cards and flowers at the store just feels tragic. Seeing happy couples feels like a slap in the face, particularly on this day.

First Wedding Anniversary

In some cruel twist of fate, on my first wedding anniversary without Reg, I woke up to the fire alarms screeching and saying, "Fire!" When I flew out of bed, I discovered flames coming out of the baseboards. I grabbed the fire extinguisher, put those flames out, and called the fire department. I had planned on visiting the site where we got married and spending the day honoring Reg. Instead, I stood outside my house in my pajamas frantic to make sure my cats were safe as I watched the firefighters and chatted with my neighbors, who had gathered to watch (and bring me a jacket and socks to stay warm).

After the firefighters left, I then had to figure out where to go, since my house was no longer livable. Thankfully, my insurance company set up a hotel that allowed cats. When I got to my hotel, I sat on the bed sobbing thinking about how November 4 (my wedding day) had once been the happiest day of my life. Now Reg was gone, and I was in a hotel room with my cats huddled close (they were quite traumatized). It was shattering. Needless to say, it wasn't how I had planned to spend my first wedding anniversary.

Thankfully, the wedding anniversary is not when Reg and I celebrated our anniversary. We had always celebrated our anniversary on the day we met, which was September 23. On my first date with Reg, we played pool at a local brewery. Therefore, on the first September 23 without him, my brother and I went to the same brewery to play pool.

As luck would have it, the brewery was closed for a private party that evening, even though it was a weeknight. I felt very disappointed, but my brother suggested that we go to a nearby bar that had arcade games from my childhood. Reg would have enjoyed the arcade place, so I felt okay switching to that. We played games and had a good time. My brother is a master with arcade games, so every time he was one of the top finishers, he put REG as the initials. That made me happy. We then went to another location and played tabletop shuffleboard, which Reg and I had also played on our first date at the brewery.

I decided that I couldn't finish this day without seeing the location where Reg and I had officially met. Therefore, we went back to the brewery, and I asked if I could briefly enter that room. The pool hall was on the top floor, and I distinctly remember walking up the stairs on that first date and seeing Reg pop around the corner. I was happy to see him and thought he was handsome. This time, as I walked up the stairs and saw the place where he had popped around the corner, I started sobbing. I kept thinking how on that first date, I just thought I was going for a first date. I didn't know I would marry the man. I certainly didn't expect that 13 years later, I would walk up those stairs as his widow.

First Anniversary of Passing

I felt especially stressed about the first anniversary of Reg's death. I thought after a year, I was supposed to be okay. But I wasn't! In fact, I was far from okay. Also, the fact I had made it through a year meant that I could live without him, and this caused me serious angst. How could I survive without him? Therefore, I felt extremely anxious for many weeks before the anniversary.

I think our society views one year as enough time to grieve. Well, let's be honest; it seems most of society believes a year is already too long. But the reality for most of my friends and for me is that one year is not enough, especially for a spouse. In fact, my grief counselor told me for many people, the second year is much harder because, in the first year, they are numb. In the second year, the numbness wears off and now they face the full reality of their spouse being gone. The idea that widows/widowers are fine after one year is unrealistic and far from the truth. But, I felt distressed and pained thinking I was supposed to be okay as Reg's death anniversary drew closer.

The actual day was relatively fine. I talked with a medium (more on that in a later chapter). I had seen this woman before and had received helpful and specific validation, so I trusted what she told me. Plus, she didn't even charge me. I ate dinner with my widower friend Laurence and my mom. We went to a pizza restaurant Reg enjoyed. It served vegan pizza and a vegan brownie. I had intended to sit in silence and concentrate on Reg at 8:50 p.m., which was exactly when Reg died one year before. However, I was so focused on my brownie that I didn't realize the time; I missed it! I think Reg would have found that perfect, as he enjoyed brownies and would probably want me eating one to commemorate his death.

I know I'm not the only widow/widower who felt stressed and anxious about the anniversary of the passing. Gina and I had a discussion about her son and her not wanting to tell his teachers a year had passed since her husband—his dad—had died. She feared the teachers would stop treating him with kid gloves and expect him to be okay. He clearly wasn't okay and still felt deep sadness. She felt sad as well, and four years later she still does.

Dakota told me what she hated most about the first anniversary was her dread that she was leaving her husband behind. It was now a new year, 2016, and he had not existed in 2016. She didn't want to tell people her husband had passed away the previous year. In fact, it was easier for her to say he died in May 2015 rather than saying it had been a year. She spent the anniversary of his death holding a mass in his memory and then going to the cemetery to spend time with him, talk with him, and cry.

My widow friend Desiree commemorated the anniversary of her husband's death by going to a river where he had enjoyed spending time ever since his childhood. He enjoyed fishing there, and she feels close to him there. So every year, she goes there on the anniversary of his death.

Reg's First Birthday

Believe it or not, I actually had a decent day on Reg's first birthday after he passed away. My house had caught on fire four days before that, and I was living in the hotel. Reg's sister had already planned to visit for his birthday, so that helped. I know I cried a lot, and it wasn't a pain-free day. But she and I hiked in a place

47

where Reg and I had also hiked. We spent a good portion of the day discussing him and how much it stinks to be a widow. Nature and few people surrounded us, so there was some degree of peace. We then went to dinner at the restaurant where Reg and I often celebrated birthdays. I wasn't alone like I normally am, which felt nice, and I got to share his birthday with someone who had shared his childhood birthdays with him. So, it wasn't an awful day, surprisingly.

On the other hand, Dakota said her husband's first birthday was unbearable. She, her kids, and her grandkids went to the cemetery to sing "Happy Birthday" to her husband and release balloons. Then they went to dinner at one of his favorite places. According to her, she "could not keep it together and was a hot mess."

My friend Gina decided to try to have fun on her husband's birthday. Coincidentally, it was also Mother's Day that year, so she and her son went roller skating. Sadly, she fell and broke her elbow. She had attempted to make something good come of that day and was rewarded with bad luck.

Yet another one of my friends, Jessica, doesn't remember her husband's first birthday; she was so traumatized by his death that her mind became a big blank for at least a year. However, she remembers making cheesecake from a box. She had done this the year before, when he was still alive. For a few years after his death, this became a tradition.

Other Firsts

In addition to the first holidays, there were other "firsts" that I found difficult. The first time I went to the grocery store after Reg passed away was immensely painful. In fact, I have a chapter specifically on the grocery store. The first time I went to Home Depot was with Reg's boss. He had volunteered to help reinstall a sink we had removed for Reg's wheelchair to fit in our bathroom. As I followed him around the store, all I could think was, "This is the wrong man. I'm at Home Depot with the wrong man. Reg is supposed to solve my home problems!"

Reg and I both had doctors at the University of Colorado Hospital. My doctor had practiced there for many years before Reg got cancer, and I had driven to that hospital by myself many times. But, the first time I drove there after Reg passed away, it was almost too much to bear. To get to my doctor's office, I had to drive by the cancer pavilion, where we had spent a lot of time. We had also spent many nights in that hospital, and we were always so optimistic that he would survive. When I drove there for the first time after he died, I sobbed uncontrollably.

My friend Gina had the same experience. She and her husband had Kaiser insurance. To this day, she still finds it difficult to visit a Kaiser office or hospital even though she still has that insurance. Sometimes just hearing the word "Kaiser" makes her want to be sick and brings quite a bit of pain.

The first time I went to a movie without Reg was also unbelievably sorrowful. Reg and I didn't go to the movies that often. But when we did, I always used the bathroom before the movie. I would exit the bathroom, and he would be standing there waiting for me. The first time I went without him, I came out of the bathroom, and my friend was standing there. It hit me in the gut and made me so incredibly sad. I started crying, of course. I can't remember what the movie was, but I remember it had a scene in the hospital. One character had the oxygen monitor hooked up to his finger and an IV stand. When I saw those, I burst into tears; a hospital scene reminded me of Reg and all the hope we had that he would live.

The first time I went to a concert without Reg, I saw the BoDeans. This band often came to Colorado, and we saw them every time they came. We loved this band. The summer after

Reg passed away, the band once again came to Denver. I debated about whether I should go, as I knew I might suffer. But, I kept thinking we always went and if the BoDeans came to town, I should go. As soon as they started to play, I cried hysterically. I pretty much cried throughout the entire concert. I almost felt sorry for the friends with me, because it couldn't have been pleasant to watch. It didn't help, of course, that couples filled the audience. At another concert much later, I actually danced for the first time (only slightly swaying my body and not my previous enthusiastic dancing while he was alive). I cried as soon as my body moved. This occurred years after he died, but it felt wrong and painful to dance without him.

My friend Dakota often went to concerts with her husband. One concert they often saw was Earth, Wind & Fire. Her husband had given her tickets to the concert for her birthday, but he passed away before the concert occurred. She decided to go anyway and took her adult daughter. She said she cried throughout the concert and was distraught.

Probably the only "first" without Reg that wasn't difficult was watching the first Olympics. Watching the Olympics actually made me feel closer to him, especially as I watched the biathlon. He had always liked the biathlon and had planned to start training for one a month before his cancer returned. Watching the biathlon made me feel close to him, especially because that is not an event I had ever watched without him. It also gave me an excuse to contact the person with whom he planned to train. I actually didn't want the Olympics to end. It felt as if getting through this "first" would take me further away from Reg. He will be even further away the next time the winter Olympics happen. So, I didn't want the Olympics to end.

In fact, I've felt this way about many of the "firsts." While experiencing things for the first time without him was—and still is—heartbreaking, at least it felt like he was still close. For me, getting through the "firsts" doesn't necessarily make me feel better. It makes me feel as if I'm leaving him behind and getting further away from him. Also, it feels as if I'm supposed to be moving on and be okay, because time is moving on.

What I discovered with these important dates—anniversaries, birthdays, holidays, etcetera—is that sometimes I had no idea what I wanted to do on the actual day until the very last minute. People would ask me what I wanted to do or I would try to plan it, but nothing felt right. Then, suddenly, it just did. Sometimes I didn't figure it out until the actual day. For example, I decided to set a place for Reg at the Christmas table just hours before the dinner. I was actually driving to the gym when I came up with this idea. For me, I couldn't necessarily preplan what I wanted to do on these important dates. Sometimes it just came to me spontaneously. I can't tell you why sometimes I could preplan the day and sometimes I couldn't. I guess that was just a part of my grief process.

As you experience your "firsts," I wish you peace and compassion. I know how agonizing these days can be, and you can't just go to sleep and skip them. If you've already experienced some—or all—of them, I hope you were able to experience them in a way that felt acceptable.

I Feel So Alone

Widowhood brings a sense of feeling alone that is almost indescribable. People told me they'd be there for me. His friends and coworkers said they missed him. My friends offered sympathy and sadness. They listened to me cry. But at the end of the day, as the widow, I felt so incredibly alone with my pain. All those people got to go back to their lives. They got to return to their spouses, their children, their jobs, and their homes. I was left to sit in my pain by myself. I couldn't escape from my new life. When I went to a new place, I couldn't make the pain go away; it came with me. It went with me everywhere I went. I knew I was alone in this. His vacancy left a hole in me that I knew was all mine, and no one could help with that.

I don't even know how to describe why widowhood feels like such a lonely experience. I knew I had my mom, who has always been a rock for me, even when Reg was alive. I knew she loved me dearly and would do whatever she could to help me. She was there for me. When I met with the minister for Reg's memorial service, my mom accompanied me. If I needed someone to do something with me, she could be my "date." She and I went for walks frequently, and I could call her whenever I needed her. To make sure I ate, she took me out to dinner almost every night after Reg died. But, I still felt so alone, like nothing I've ever experienced before or like nothing I can even begin to describe. It's as if a temporary insanity came over me; even though I had my mom and other friends who cared about me, it didn't matter. I couldn't see or feel them. Instead, I felt completely alone.

My widow friend Jennifer describes being a widow like being an alien. You feel as if you aren't really part of this world. Everyone seems different from you. You're this species that can't relate to others, and they can't relate to you. I like that analogy. I did—and often still do—feel like an alien species.

I've talked to other widows with children who have said they feel all alone in this world. Logically, they have kids, so there are other people in their houses, thereby ensuring they aren't physically isolated. Yet, they feel entirely alone. Widowhood has this ability to make you feel this way even if you're surrounded by other people.

After Reg died, I even had a few different people overnight at my house just so I wasn't alone. But it didn't matter. It wasn't the physical presence that mattered. It was this sense that I'm now all alone in the world. I thought my future had Reg in it, and we would grow old together. I belonged somewhere and with someone. I knew I wasn't on my own. Now, I am.

Being alone often made me wonder if my death would affect anyone that deeply. Would anyone even care if I died? Would anyone put together a video slideshow of my life like I had done with Reg's life for his memorial service? Not long after Reg died, I found my old yearbooks. I had never shown them to Reg and as I looked at them, I felt a profound sadness. I felt as if there is no one who now cares about my past. There is no one to show these yearbooks to or to show photos of me as a baby with crazy, curly hair. It made me feel as if I don't truly matter to anyone. It made me feel alone.

In the introduction to this book, I told you I would share experiences and emotions about myself that aren't necessarily pretty. They don't make me sound like a good person all the time. Here is one of those examples. I felt so alone after Reg died that

I liked hearing on the news about other people dying. I liked to know I wasn't the only one suffering. I wasn't the only one leading a happy life and then had it all ripped away. I wasn't the only one who hated waking up every day.

I remember one day in particular hearing about a young woman who'd been shot. She was in the hospital, and then the news announced she had died. Her family and friends talked about what a good person she was and how she didn't deserve to die. I remember not feeling sad about this. I almost felt a little bit happy because I knew there was now another family suffering. I wasn't all alone in my suffering. At least one other person in the world also felt pain.

Similarly, there was a plane crash where everyone on board died. In my past, I didn't watch the news because I found it depressing. I never had any idea what was going on in the world. But after Reg died, I was glued to the TV as the airplane story unfolded. Once again, I wasn't alone in the suffering. Family members and spouses of all the people who died on the plane now were in pain as well.

I'm not proud of this and feel bad I felt this way. But, watching these news stories relieved the sense of feeling so alone in the world for just a minute. I knew someone else out there was grieving and missing their loved one. My husband wasn't the only good person taken; this woman who was shot and the people on that airplane were also good people. Reg's death wasn't the only senseless one, and his life wasn't the only one taken too early. Their families felt just as baffled as I felt. Their families hurt just as badly as I did, so in that moment, I wasn't alone.

My widow friend Gina says when she talks to her friends who are married, in her mind she thinks, "You'll be a widow soon." She doesn't like to admit it, but she wants or hopes something bad will happen to them, or she wants them to become widows as well. This woman is one of the kindest women I know. But that part of her that had her heart ripped out and grieves the loss of her husband is tired of being alone in her suffering. She doesn't want to be the only person to have tragedy in her life. She feels better knowing that someday her friends and other women will become widows too.

In addition to feeling emotionally alone, Reg's death also led to my feeling physically alone. Because we didn't have children, it was just the two of us in the house. Our house is small, so we could always hear the other person. When he died, the house was silent. Thankfully, our cats were—and still are—excited when I arrived home and greeted me at the door. But, they are quiet. The TV became my saving grace; I had it on constantly in order to hear voices, so I wouldn't feel so physically alone.

When I was living in a hotel after my house caught on fire (eleven months after Reg died), I went into the whirlpool to help relax. I was, of course, all by myself. I looked up on the wall and saw a sign that said, "Don't go into the spa alone." Ha! What choice did I have? That sign seemed so symbolic of my new life, of being all alone now.

In the summer after Reg passed away, my grief counselor suggested I go on vacation to try to temporarily escape from my grief. That just made me feel even more alone. I used to take my vacations with him. Now, whom would I go on vacation with, given that all of my friends have their own spouses and children? My mom had an older dog that wouldn't eat if she left for too long, so I couldn't go with my mom either. I was left with the choice of either not going on vacation or going alone. Going alone felt too symbolic of my life. I'm sure there are people who wouldn't mind going on vacation alone and may even look forward to the time. But not me. It was once again shoved in my face that I'm now all alone. Needless to say, I didn't go on vacation.

My calendar is now wide open. When I make plans with

other people, they have to find room for me. I'm generally open, especially on the weekends. In the past, when I didn't have plans, I was home with him, so I didn't notice. Now, my wide-open calendar just makes me feel alone. And it makes me feel like I'm a third wheel when I do make plans with other people, as they have to somehow squeeze me into their busy lives. It makes me feel pathetic, and it hurts deeply.

When I was living in the hotel, I became friends with a woman living down the hall from me. Her house had a bad flood, which caused her to live in the same hotel. She and her husband watched the Oscars and invited me to their room to watch with them. In the past, Reg and I didn't watch the Oscars. I didn't care about the Oscars, but now I felt thankful that someone was willing to do something with me and invite me over. I hate that my life now includes being thankful to people for including me, for not forgetting about me, and for caring I'm all alone.

If you're feeling alone, even if you're surrounded by people, I understand. I am sorry.

I'm now a "me" or "I" and not an "us" or "we"

As I discussed earlier in this chapter, widowhood caused a deep feeling of isolation inside me. Tied to that is the sadness that I'm no longer part of a "we" or "us." I'm now an "I" or "me."

Reg and I were a team. We lived together, we vacationed together, we exercised together, we ate our meals together, we "raised" our animals together, we volunteered together, and sometimes we worked together. We even fought cancer together. When he went to the doctor, I always accompanied him. On his last four hospital stays, I stayed in the hospital room with him. I even climbed into the hospital bed with him. When it was time to go to chemotherapy or for a PET or CT scan, he would say,

"We have chemotherapy" or "We have a scan." It was always "We . . ." and not "I . . ." We were a team. We did this together.

When Reg died, we were no longer a team. I was all alone. And no matter how many people surrounded me, that sense of being alone wouldn't go away and hurt tremendously. During my greatest need, my teammate—my buddy—was gone. I was all alone! I used to be part of a "we." Now I'm just an "I."

One of the first times I realized I was now just an "I" occurred when I needed to repair my house's main water line, which broke six months after Reg passed away. I had asked for advice from my neighbor, who is a builder. He said he would talk to the plumber for me because people take advantage of a "single woman." I guess at some level I knew I was now a single woman, but that was incredibly hard to hear. It felt like a sucker punch. I don't want to be a single woman. I want to be Reg's wife.

Another time, two of Reg's coworkers came to dinner. One of them talked about how his wife had gotten into a car accident. He talked about how he arrived on the scene to help his wife. As he talked, I kept thinking about how Reg had once come to get me from my car accident and how happy and relieved I felt to see him when he arrived. More importantly, I kept thinking, "I used to be someone's wife." Now I'm not.

Another time I noticed I'm now an "I" or "me" occurred when I went to Home Depot to purchase a washer and dryer. I told the sales clerk I had considered retiring someday in Vail, one of Colorado's ski resort towns where I had lived in my early twenties. Reg and I had often talked about retiring there. When I talked to the sales clerk, I said, "Maybe *I* will retire there." I used to say, "Maybe *we* will retire there." I was so upset to realize it will now be *me* retiring and not *us* retiring.

Yet another area where I notice I'm now a "me" or "I" relates to other couples. In the past, Reg and I sometimes got invited to other couples' houses for dinner, and we invited them to our house. Now that I'm no longer part of a couple, I no longer receive dinner invitations. That is okay; I don't want to sit across from another couple and be reminded of what I lost. But it definitely shows me I'm no longer a couple or a "we."

Similarly, when we entertained in the past, I cleaned and chatted with the guests, and Reg cooked. Now, on the rare occasion when I've invited people for dinner, it's no longer the two of us entertaining. I now have to talk with people as I try to cook, which overwhelms me. I can't talk and cook at the same time. Plus, we used to do cleanup together, and now I have to do it all myself. I miss hosting dinner parties together. I miss being part of a well-oiled team. I hate that I'm no longer technically married!

About six months after Reg passed away, I filled out an online survey for a 10K (6.2 miles) running race I had just completed. As part of the demographic information, the survey asked for marital status. The choices included single, married, divorced, living with a significant other, and other. There was no widowed. I stared at it for the longest time because I didn't know what to pick. Should I pick other or single? I finally chose single but with much reluctance.

Since that time, anytime I've filled out demographic information, and the choices haven't included widowed, I've chosen "other." I don't like single, as I don't truly feel single. My husband is just gone. For me, it feels better to be married to a dead man than to be alone. I still wear my wedding ring because I can't imagine thinking I'm not married to Reg anymore. My friend Dakota has a T-shirt that says, "I'm not a widow. My husband waits for me on the other side." I like that!

Gina told me she felt so devastated the first time someone told her she is no longer married. She understood she was a widow but didn't realize or understand that meant she was no longer married. She has actually written "widowed" on forms asking for marital status when the forms haven't included widowed. She refuses to pick single. My friend Desiree says emphatically she is still married. In fact, she dated a man for almost two years after her husband died, but she still says she is married.

I must admit that even though Reg is no longer here, I still include him frequently. For example, I talk about "our house" or "our cats." I was—and often still am—unable to call things "mine." In my mind, we are still one and a "we." It feels too much for me to have sole responsibility for and ownership of the house, cats, and everything else that used to be ours together. It's truly too much for me to think I'm now all alone.

I know I'm not alone in feeling this way. Dakota recently purchased a frame to hold a photograph of her grandchildren. The frame has an engraving that says, "Our Grandchildren." Even though she is now on her own, she specifically bought this frame because they are not *her* grandchildren; she includes her husband, so the kids are "*our* grandchildren." Like me, she hates that she is no longer a "we" or "us."

I realize you may not feel this way. I believe every widow I know has had a hard time coming to grips with the idea of not being married anymore or part of a team. But, this probably isn't a universal feeling.

I'm Angry

According to Dr. Elisabeth Kübler-Ross, who wrote *On Death and Dying*, there are five stages of grief: denial, bargaining, anger, depression, and acceptance. Yes, I've felt all of those (and not in any linear fashion). Anger, in particular, is definitely an emotion I've become intimate with since Reg passed away.

I didn't use to cuss. Reg used to tease me, look me in the eye, and say, "Say it Kim. Say it." He was trying to get me to say "fuck," which is a word I almost never used. I was taught girls don't cuss. Once he died, however, I became a cussing machine and said the f-bomb constantly. My widow friend Gina even said when she was around me, she had this huge desire to say "fuck." I don't know if I gave her permission to say it or if so much anger was resonating off me that she wanted to cuss too.

One day, I went to Home Depot. I was there by myself, of course, and saw a couple with a flatbed cart. The woman pulled the cart but not with much effort. Instead, the man pushed the cart and did all the work. As I passed them, the woman said, "Hi." She was being friendly and nice, and I wanted to say, "Fuck you." I felt so angry and jealous that she got to have her man there and that he was doing the work. I think I probably smiled at her, but anger was seeping through every pore of my body.

Like a lot of grieving people, I was—and still sometimes am—outraged with God. How could God take this wonderful man? Why does God let assholes and cruel people live but took my

Reg? Reg had tumors in his spine, which caused excruciating pain. These same tumors caused him to become paralyzed and wheelchair-bound. This strong, independent man had needed my help to survive. Despite strong pain medications, his pain was often so unbearable that he hyperventilated from pain. Why did he have to suffer so much? I hate God for letting that happen, and I hate God for taking him from me. Yes, God is definitely a target for some of my anger. Many people cannot understand that. I realize that fury with God conflicts with many individuals' religious beliefs. But I don't apologize for my anger. God deserves my wrath!

Another target for my anger is Reg himself. Friends and family can't understand why I feel angry with Reg, and they tell me I shouldn't be angry with him. They tell me he didn't want to die, he fought cancer with everything he had, he hung on as long as he could, and he loved me. I understand that. I logically comprehend that. Yet I feel as if he abandoned me. I feel he left me behind. I feel if he truly loved me, he would have tried even harder; he would have lived! He wouldn't have wrecked our lives. He would have done more.

When we got married, we didn't say wedding vows. Instead, we made wedding promises. I feel angry he hasn't held up his promises, such as listening to my stories no matter how boring they may seem and being my best friend forever. During our wedding, he held my hands and said, "From this day forward, you shall not walk alone." Yet now when I need him the most and when I'm in the most pain, he is gone; I'm walking alone. I'm angry with him for that. I know not every widowed person feels anger toward their spouse. But for me, anger toward him was—and still is—a strong emotion.

My anger has caused me to nickname Reg "fucker." I often tell someone about him and say, "That fucker . . ." Or I tell a story or say something about him and finish it with "Fucker!"

Many who haven't experienced widowhood—even some who have—don't understand this nickname. But that is how I feel; he is a fucker for leaving me. He is a fucker for dying. He is a fucker for causing me this much pain. How dare he worm his way into my life just to take my heart and squash it. How dare he leave me so broken. He had no right to do that. He is a fucker!

Frequently, I say I hate him. I hate him for doing this to me. I hate him for causing me this much pain. One day I told my mom I hated Reg. She told me I didn't hate him. I hated that he made me love him. He was such a good man, and he treated me so well that I loved him so much. I opened my heart to him, and it left me crushed. So yes, I often hate him. After all, isn't it reasonable to hate someone who ripped my heart out and left me broken? Isn't it reasonable to hate someone who left me a shadow of the person I used to be? I guess sometimes hate is easier to handle. It doesn't feel as awful as the deep sadness and pain of loving someone and losing him.

Also, I often say I wish I had never met him. If I hadn't, I wouldn't have all this pain. When I tell people that, they say it's better to have had the love I had than to never have had it at all. In my opinion, these people have never experienced this much loss and sadness, or they couldn't say that so unequivocally.

I may be unusual in feeling this way though. Most of my widow and widower friends say they are glad they met their spouses despite the deep pain. However, almost all of them have felt a deep anger. When I first met Desiree, I remember her declaring that she was angry with her husband. She didn't wish she had never met him, but she was mad at him for dying, and the anger caused deep pain. Gina is glad she met her husband, but like me, she calls her husband "fucker" because she too is angry with him for dying.

Dakota says she doesn't feel any anger with her husband or God. She doesn't hate her husband for giving her all this pain.

However, she is extremely angry with her husband's doctors. She feels they didn't try hard enough to save him or make him better.

In the spring after Reg passed away, Laurence and I discussed our anger. His wife passed away roughly a month before Reg. So, we generally went through the same stages of grief and emotions at the same time. We decided to go to a shooting range to try to relieve our anger. The people who know me well find this shocking, as I'm a vegan and tend to be a pretty passive and loving person. But, I felt so much anger that I needed somewhere to put it. Laurence was one of the nicest, calmest, and most spiritual men you could meet. He had even enrolled in ministerial school. But like me, he had to do something with his anger.

So, we headed to an indoor shooting range. He rented a Glock, and I rented an assault rifle. I needed the power to repeatedly shoot the target, which was a paper outline of a human body, without stopping to reload. Because the cancer had spread to Reg's spine, I focused a lot of my anger in the target's spine area. In fact, I pretty much obliterated the paper in the spine area. Laurence's wife had a brain tumor, so he shot the head. At the same time, while I imagined I was annihilating the cancer as I shot the target, I also thought about Reg's doctors. I felt furious with them, so I imagined I was shooting them while I repeated in my head, "Fuck you!" I shot God too. I can't say this experience made my anger go away. But at least for that day, I had an outlet.

Jessica told me that one day she felt so angry that she went down to her husband's workbench in the basement, took a sledgehammer, and pounded everything on the workbench. Like me, it gave her a place to put her anger for the day. It didn't take it away permanently though.

We have an organization here in Denver called Judi's House. It's a place where people can take their children when they have experienced a loss. The children get counseling, and the parents or guardians also get counseling, so they can help the children with the loss. At Judi's House, there is a padded room where kids can throw plates and dishes at the walls to help with the anger. Unfortunately, they don't allow adults to use the room. Trust me, I inquired.

I'm sure someday I will only feel glad I met Reg and feel only love for him. Maybe someday I won't be angry with God. But for now, I often still feel angry. If you feel angry, please take comfort in knowing it's normal. And if you don't feel angry, that's acceptable too. Not everyone does; again, we all grieve differently.

I Hate Seeing Couples

When Reg was alive, I never noticed the world is full of couples. I know that not every widow and widower feels this way, but I absolutely hate to see couples. When I observe them, it feels like a gigantic reminder that I'm no longer part of one. I was part of a happy couple and now I'm alone. If I had it my way, couples would have to stay in their houses. I truly detest seeing them! I dislike seeing couples who are my age, as they show me what I lost. I also despise seeing older pairs, as I thought someday I would grow old with my husband. Why did they get to grow old together, and I didn't get that chance?

Spring and summer seem particularly dangerous for noticing couples. I live three blocks from a park and in the spring and summer, I often see couples there. They walk and hold hands, ride their bikes together, or sit on a park bench enjoying time together. Thankfully, there are many dogs in the park, which makes me happy. So I try to focus on the dogs and ignore the couples. But they are everywhere! It hurts my heart to see all of them. Reg and I used to take daily walks in the park. We had sat on the park benches just chatting and observing the scenery. Now, I have to witness other couples doing that.

I distinctly remember one summer Friday night when I was sitting on my front porch. I watched as the couple next door walked to their car, got in, and drove off somewhere. Who knows where they went. Maybe it wasn't even anywhere interesting or exciting. But, the destination didn't matter; they were together. I used to get in the car with my husband and go somewhere on a Friday night. The woman got in the passenger seat just like I used to get into the passenger seat. Now, I watched another couple do what we used to do while I sat at home alone on a Friday night.

Similarly, I remember walking down the street on a summer night and seeing the couple two doors down sitting on their front porch. Reg and I used to sit on our front porch. It was such a mundane thing to do and certainly not exciting. But, it made me so sad to think we will never sit on the front porch and watch the world go by like we had done in the past. Sure, I can sit on the porch by myself and watch the world, but that just feels pathetic and sad.

As I said, I also detest seeing older couples. I love to hike and often go to an area situated right off I-70, the highway that travels into the Rocky Mountains from Denver. There is a small town with a nice visitors center right near the places where I enjoy hiking. So, I usually stop there to use the restroom before starting my hike. While I appreciate this visitors center because it's clean, I find it painful every time I go there. This is because there are always older couples who also stop at the visitors center. They always look retired and on a road trip. It makes me incredibly sad to see these couples who got to retire and enjoy their travels, vacations, and time together. I look at them and wonder why I never got that chance. Reg and I had talked about traveling when we retired, and we once went on a month-long road trip through the national parks in the West. We planned to do that in our future; so when I see these couples, it brings so much pain.

My widow friend Gina told me she felt okay being around couples. Therefore, when one of her friends had a birthday trip with two couples to Lake Havasu, she believed she could handle it. It had been almost three years since her husband passed away, so she thought she would be fine. However, it was a trip from hell for her. She was on a boat watching two sets of couples snuggle together under the night sky. They went into town and visited a bar with dancing. She sat there while they danced until they finally came over and insisted she join them on the dance floor. But by that time, she already felt truly awful. She was the fifth wheel. As she watched these couples on the boat and the dance floor, her loss became even more obvious and painful. Her husband should have been there with her. Upon returning home, she felt depressed for a while and emotionally exhausted.

Tara told me she didn't mind seeing couples. This surprised me, but she is a sweet lady. I thought maybe she felt happy for all the couples and didn't let her own loss tarnish her joy for others. Then, she went to a wedding. She was the only person there alone and couples, or at least people who attended with some-one else, surrounded her. Needless to say, she felt tremendous pain and hightailed it out of there right after the ceremony. Kind of like the go-to-jail spot on the Monopoly board; she didn't pass go—the reception—and went straight to jail—a.k.a. home.

When I lived in the hotel after my house caught on fire, cou-ples constantly bombarded me. I dreaded seeing them in the breakfast room every morning. Reg and I had sat in the breakfast room at hotels when we had traveled on vacation, and now I had to watch other couples. It felt so cruel. One time, I even had a couple in the room next to me having sex at 11 o'clock at night. I felt jealous that they were a couple on vacation. The next day, I stayed in bed all day and even ate my meals in bed because I was so depressed. Listening to this couple next door having sex on vacation felt like such a contrast to my new life.

It isn't just seeing couples that pains me; it's also hearing about them. Before Reg passed away, I never noticed how often people talk about their spouses. I suspect I probably talked about Reg a lot in the past as part of normal conversation. I don't know. But I know that people talk about their spouses incessantly. I have to hear all about them. Sometimes, I find this so unbearable that I would rather be alone than have to sit there and listen to people talk about their husbands.

The summer after Reg passed away, I frequently hiked with an acquaintance. I enjoyed her, but she constantly talked about the hikes she and her husband enjoyed and about their life together. Also, he frequently called while we hiked. She would answer the phone, and I would have to hear her say, "I love you" at the end of the calls. I wanted to say, "Don't you know I no longer have my spouse? I don't want to hear all about your wonderful hikes with your husband. I don't want to listen to your talking with him on the phone!"

I belong to a book club with a group of women. I know all their husbands, but the club is only for women. Even though I don't have to see the couples, the women always talk about their spouses. One woman in the book club lost her husband a year and a half after Reg died. So, I want to tell the other women that there are now two widows in the club, and we would appreciate not having to hear about their husbands. But, of course, I can't do that. I just sit there and listen.

My widow friend Gina actually got up and walked away when people kept talking about their spouses at a party. It was hurting her soul, and she was smart enough to take care of herself and walk away. I was proud of her for that. Dakota told me that when she said she didn't like winter, someone told her, "We get to snuggle in winter. This is snuggle weather." Dakota lifted her hand in a fist position (as if she were going to flip the person off or hit her) and said, "Snuggle this!"

Jessica said her friends have complained to her about their husbands. She said when they do that, she wants to yell at them that at least they still have their husbands. One friend even went so far as to tell Jessica that she and her husband are like two birds passing in the night; they see each other infrequently. Therefore, she believed her life is not so different from Jessica's. Are you kidding me? Thankfully, none of my friends have been that insensitive, but I, too, have had friends complain about their husbands. I want to shout at them to stop being insensitive and realize that even with their flaws, their husbands still exist while mine doesn't!

One of Reg's friends is great about keeping in contact. I probably talk to him on the phone a few times per year. While I love talking to him, it drives me crazy because when I ask him a question, he turns to his wife and asks her. I want to say to him, "Don't you realize that I can never ask questions of Reg? I can no longer consult my spouse on anything! Can't you answer the questions yourself?"

It isn't just couples in person that bother me. I also dislike seeing them on TV. Reg and I used to enjoy watching the Tour de France and other bike races together. After Reg passed away, I continued to watch the races. During one race, the day's stage was a strenuous mountain stage that pushed the riders to their limits. The man who won the stage said he had pushed even harder because his wife was waiting at the end. That statement caused tremendous pain for me. In 2009, Reg had run a half marathon. I had waited for him and cheered for him at the finish line. When the bike rider said he pushed harder because his wife was at the finish line, I burst into tears. I felt despondent knowing I will never wait at the finish line for Reg again. I will never be his inspiration again. In my past, I was someone's wife and inspiration; now, I'm no one.

The same man not only won that stage, but he won the entire eight-day race. When he found out he won, the cameras zoomed in on him. He was so excited. Then his wife came over to him, and they kissed. I once again burst into tears and felt so incredibly sad. All I could think was, "Why does he get his wife and, more importantly, why does she get to keep her husband?"

Watching sports on TV should be a break from having to see couples, but it's not. As I explained above, I'm forced to see them even there. And it's not just sports; it's other shows as well. I don't know why, but writers of TV programs seem to think shows are better with couples. I prefer to watch crime shows, but even those usually have happy couples in them. Why can't two police partners just be partners? Why do they have to become romantically involved? I seriously don't understand why. Worse yet is when a character is widowed, and the show has the widow/widower become romantically involved with someone pretty quickly. It's offensive to me. I know TV is fake, and the shows aren't supposed to be realistic. But for some reason, this script-writing makes me angry.

Similarly, there don't seem to be any comedy shows that don't have couples. Reg and I used to watch *The Big Bang Theory*, a popular show with four scientists who have always been awkward around women. It's a hilarious show I've always enjoyed. But, even that show now has the men matched up with serious girlfriends or wives. Why? If I can't even get a break from having to see couples on *The Big Bang Theory*, then where can I catch a break?

One comment I've frequently made since Reg passed away is that supposedly the divorce rate in the United States is 50 percent. That means there are many people who are alone in this world. Do those people want to see TV shows with couples? I can't be the only person who doesn't want to see so much romance.

The radio is not much better. Songs about couples fill the airwaves. I can't even begin to count the number of times I've driven in my car listening to the radio while I sobbed.

I wish I could just go somewhere where couples don't exist. I'm tired of watching them on the television, hearing about them on the radio, or seeing them in person. It feels as if every time someone talks about their spouse or I see a happy-looking couple, it puts a little ding in my heart and soul; I'm like a car with dents in it from a hammer that chips away at the metal over and over again.

As I said, I know not every widow and widower feels this way. Perhaps you are fine seeing couples and interacting with them. If you are, I congratulate you and am envious. It's probably a little easier to get through life if your heart isn't punctured every time you see a couple. On the other hand, if you wish all couples lived in another city so you wouldn't have to face them daily, I understand.

Are You Dating Yet?

If you're like me, you've possibly had friends and family members ask if you're dating yet. I'm not opposed to dating and understand why some widows/widowers start dating pretty quickly. For example, I had an acquaintance whose mom passed away. Within a month or two, her dad started a romantic relationship with a family friend. At the time, I found that sort of shocking. However, when Reg died six months later, I understood. Especially at the start, the grief was so debilitating and heart-wrenching that I appreciated why some widows/widowers would want to date and maybe lessen the pain a little. In fact, my grief counselor told me the average widower starts dating about a year after losing his wife.

That being said, I've found it extremely frustrating and get irate when people tell me I should date. There seems to be a notion that widowed people should become romantically available, especially young widowed people. I've repeatedly heard something along the lines of, "You're young. You'll find love again." I want to scream at people when they tell me this.

Six weeks after Reg passed away, I had a doctor's appointment. My doctor, whom I've known since I was eighteen, asked me if I still wore my wedding ring. I said I did. He told me I should take it off because I was "available" now. Are you kidding me? I was so shocked that I didn't feel angry with him. But, his attitude represents how people feel and how they think it's appropriate and fine to tell me I should date again. There seems to be an opinion in our society that after a respectable amount of time—often one year—widowed people should be ready for another romantic relationship or spouse.

Reg wasn't a car that died and that I need to replace. He wasn't an old piece of clothing whose time had come and can just be substituted with a new piece of clothing. He was the love of my life and the man I thought I would grow old with. He was my soul mate. How could anyone replace him? It stresses me out to think about having to start all over again and date. I opened my heart to him and made a life with him. How can I possibly do that again?

And it's not just well-meaning friends who seem to think I should date again. Within a few months of Reg's death, a male friend declared that now he could date me. This dumbfounded me, and I felt I needed to avoid him. I know my widow friend Desiree had the same experience. A man she'd known for years propositioned her not long after her husband passed away. She, too, felt baffled her friend thought that was acceptable and appropriate. She felt uncomfortable and lost that person as a friend.

What further complicates dating for me is the thought that dating would mean betraying Reg. His mom remarried roughly three years after Reg's dad died. When Reg was dying, I remember looking at his mom and thinking she had found love again. I told her she showed me it was possible to remarry and live a happy life again. But once Reg died, I no longer felt that way. I felt—and still feel—that I couldn't date. Logically, I know dating would not mean betrayal. But emotionally, I feel dating would somehow equate to cheating on Reg. Yes, I know he's dead. Yes, I believe he'd want me to be happy and find love again. But I can't stand the idea of betraying him or hurting him. So for now, I avoid dating. Maybe someday I won't feel this way. For now, though, I feel uncomfortable with the idea.

I feel envious of older widows/widowers who seem to have an excuse to not date. My friend Tara became a widow in her 70s, and she tells me she never plans to date again. Although we have mutual non-widowed friends, none of those friends have suggested she should date again. Yet, I've heard comments about dating from many of them. I'm not suggesting widowed people can't or wouldn't date again in their senior years. In fact, not long after Reg died, I watched a story on the news about two people who met in their 90s and fell in love. I'm merely suggesting that I think I would get less pressure to date if I were older.

I know every widow/widower is different. Two of the widowers I know started dating right around one year after their wives passed away. Four of my widow friends have also dated. That's fine for them. I completely understand. On the other hand, I have a friend whose dad passed away in his forties, and her mother never dated again (she died at 97). She promised her husband she would never remarry and despite having many suitors, she was never interested. I understand this too.

It's possible I may date again. After all, I became a widow at 42 years old, and both my grandmothers were older when they died (at 97 and 102). If I'm anything like my grandmothers, I could live a long life and be alone for a long time if I never date again. I'm not closed to the idea, but I honestly can't imagine doing it now and have no desire to get into another relationship now. And I absolutely hate when people tell me I should or that Reg would want me to date again. I wish people would leave me alone. My friend Meg once told me that she hoped someday maybe I would date. But, she lovingly said, "I will be more than happy to have you as my friend whether you sign up for Match [an online dating website] right now or whether you swear off dating for the rest of your life." I really appreciated her saying that and accepting me for whatever I decide.

Please understand that I'm not saying dating is bad or that

widows and widowers should not have romantic relationships. Perhaps no one has judged you on your decision to date or not date, so you can't relate. But what I want for all of us is the right to make the dating decision on our own. I wish friends, family, and society would not judge us, regardless of if and when we decide to enter the dating world again. After all, only we know if dating is right for us and when the timing is best.

Regrets

Like probably anyone who has experienced the loss of a loved one, I have a lot of regrets. Dealing with the regrets has been challenging and painful. Probably my biggest regret is taking Reg for granted. It never occurred to me that he would be gone. I have tremendous regret for all the times I ignored him or focused on other things. I understand it's unrealistic, but I wish I had spent all of my time with him. I didn't know we had so little of it left, so I was busy doing other activities.

I was particularly devoted to my volunteer work at an animal shelter. (I volunteered there for eight years before he died.) On Saturdays and Sundays, I often visited the shelter to train new volunteers or interact with the cats. This was an important part of my life, and Reg loved my compassion and love for animals. But, I wish more than anything I had spent those Saturdays and Sundays at home with him. Similarly, I often called new adopters or took their phone calls when they had trouble with their new pets at times when I now wish I had been with Reg.

Reg sometimes had wanted to hang out at the coffee shop that is a block from our house. Somehow, though, we only did this twice. I don't know why I was so busy and didn't make time for this. Ironically, since he has passed away, I've frequently walked to the coffee shop to meet people. I regret so much that I didn't make more time to do this with him.

Similarly, I regret I wasn't more carefree about food when he was alive. There is an ice cream shop a little over a mile away from our house that carries two vegan ice cream flavors every day. He liked the idea of walking down there, but I always worried about the calories involved in ice cream. Therefore, we only walked down there once. Since his death, I've walked there at least three times. Why didn't I do this with him? Why didn't I just relax and enjoy life and some of life's pleasures? It pains me to think about all the lost opportunities. It also makes me mad at myself.

One day, I went for a walk with Laurence, and we ended up sitting on a bench in the park. Reg had wanted to do this, but it wasn't until he was dying that I sat with him. Instead, for me, being in the park was about exercising and burning calories. I, therefore, was rarely willing to just "hang out." When I sat on the bench with Laurence, I felt tremendous guilt and regret that I hadn't done that more with Reg. Granted, it was Laurence's wife's birthday, the first birthday after her passing. But as I sat on that bench, I kept thinking I was with the wrong man. I should've been sitting with Reg and just enjoying the beautiful scenery. I regret so much that I had not been willing to do that more when he was alive.

I also regret tremendously that we didn't remove his thyroid sooner. A lump developed on his thyroid, and the doctor suggested we have the thyroid removed. Two different biopsies indicated there was no cancer in the lump, so I stubbornly resisted getting his thyroid out. I told Reg not to remove the thyroid. I believed in healing things naturally. After all, we have a thyroid for a reason. Why would we remove his thyroid when there wasn't a reason? But, it turns out that an aggressive form of cancer developed on his thyroid and as you know, I've now lost him. I ask all the time if he would still be alive if we had just taken his thyroid sooner.

I regret that I didn't do enough to make his life easier. I wish I had kept the house cleaner and cooked for him. I despised cooking, so I rarely made him dinner. Instead, after a long day at work, he had to cook for himself. Similarly, I was perfectly content sitting in our backyard even though there were weeds. He hated the weeds and would be the one to pull them up and to handle all the gardening work. Now, of course, I have to handle all the gardening and weeds, so clearly I am—and was—capable. Yet, I let him do it. Why didn't I do everything I could to minimize his stress? I often wonder if he would be alive if maybe I had made his life less taxing and made our home a sanctuary, a place where he could have physically relaxed. That makes my stomach hurt to even ponder, as the guilt is tremendous.

Among other regrets, I'm sorry I refused to listen to his music, as he often requested. I told him his music was boring. Now, I listen to his music all the time and enjoy it. Why wouldn't I listen when he was alive, so we could have had yet another shared experience?

I regret I never understood why he was fine with just being content and okay. I had attended enough self-help seminars and lectures that I wanted to have a "great" or "amazing" life. But after he died, I realized contentment was the best I could shoot for; that was just fine. Reg's dad died when Reg was only 13; he had been sick for many years before that. I never realized how a death could change you so much that just being content was "good." When Reg died, I finally understood. I realized contentment is good. Contentment makes for a pleasant life. I wish I had understood that rather than harassing him about being happier and wanting more.

I regret I didn't realize how lucky I was to have him by my side. For example, one of his friends got married in Sedona, so we traveled there for the wedding. Most of the bride's friends knew each other and were a close-knit group. Reg and I were not close to them. He knew them but wasn't close to them. At the wedding, I felt left out; I wanted to be with the "in crowd" and hated that he and I stood on the outside of the group. In particular, I remember watching the group dance joyously to the Journey song "Don't Stop Believing." I wanted to dance and feel included too. Now, every time I hear that song (which still plays frequently on the radio), I think, "I would do anything—*anything*—to stand in a corner alone with him. I just want to be in a bubble with him and no one else." I wouldn't even want others around us now; I would be so happy to have him by my side.

Something similar happened at my friend's wedding in Puerto Vallarta. Her friends all knew each other and visited a local nightclub. Reg and I stayed at the hotel alone. I felt jealous and left out of the fun. Now, I would do anything to go to Mexico with him and would actually choose to be isolated; we could just enjoy each other and make our own fun. I wouldn't want anyone around us. I wish I had appreciated him and realized how lucky I was to be his date and stand alone with him.

I regret when he was dying, I got frustrated because I wanted to go outside to the park, and he didn't. Or sometimes we went to the park, but then his pain became so intense we had to immediately return home. I wanted to be in the sunshine and got frustrated when we had to return home. I wish I had had more patience and understanding. I wish I had put my own desires aside and appreciated the time I had with him wherever we were.

My widow friend Gina regrets this same thing. She wanted to go into the sunshine and was sure that being in the sun would help her husband. She got frustrated that sometimes all he wanted to do was sit on the couch watching TV. As she and I have discussed, we obviously didn't understand the amount of energy it took to die, and that our husbands didn't possess the energy to go outside with us. With 20/20 hindsight, we both regret this now.

Gina also regrets that she told her husband it was okay to let go. In some way, she feels as if she gave him permission to die and regrets that. Sadly, I think he would have gone regardless, and she just helped him to have a little more peace. But, I definitely understand this regret. She also regrets that she frequently spent time with her friends rather than spending all her time with her husband. Dakota has tremendous remorse and pain thinking about how she hadn't stayed with her husband 24/7 during his last week of life (which she didn't know was his last week). She has cried and told me, "I should have been with him always. I should never have left his side!"

Like any person who has survived a loss, regret is inevitable. I think we all experience it. Just yesterday, I received an email from my friend Dakota saying how she feels overwhelming guilt. She wishes she could go back in time, give her husband more, and do things differently. She said all the guilt and regret make her feel much sadder and even more lonely; they make her miss him that much more.

Overall, I wish I had not taken our life for granted. I wish I had known and understood how lucky I was. I always wanted more: more income for myself, to lose weight, a bigger house, etcetera. I should have just been happy. I should not have taken Reg and our life for granted. It fills me with tremendous pain, guilt, and regret. If only I could have another chance or just a few more days…

As I mentioned earlier in the chapter, I think it's probably impossible to lose a loved one and not have regrets. I don't think they serve us, though; instead, they torment us. Therefore, I hope you don't have many regrets. If you do, however, I understand and am sorry. Please have compassion for yourself.

Reg Is My Favorite Topic

I have no idea if I frequently talked about Reg when he was alive, but now he's practically my favorite topic. I like to tell people all about him, and I often compare him with others and share his opinions. Talking about Reg brings me peace and some degree of happiness. I suppose in some ways, talking about him keeps him alive for me and keeps us connected.

I also like to talk about him because I want people to understand why widowhood has been so hard for me. If they hear about our happy life together—his personality and intelligence, his love for me, how well he took care of me, the activities we did together, and so much more—then maybe they'll understand why I miss him so much. I want people to understand that I don't want that chapter of my life to be over and that for me, it's not.

On the night Reg passed away, the hospice sent a chaplain to my house. As I laid my head on Reg's chest and sobbed, the chaplain said, "Tell me about Reg." I can't remember what I said. But I remember appreciating that he asked me to tell him about Reg. I can picture the chaplain standing in the corner as he asked. I think that might be the only time I felt calm that night.

A year after Reg passed away, I ran into a woman who used to volunteer at the animal shelter with me. She had met Reg and knew he'd passed away. She asked me if I still talked about him. Are you *kidding* me? Of course I did—and still do! Why wouldn't

.? I realize not every widow/widower wants to talk about their spouse; for some, it hurts too much, and that's perfectly acceptable. But for me, talking about Reg brings me peace and happiness, and I could talk about him all day long.

Interestingly, though, even in my early widowhood, I found that some people didn't want to talk about him. For example, I had friends visit a couple of weeks after Reg passed away. Anytime I mentioned his name, one of them quickly changed the subject. It was as if my friend was uncomfortable or afraid to talk about Reg and thought it would be better to pretend as if he had never existed. I understand that many people don't know how to handle grief and choose to change the subject or ignore the proverbial elephant in the room. Or maybe they think their job is to distract from the grief. I realize this is normal behavior. But, this truly annoyed me.

Even one of Reg's best friends seems uncomfortable if I talk about Reg too much, especially if I become emotional. I noticed one day that when I was upset and mentioned I'd been crying, he sort of shut down. Even though this man is a compassionate and emotional guy, he couldn't handle my deep sadness and chose instead to avoid it by changing the subject. Again, I realize in our culture that we aren't taught to understand and handle grief, and most people just want it to go away. But rather than switch the subject, I wish his friend had told me if and how he missed Reg, shared stories of their past, or even just let me talk about him.

Within the first few months after Reg died, I read an article by a woman whose mother had died the previous year. The writer said it brought her peace to talk about her mom, and yet no one, not even her friends, would let her. They avoided the subject of her mother altogether and changed the subject if she came up. They thought their friend should just move on and that talking about her mom stopped her from doing that. She wanted them to understand that talking about her mom was the only thing that brought her peace. My widow friend Tara recently told me her son had lost friends for this exact reason. Anytime he brought up his dad, his friends became uncomfortable. So rather than face the discomfort, they avoided him.

Because I know how much I like to talk about Reg, when I meet a new widow or widower, I always ask them to tell me about their spouse. Not long ago, I met a woman at the doctor's office whose husband had passed away the previous year. I asked her about her husband and just listened as she spoke about him. She lived in Texas and had come to Denver for some specialized treatments. I asked her if she had anyone at home she could chat with, especially who had known her husband. She immediately burst into tears and said no one would talk about him. She wanted to talk about him, but everyone changed the subject when she tried. This was painful for her. The last thing I said to her as we parted was to make sure she kept speaking about her husband even if it made people feel uncomfortable. She had the right to talk about him, and it didn't matter if other people didn't like it!

Dakota recently told me her husband continues to be her favorite subject—over two years after his death—and she feels hurt that people switch subjects when she brings him up in conversation. She expressed that people seem afraid to talk about her husband and change the subject quickly if she talks about him. So rather than feel judged by her family and friends, she often just shuts down and stays quiet.

Similarly, Dakota met another widow in a support group. Just the other day, the other widow told Dakota that she had recently started dating someone and said she was happy. Dakota sadly told me, "Now I can't talk to her about [my husband]." Like me, her husband is Dakota's favorite topic. I told her she could always talk to me about her husband. Similarly, my widower friend Laurence said he just could not help but talk about his wife.

Queen Victoria also liked to talk about her late husband. A duke, the Duke of Argyll, noted Albert was the only topic of conversation that interested Victoria. When the duke visited her, he tried to steer the conversation to the "hills, birds, and waterfalls." Victoria directed the conversation back to Albert by saying things like, "... the birds he had liked, the roads he had made, his speeches, etc." It was as if Albert were still with her. When Queen Victoria was being pressured to return to her official duties, she told one of the English lords, Lord John Russell, that "the things of this life are of no interest to the Queen."[iii] Instead, she seemed to prefer to take short walks in her garden and talk about Albert.

Every single widow and widower I know likes to talk about their spouse. They all like to share stories, discuss how hard widowhood has been, talk about their lives together, and give descriptions. I encourage you to talk about your spouse as well. Yes, most people probably will be uncomfortable with that, as our society doesn't do well with death and grief. But they are not the widow/widower; you are. So if it makes you happy and brings you peace to discuss your spouse, do it. If talking about your loved one brings too much pain, then don't.

Feeling Blindsided

According to the Merriam-Webster dictionary, the definition of "blindside" is:

1) to hit (someone who is facing in another direction) suddenly and very hard

2) to surprise or shock (someone) in a very unpleasant way

One of the hardest things about being a widow or widower is what I call the blindsiding moments. When you lose someone you care about, you expect certain things to be hard, such as holidays, anniversaries, birthdays, the first time you go to a restaurant without the person, the first time you take a trip without your loved one, and many more. In a way, you prepare for these. You protect yourself from those days and moments, and you know how to handle them. Or maybe you don't know how to handle them, but you know they are coming; you prepare to be sad and upset these days. You expect to cry.

For example, I knew on my first birthday without Reg, I would probably be a mess. I knew my first Christmas without him would be god-awful, and I was prepared for that. I knew I would be an emotional wreck on the anniversary of his passing. I didn't expect to have a good day; I didn't expect to get through the day without tears.

When you read newsletters from organizations, such as hospices or grief groups, they tell you how to prepare or give suggestions for these big, important dates. They tell you they know these dates will be hard. If you're lucky, you may have friends or family members who reach out to you on those important days to make sure you're okay or just to tell you they're thinking of you and love you.

But what no one tells you about or warns you about are the moments when you're blindsided. These are the times when you're just going about your business and are not expecting to be overcome with grief. These are the moments when you feel like you've been smacked across the face, when you're sucker punched. These are the instances when you fit the dictionary definition of blindsided: being hit suddenly and hard, and surprised and shocked in a very unpleasant way.

Let me give you some examples. As a grieving person, we all have them. I could fill this entire book on the occasions when I've been blindsided, on the moments where I was just living my life and then BOOM, I got smacked across the face. But I will give you just a few to let you know that you're not alone in being blindsided. It happens to the best of us.

One day I drove to the gym the same way I've driven to the gym for years. When I stopped at the stoplight, there was a man on a bike in front of me waiting to cross the street. When the light changed to green, he clipped his bike shoes into the clips and crossed the street. I immediately burst into tears. The man clipped his shoes into the pedals the same way my husband did. I had seen Reg clip into his pedals, and somehow watching this man brought up all those memories. As I watched this man ride across the street, I thought, "That should be Reg. He should be on his bike. He will never ride his bike again. I will never see him clip into his pedals again. Why does this man get to ride his bike, and Reg doesn't?"

This was blindsiding because I was completely unprepared. I was just going about my business, going to the gym the same way I always drive. I had not been thinking about Reg in that moment and then out of nowhere, I became overwhelmed with grief.

Speaking of sucker punches that involve bicycling, I had yet another shocking and unexpected experience at the bike store. After Reg died, I took up bicycling (using his bike), so I could participate in a charity ride he had wanted to do. I brought his bike into the store to get a tune-up. The bike mechanic lowered the seat, so it would now fit me. Perhaps I should have been prepared, but I felt blindsided with the emotion that came over me as he lowered the seat. Lowering the seat meant the bike now belonged to me and not to Reg. Lowering the seat meant Reg was never going to ride it again. I unexpectedly became overwhelmed with grief while I watched the mechanic maneuver the seat.

I was similarly blindsided when I ran in a 5K race for lung disease. I used to run in 5k or 10k races once or twice per month and always wore a Road ID on my wrist to identify myself in case of an emergency. The contact information listed Reg, our home phone number, his cell phone number, and my mom's cell phone number. At this race, I remember standing at the start line waiting to go, and I looked down at my Road ID. I had put it on that morning and obviously not looked at it. When I gazed at it and saw his information as my emergency contact, I burst into tears.

I had never raced this course before, so I had been focused on that and had not been thinking about Reg. I was just going about my business when, wham! I was once again blindsided. Here I was surrounded by people excited to race, and I was in tears. I couldn't believe he is no longer my emergency contact person. If something happens to me, he won't pick up the phone and come get me. If something happens, he won't be on the other end of the phone to help me or to take care of me.

Yet another example happened when I attended a University of Colorado football game. A woman sat next to me who looked like Reg. I had never seen anyone who looked like him. This woman looked more like him than Reg's sister. I kept staring at this woman during the game. I asked my mom (who was with me) if the woman looked like Reg, because I thought maybe I desperately wanted to see him. My mom agreed the woman looked similar. When the game ended, and we exited the stadium, the woman went left, and we went right. I started crying hard because watching this woman walk away felt as if I was losing Reg yet again. This woman was the closest I've come to seeing him, and watching her walk away felt like another loss. I certainly didn't expect to go to the football game and be blindsided by what felt like another loss!

Blindsided watching TV

When I watch TV, I expect to escape and to not have to deal with my pain and grief. Yet I find I'm often blindsided the most when I'm viewing it. For example, one day I watched a TV show called *Bones*. It's a fictional crime show with a forensic anthropologist and an FBI agent who partner together to solve murders. They are also married. The FBI agent, otherwise known as the husband and named Booth, got kidnapped in one episode. The anthropologist, otherwise known as the wife, said, "I cannot imagine a day when Booth does not come home." I burst into tears because that is my life! Reg will never come home. I never thought I would see the day when he wouldn't be here. But he will never, ever come home. I will never, ever be able to greet him at the door again. I will never eat dinner with him again. I will never watch this TV show with him again. So when the character on this TV program made that comment, I burst into tears and sobbed for a while.

In another TV show, the main character was also kidnapped. When the kidnappers released her, the husband called their kids and said, "Mom is coming home." Once again, I burst into tears. I would give anything to hear someone say Reg was coming home. No one will ever call me and say that though.

In both these instances, I was just trying to watch TV and escape into it. Since these were crime shows, they weren't supposed to elicit any emotion. I should have been safe watching the TV. And yet, I was blindsided and ended up wracked with grief.

Another example of how TV has blindsided me is when I was watching the *CBS Sunday Morning* show. This is a TV show that has different segments highlighting special interest stories and sometimes famous people. It's certainly not a show designed to elicit emotion. It's just a feel-good program where you learn at the same time. As I watched an episode, a commercial appeared for Subaru and its commitment to helping the national parks clean up the trash that tourists leave behind. The commercial had a scene where the camera looks out the windshield of the Subaru at one of the national parks. Reg and I had spent a month traveling around the national parks in the West and had driven in his Subaru. When this commercial came on, I was immediately taken back to our trip and to the knowledge that I will never go on a road trip with him again. I will never hike in a national park with him again. On that trip, I was the passenger the entire time. So when I saw that commercial, this overwhelming grief came over me with the understanding that I'll never be a passenger in his Subaru again. Therefore, I started sobbing. Once again, this was an example of just trying to watch TV and being blindsided by grief.

Another example happened when I watched *NFL Countdown* one Sunday morning. This show certainly should have been safe, right? It's about football. But on this particular Sunday, the show featured a feel-good story about one of the NFL players. His mom had died of thyroid cancer, which is how Reg died. His dad completely fell apart and lost their home and business after his mom died. They had to move to an apartment with cockroaches and in a bad neighborhood.

This NFL player had talent, though, and got mentored and coached by people who helped him ultimately get to college and the NFL. It was a truly touching and great story. But I felt completely blindsided. I had expected to just watch the broadcasters talk about football. This story about a woman dying of the same type of cancer that took my husband left me sobbing. I wasn't prepared for that!

I also was blindsided during yet another sporting broadcast. One day I turned on the NCAA basketball championship, and Wisconsin happened to be playing. As the broadcasters introduced the players, one player was from Sheboygan. Sheboygan is a town not far from where Reg grew up and certainly not a town I had ever heard of before I met him. As soon as the broadcasters said "Sheboygan," I burst into tears. Then they introduced someone from La Crosse, which is where Reg went to college. So I once again cried. I had not been thinking about Reg and wasn't expecting to double over in grief in that moment. But, I was once again blindsided.

Music has an ability to really blindside

Music can be emotional and frequently blindsides me. Music can take me right back to good memories I spent with Reg and make me so sad that those times are over. Music can also take me right back to the painful moments, such as his memorial service. Usually, I hear the songs when I least expect them, and I'm blindsided.

I had one of my favorite songs as the ringtone when Reg called me. After he passed away, I had his cell phone forwarded to my cell phone. The mortgage company had his cell phone as the contact number, so one day they called his cell phone. I was at the doctor's office and was checking out after my appointment when my phone rang. It was his ringtone! I was completely blindsided! I just stared at my phone and burst into tears. The poor woman behind the desk was surprised and had no idea what to do with me.

In another example, I completely lost it when I had to call the Colorado Division of Labor to check on how to submit self-employment tax reports. This shouldn't have been an emotional call. But, the hold music was the exact music Reg's insurance company used. Shortly after he died, I had been forced to listen to this music when I called the insurance company. I was in so much pain when I made that call that the hold music is forever implanted in my brain. So when I called the Colorado Division of Labor and heard the same hold music, I started to sob. By the time the voicemail came on for the person I needed to speak with, I was hysterically crying and could barely get through my message. I was completely blindsided.

Even sounds—not necessarily songs or music—can send me right over the edge. Reg and I used to play Words with Friends (an application that resembles Scrabble) on our cell phones. We only played each other, so when he died, I stopped playing or even thinking about the game. But one day, I had dinner with one of his coworkers. Unbeknownst to me, she plays Words with Friends. While I sat with her, her phone gave the alert that it was her turn to play. Of course, it was the same alert I used to receive when Reg had entered a word, and it was my turn to play. When this woman's phone sounded, I felt sucker punched!

Tara told me one day she was at the grocery store and heard a song that her husband had liked. She became so emotional she left her cart exactly where it was and exited the store. She was blindsided by the music and became so overwhelmed with

91

grief that she couldn't even check out her groceries. Dakota also felt blindsided at the grocery store. As she rounded the corner of an aisle, she saw a man who looked strikingly similar to her husband. She started crying and quickly turned around to head back to where her adult daughter was standing. You can imagine how shocked her daughter was to see Dakota when one minute earlier, Dakota had been fine. She was just trying to purchase butter and hadn't expected to be sucker punched at the store.

Yes, blindsiding moments happen to all of us! I don't know a single grieving person who has not been blindsided. I wish I could give you advice on how to handle them. But since they come out of the blue and sucker punch you, there's no way to prepare. Just know they will come; you can't avoid them, and that's okay.

Loss of Self

When Reg passed away, I felt that not only did I lose him but also myself. Being Reg's wife was only part of my life and identity. I also was a writer, editor, coach, committed volunteer at an animal shelter, friend, daughter, aunt, and huge advocate for animals and the environment. Yet when he died, I felt as if I didn't even know who I was anymore. All those other pieces of me seemed to go out the window, and I felt as if I had lost myself.

Not long after Reg passed away, I watched an episode of *Downton Abbey*, a British TV show popular in the United States. In the show, one of the main characters died in a car crash. In one particular episode, the dead man's mother declared, "When your only child dies, then you aren't a mother anymore. You aren't anything really, and that's what I'm trying to get used to." That's exactly how I felt! I'm not a wife anymore. This felt especially true after taking care of Reg for six months. Like the mother in the show, I felt as if I was "not anything really." I was—and often still am—just going through the days and have no identity.

In the summer after Reg died, one of his previous coworkers came to dinner. While eating, he told me his wife had been in a car accident. He talked about how he arrived on the scene to help her. As he talked, I kept thinking, "I used to be someone's wife. I once belonged to someone. Someone once talked about me with pride. Someone once referred to me as 'my wife.'"

Now who am I? I miss that sense of belonging and security. I want someone to feel proud of me. I want the normalcy of having a day-to-day—maybe sometimes boring—life. I miss being Reg's wife and his companion. I used to be the most significant person in Reg's life. Now, I've often wondered if I'm even important to anyone, let alone the *most important* person.

Reg used to say we didn't fit in the world. Our values differed from most people's. We lived a vegan lifestyle, we rarely drank, we looked out for the environment, and we rarely bought material things (except electronics). We didn't "fit." But the thing is, we fit together. Now, I don't fit. I don't fit in the world or with anyone. I feel like an outsider. Because my beliefs and values have always been different from most people's, I had already felt that way. But now, I especially feel adrift. I feel like I don't fit anywhere. Reg and I were like puzzle pieces that fit together, and now I'm just a puzzle piece alone.

I was raised by a mom who was extremely positive and always believed you could get what you want if you tried hard and believed you could. In high school, my teachers taught me to work hard and that life was for the taking. No one—not my mom and not my teachers—taught me life could knock you down. I felt angry with my teachers and my mom for not teaching me life could be unfair, you could feel heartache, and you could have your whole world turned upside down no matter what you did. You see, a big part of my identity had been as an optimist, as someone who believed she could conquer the world. Then Reg died, and I lost that part of myself.

I often cry when I see pictures of myself from before his death. I looked happy and had a sparkle in my eyes. In many photos, I even glowed. After he died, I mourned the loss of that woman—the old me. I would look—and still look—at her and think she was so naïve. She had no idea what was coming down the pike. I would also get mad at her. How could she not have known? How could she have been so naïve? It was as if I turned into two people: the me before and the me after his death.

This was particularly obvious when my mom and I did a fundraising walk for the Peaceful Prairie Farm Sanctuary seven months after Reg passed away. Because the sanctuary had named a rooster after Reg, we formed a team called "Team Reg" to honor him and to raise funds for Reg the rooster. At the walk, I heard my mom say to the founder that I was Kim, and my husband was Reg. He said, "I know Kim." When I heard that, I burst into tears. That man had known me when I volunteered at the farm sanctuary, which was a happy time in my life, a time when I could help animals and had the emotional capacity to do that, a time when Reg was either with me volunteering or at home waiting for me to come home, a time when I could think beyond myself, and a time when I wanted to be in the world and contribute to the world. When the founder said he knew me, I wanted to say, "You used to know me. That woman is gone now."

Not long ago, I watched a TV show where the characters traveled back in time to 1983. In 1983, I was in middle school and felt like the world was there for my taking. I knew I would have a great life. During the TV show, a song from the 1980s played, and I burst into tears. At first I couldn't figure out why I cried and had such a strong reaction. Then I realized the song brought up the loss of that naïveté and the loss of the optimistic, happy person I used to be.

I know I'm not the only widow who feels this way. Just recently, I chatted with my friend Desiree, whose husband passed away four years ago. She told me when her husband died, she felt she lost herself. Like me, being a wife was only one of her roles. She has children, owned a retail business, had another business on the side, and had and still has many friends. Yet, she felt a loss of herself when her husband died. She said she used to be spontaneous. Now she is not, nor is she as happy as she had been in her past. She now has to work in a job she never wanted to do because now she is fully financially responsible. Her husband had been her greatest cheerleader, would encourage her to push herself, and served as a soft place to land. He knew her well enough to know what her strengths and weaknesses were and encouraged her when he thought she would succeed. Now, she has lost her cheerleader and herself. As we chatted, I told her I felt the same way, that I had lost myself. She said, "We will never be the same again. How can we be?"

My widow friend Dakota told me she doesn't know who she is without her husband. She has children and grandchildren. But, she still feels as if she lost herself after her husband died and doesn't know who she is without him. Tara told me what comforts her is focusing on her other roles. She is no longer a wife. However, she is still a mother, so she feels comforted in knowing she still has at least one other role.

I don't know about my friends, but sometimes it almost feels as if I have to consciously *choose* to be myself. My grief counselor assured me I wasn't alone; that is part of the grief process. I have to define who I am now. Who am I without Reg? Honestly, I don't want to know. I want to be Kim, Reg's wife.

Perhaps you're similar to Tara and still know who you are without your spouse. Perhaps you've been able to focus on other areas in life and other roles. I would guess many widowed people can do that. On the other hand, if you're having to redefine who you are now, I understand how difficult that can feel and how much you may want to rebel against that. I suspect that with time, defining who you are—and who I am—will become easier.

Loss of Security

When Reg passed away, a lot of the security I took for granted disappeared. With him, I had physical, financial, and emotional security. Now, I've lost all of those. I know this doesn't happen with every widow and widower (especially widowers), but this has been a part of my new life.

Physical security

Reg wasn't a huge man, but he was athletic. If someone broke into our house with a gun, Reg probably could not have defended us. But I always felt safe with him. We slept with our windows wide open during the summer, and it never occurred to me to even worry. He was sleeping next to me, so I had no need to fear.

Toward the end of his life, tumors invaded his spine, and he became paralyzed. He had to use a wheelchair, and he was taking serious pain medications and became pretty weak. We went to the mountains and stayed with someone whose house was surrounded by wilderness. Reg was in so much pain he would often moan in the night, making it problematic for me to sleep. This house had an extra bedroom, so I decided to sleep in the spare room just so I could get some sleep. But, then the dog in the house started barking, and it scared me because I didn't know what potentially huge animal was outside. I went back into the bedroom where Reg was. He said, "You realize if an animal breaks in or something happens, I can't do anything." My response to him was, "Even paralyzed, I still feel safer in here with you than without you."

Now, I'm entirely alone. I don't have that security anymore. Reg took a trip to see the Green Bay Packers play in a different city each year. Other than that weekend, I never slept alone in our house. Whenever he left for that weekend, my imagination would always go wild thinking about the bad things that could happen, and I couldn't wait for him to get home. Now he will never come home.

After he passed away, I placed a baseball bat next to my bed and mace on the nightstand. I hadn't even thought about security before (other than his once-a-year trip), but now I had to think about it. I remember one night realizing I had to either let go of the fear, or I would be fearful every night, which is not how I want to spend my life. So, I let the fear go and now generally feel safe and don't worry about intruders. But I no longer sleep with the windows open during the summer. I don't like to go outside in the summer when it's late and dark to water the lawn, because I'm scared someone will go in the house. I don't have the same sense of physical security I used to have.

A few weeks after he died, the SWAT team was in our alley with guns because someone had broken into a house with a gun. Are you kidding me? About a year later, I saw the police across the street. Once again, there had been a home break-in. Those events wouldn't have thrilled me even when Reg was alive, but now such occurrences caused extreme nervousness. I feel vulnerable now, where I hadn't felt vulnerable in my past.

Let me give you another example of my feeling vulnerable now. In the summer after Reg died, I had raccoons in my cat enclosure. Many years ago, I had an enclosure built for my cats, so they could go outside while staying safe. (It's basically a big cage with a doggie door that goes between the enclosure and the house.) Raccoons had never gotten into it when Reg was alive but, sure enough, a baby raccoon slipped through the wiring and got trapped in the enclosure. It happened in the middle of the night when I was sound asleep. When I went outside to hear what all the commotion was, I completely freaked out. I opened the cage door, so the raccoon could get out and run away with his mom, who was standing on top of the cage. Sure, I wasn't in any danger, but I would rather deal with wild animals with Reg by my side than alone. I felt so sad that I could not climb back into bed and feel safe next to him after this experience.

Similarly, last spring a huge tree next door toppled under the weight of the heavy snow and landed in my yard. It pulled the electricity box off my house and caused other damage to my house. I felt terrified that the wire now exposed from the electricity box would catch on fire. The electricity company told me there wasn't anything they could do, and I needed to call an electrician in the morning. Had Reg been here, I wouldn't have been frightened. But because I no longer feel physically secure, especially because my house had already caught on fire, I felt terrified. I finally climbed into bed and wrapped myself in the quilt I had made from Reg's T-shirts, so I could pretend he was comforting me. Sadly, that wasn't the same as having him there to protect me.

Finally, I've lost physical security with other men. For example, a male friend helped me with some work around the house. One day, he asked me to kiss him. What? I had hugged him many times as he is a good friend. But now he wanted me to kiss him, which made me feel physically violated. Is this what I had to do to get handyman help? It made me feel as if I was no longer safe around him. In fact, I avoided him for quite a long time. That kind of thing would never have happened when Reg was alive!

Similarly, as I stated in an earlier chapter, another male friend declared one day that now he could date me. Again, this would never have happened if Reg were alive. It made me feel like I needed to avoid this man. I had never worried about men when I was with Reg. Now, I felt vulnerable. Now, I felt I couldn't just be friends with a man and be left alone. I had to keep up my radar. I no longer felt physically safe.

As stated in an earlier chapter, my widow friend Desiree had the same experience. A man she had known for years proposi-tioned her not long after her husband passed away. She, too, felt uncomfortable and lost that person as a friend. She also said she no longer feels physically safe doing some activities she used to do. For example, she used to go dancing with her girlfriends. She would innocently dance with men knowing she would go home to her husband. She felt completely safe doing that; both she and the men understood she was married, and they were just having fun dancing—nothing more. Now, she no longer feels comfortable going dancing with her girlfriends. That physical safety is gone.

Financial security

Besides physical security, I also lost my sense of financial security after Reg passed away. He was the main breadwinner and paid for all the big bills, including the mortgage, cell phones, inter-net, satellite television, electricity and heat, and water. Now, I'm responsible for all those bills. Reg was a software developer and according to many people who worked with him at different companies, he was the best software developer they had ever worked with. He was the guy his coworkers turned to when they needed help and couldn't solve an issue on their own. Even when the tumors invaded his spine and he was highly drugged up with pain medications, he was still smart enough to solve an issue that the rest of his department was frantically working on and couldn't solve together. Therefore, his company wanted to keep him. I never worried about his getting laid off, even in economic downturns.

Now, I frequently worry about finances. I do contract work and have felt vulnerable with my clients. With one client in particular, I felt as if I had to be careful, so I wouldn't upset anyone and get fired. Interestingly enough, I got fired when I asked for work early in order to go to Reg's memorial service in Wisconsin. In my past, I would have been able to say, "Fuck you. I'm going to my husband's memorial service; if you can't be sympathetic to that, then you can take this job and shove it." Instead, now that I have financial insecurity, losing this job devastated me.

A symbol of my new financial insecurity is a database Reg had for his passwords. Reg believed in having a different password for each online financial institution, such as the mortgage company, credit cards, and bank accounts. Because he didn't trust himself to remember the passwords and because he had them randomly generated, he had a database with all his passwords. Due to his intense pain, I had been paying the bills for many months before his death and was familiar with this password database. But somehow, when I opened that password database after he died, I couldn't stop crying. I saw my life disappearing. Seeing his password database felt like another part of my life— my financial security—had been taken away.

Similarly, Reg had always paid a little extra each month toward our mortgage, so he could minimize the amount of interest we paid. After he passed away, I didn't feel secure enough to pay any extra and instead have just paid the amount I owe. Once again, when I made that change, I was overcome with grief because being able to pay only the amount I owed felt as if it represented my new life, my life without him and financial security.

I know I'm not the only widow who has felt this way. A couple of my widow friends receive their husbands' pensions or

Social Security, yet they still worry about finances. In addition to Social Security, Gina received enough life insurance that she could pay the mortgage on her house. But, she still has to budget each month, whereas she didn't need to budget before. Sadly, Desiree lost her house not too long after her husband passed away. I know Tara constantly worries about money.

One widower I know, Bill, became homeless after his wife died. His wife spent six months in the hospital, resulting in roughly $250,000 in medical bills, which Bill couldn't pay. When she died, he became so distraught that he started to drink and lost his job and home. He is sober now and working, but he is still homeless and has no financial stability. On the other hand, the other two widowers I know haven't felt financial insecurity. Therefore, if you're a widower reading this book, you may not relate to this chapter. More and more women are becoming the family breadwinners, so you may not relate to the chapter as a widow either. But in general, I think a loss of financial security is relatively common.

Emotional security

Even worse than the loss of the physical and financial security has been the loss of emotional security. I was living a nice life with a man I loved. Our life was far from perfect, but we were happy. Then, he was gone. I became a 42-year-old widow! My heart felt as if it shattered into a million pieces when he died, and my emotional security vanished.

A symbol of my emotional insecurity disappearing was Reg's Green Bay Packers garden gnome. He loved that gnome and when the Packers played poorly, Reg would place the gnome on the table facing the TV, as if the gnome were giving the Packers a reprimand. One day after he died, I moved the table to clean the floor and broke the Packers gnome. It broke into many pieces, and I sobbed uncontrollably. I was absolutely crushed. Reg loved this gnome, and now it was shattered. The gnome also was symbolic because I felt as if his death shattered my life. This gnome and my heart were in pieces. My emotional security was gone!

Over a year after Reg passed away, my grief counselor did EMDR with me. EMDR is a technique used to help people release trauma. Because it's often used in instances such as war and rape, the trauma of reliving the incident during the session can become pretty intense. Before starting, the practitioner helps the client come up with a "safe place," a place where the client can mentally go if the emotion gets too intense. In my past, I had a "safe place" on a rock in the mountains that I would picture when I meditated. But, that was the old me. That person died when Reg died. When I tried to think of the mountains as my safe place, I felt Reg should be there with me. So, the mountains brought up sadness and no longer enveloped me in safety.

My grief counselor asked if I could come up with another safe place besides the mountains, but I couldn't come up with one. My counselor suggested maybe a childhood room where I had felt safe. I pondered that, but when I tried to picture myself as a little girl in her room, I realized she wasn't safe either. No, not because that child suffered trauma as a child but because that child had no idea how much was coming down the pike for her and how much heartache awaited. Rather than feel safe, I just felt sad for her. Finally, I told my grief counselor, "Nowhere is safe."

As a side note, Reg had a practitioner work with him after his doctor told him he wouldn't be able to get rid of the tumors. He was so traumatized and anxious we thought EMDR could assist in releasing that trauma and help him. When the practitioner told him to think of a safe place, he imagined the time when he asked me to marry him. I was his emotional safety! Now, because of his death, nowhere felt emotionally safe to me.

Eventually, I came up with a place. I pictured an empty beach with the sun beating down on me. Reg hated the intense heat, so he wouldn't want to be there. Therefore, it was a place where it didn't feel like he needed to be with me. But, the fact I took so long to find a place and the fact I didn't feel safe anywhere is quite telling of my loss of emotional security.

Let me give you another example of the loss of emotional security. About ten months after Reg died, a group of women with whom I had taken yoga in my past invited me to attend a yoga retreat center. One woman had reserved a spot and paid but couldn't go, so she offered me her spot for free. You would think going would've been an easy decision for me; after all, I could spend the night in a beautiful, mountainous place doing yoga and eating healthy, vegan food. The women were all kind, and many of them had been at Reg's memorial service. They, therefore, knew I was vulnerable.

But when I thought about going to this place, it didn't feel safe. I had planned on hiking with my friend Vicki—who knew Reg well, was single, and knew my emotional state—and her loving dog, Moby. That felt safe. On the other hand, it felt dreadfully risky and unsafe for me to go to this yoga retreat center with these women who were happy, whose lives were intact, and whose husbands were alive. Would it be okay if I cried? Would it be okay if I had to leave and isolate myself? Would I be okay if I had to listen to these women?

I desperately wanted to stay home and stay safe. I wanted to cocoon myself in my house with my cats, where I wouldn't have to worry if I cried or became emotional, or where I wouldn't have to interact with happy people. In my past, I would have jumped at the opportunity to visit this place, even if I had to pay. But now, I felt terrified because I no longer felt emotionally safe out in the world. Ultimately, I decided I should go and pretty much sobbed through the whole drive to the place. I cried a lot while I was there but did enjoy the setting's peace and beauty.

One day I told my widow friend Gina that she felt emotionally safe for me. As soon as I said it, I burst into tears. Why did I have such a strong reaction? When I told my grief counselor about it and said I couldn't figure out why I had such a strong reaction and cried, she said, "Well, when you talk to [Gina], you don't have salt poured in your wounds." I hadn't realized it, but talking with and being around non-widowed people didn't feel emotionally safe. It constantly felt as if salt was being poured into my wounds! They inevitably talked about their husbands and their pleasant lives. Even if they complained about their husbands, it was a constant reminder that my husband is gone and that my life had been shattered! With Gina, I wasn't forced to hear about her happy life; I didn't have salt poured on my wounds, so she felt emotionally safe.

In addition to feeling emotionally unsafe with friends due to having to hear about their happiness, I also became more emotionally insecure about friends. In my past, I didn't worry about whether I alienated someone. Honestly, it's not in my makeup to alienate people. I'm a person who tends to make friends and keep them. But, in my past, it didn't matter. I would always have Reg. Even if everyone went away, he would still be my best friend, and we would have each other. I wouldn't be alone.

After he passed away, however, I felt vulnerable to losing friends and rejection. Sadly, one of my friends and I had a misunderstanding a little over a year after Reg passed away. It sent me right over the edge, and I was despondent for days. In my past, losing a friend would have upset me, but I wouldn't have become despondent. Now, I'm vulnerable, and losing anyone is distressing. In fact, when I lost this friend, I had to spend two sessions with my grief counselor dealing with it.

I know it makes me sound like the stereotypical crazy cat lady, but my cats make me feel more emotionally secure than pretty much any human I know. Often, I can't wait to get home to be with them. I feel loved by them. They greet me at the door and when I'm feeling so alone, they sit in my lap and remind me I'm loved. They don't talk about their spouses or tell me to move on or that I should be okay. They never tell me they are too busy for me or make me feel like a third wheel. Instead, they just love and accept me. I do, however, worry they will die. I worry the stress of losing Reg and then our fire and subsequent six-month stint in the hotel caused them enough stress that they will get sick and leave me too. Therefore, I guess even they don't provide absolute emotional security for me. Nothing does.

I don't know if a loss of physical, financial, and emotional security is common for widowed people. Maybe you've felt all three. Possibly you've felt just one. Regardless, if you've lost any security, I'm sorry. I suspect with time this will get better (at least emotional security).

Desire to Isolate Myself

My grief counselor once told me when she works with clients, she watches to make sure they don't isolate themselves too much. I understand from a clinical point of view that isolating oneself and staying in the house too often are probably not good. But I know from my experience that sometimes all I wanted—and still want—was to cocoon myself in my house, where I feel safe.

As I explained in the previous chapter, after Reg passed away, the world didn't feel emotionally safe to me. It seemed as if every time I left the house, I ran into couples. Or I would meet my friends, and they would talk about their husbands. Being around happy people just felt emotionally unsafe. It felt safer and much easier to stay in my house, where I wasn't bombarded with reminders of what I was now missing.

For example, I remember visiting a friend's house one Sunday. While I was there, her husband handed her a piece of mail and said, "Look at this." I have absolutely no idea who sent the envelope or what it was about, but I felt depressed knowing Reg will never hand me mail again and say, "Look at this." It was as if my friend and her husband were sharing a secret or some issue they had discussed, which is something I will never do with Reg again.

Then as I drove home from their house, I stopped at a stoplight by a church. It was Easter, and there was an Easter egg hunt taking place. I saw a family with a man, woman, and little girl. Again, Reg and I didn't have kids, but just seeing this family made me sad. They had an intact family and relationship. In my mind, they were just doing something routine that they did on any Easter; their life was proceeding as planned. Mine no longer was. Between watching my friend and her husband, and seeing this family at the church, I couldn't get home fast enough! As much as it makes me sound antisocial or like a crazy cat lady, I remember thinking I couldn't wait to get home to my cats. I felt as if they were also grieving Reg and understood I felt sorrow and was not okay. They would greet me at the door, sit in my lap, and expect nothing from me. They, and my house, were safe!

I remember another distinct time when I couldn't wait to get home and isolate myself. I attended a football game between the University of Colorado and Colorado State University. These teams play a rivalry game yearly, and I had attended many times. But, the first time I attended the game after Reg passed away, I felt miserable. I saw couples everywhere. I saw young couples with their lives ahead of them, and I felt envious. I observed couples who had grown old together and still get to attend the game in their old age. Everywhere I looked, I saw the life I once had and no longer get to have. I decided I'd rather be home alone than having to see the life I no longer have.

Seven months after Reg passed away, a woman I've known for years invited me to the mountains with her. She was pet sitting for her sister, who lived in a pretty isolated section of the mountains. I felt tempted but also afraid to leave my house for two or three nights. Would I survive? I used to take whatever opportunity I could to spend time in the mountains. In my past, I would have jumped immediately at this opportunity. However, I felt panicked being in the mountains without Reg and being gone from my sanctuary for so long. Ultimately, I went because this woman is an exceptionally calm, spiritual, and loving person.

I felt as if I would be emotionally safe with her. But I had to make myself go when my desire was to stay home cocooned in my safe haven.

I know I'm not the only widowed person who feels this way. I think pretty much all the ones I know have desired to isolate themselves in their houses. For example, Gina told me she stopped going to parties. She said she didn't want to listen to people's "stupid, happy lives" and listen to them complain about their biggest concerns, which were whether their children's sports teams made the playoff. I agree; when your spouse dies, hearing people's problems seems so trivial. Like her, I rarely felt like listening to people and found it easier just to isolate myself and be alone.

A year and a half after her husband passed away, Gina went to dinner with friends from out of town. They asked if she had started to date yet. She told them it took a ton of energy for her to even get herself out to dinner with them. Yes, staying isolated in the house is much easier!

Queen Victoria secluded herself for many years after Prince Albert died in 1861. In October 1863, almost two years after he died, she made her first public appearance to unveil a statue of Albert in Scotland. She didn't appear publicly in London until 1864, and she didn't personally open Parliament until the 1866 session. She pretty much didn't come out of seclusion until 1872.

My widow friend Jessica told me that winter feels easier because she can hibernate in the house and not have to see happy couples and intact families. When spring and summer roll around, that becomes more difficult. Tara told me it's easier just to stay home, and I know she pretty much only leaves her house to run errands or to do activities with her children. She has avoided most social engagements. Yet another friend, Dakota, told me even after two and a half years, she often has to force herself to visit family and friends. Their lives are the same or better than when her husband died, so she doesn't want to be around them.

I recently brought food to an acquaintance who had a transplant and needed food and help while she recovered. Her husband was her donor. When I arrived with the food, she introduced me to her husband and said they had just celebrated their 33-year anniversary. She said, "He loves me enough that he wants to spend another 33 years with me and gave me his kidney." Ouch! That was a dagger to my heart. I could not get home to my safe haven fast enough! I think I sped all the way home.

Other than being alone, I prefer to spend my time with my mom, who is not married, or other widows and widowers. They understand how difficult losing a spouse is, and they don't talk about their happy lives and spouses. I actually like to learn about their spouses, but unlike with people still married, it's not a slap in the face to hear about their spouses. When I discuss their spouses, I don't feel jealous; I don't feel it's unfair they still get to keep their husbands while mine is gone. I know they share my pain. It feels safe to be with these people. Otherwise, I often just prefer to isolate myself in my house.

Of course, the irony is sometimes we widows/widowers don't want to isolate ourselves but have no choice. Laurence told me people stopped inviting him to dinner. He and his wife used to attend dinner parties, but when she died, people stopped inviting him. I, too, have experienced that. Reg and I occasionally went to other couples' houses for a meal, and they came to our house. When I was no longer a couple, those invitations stopped. This has especially been true with his friends and coworkers. Of course, I would feel extremely awkward going to a couple's house by myself. I would struggle to engage with a couple alone when I used to engage with them as a pair. I would find it painful to have them at my house without Reg. But, it definitely hasn't escaped my notice that in addition to losing Reg, I also lost friends because I'm no longer part of a couple.

My friend Meg (who isn't a widow) told me she read an article about an 80-year-old woman whose husband passed away. The article discussed how the woman lost her friends at the same time because she was no longer invited to people's houses for dinner or parties. I understand that. I would have thought by the time you reach 80 years old, quite a few of your friends would be widows or widowers and would still invite you. But apparently not.

One of my friends told me when her dad passed away, people stopped inviting her mom to social events. She thought her mom's friends were afraid because her mom was now single and would try to steal their husbands. I don't believe that is why people don't invite me, nor did Laurence. But regardless of the reason why widows/widowers stop getting invited, I think it's relatively common. So, even when we don't want to isolate ourselves, sometimes isolation is almost forced upon us once we are no longer part of a couple.

It makes me sad that I no longer have those social opportunities, but I guess I've gotten used to it. I do my best not to isolate myself. But, I'm also careful where I go. I don't force myself to go to places where I know there is a high likelihood I will leave feeling sad and depressed. I pick and choose my social engagements.

As I said at the start of the chapter, according to my grief counselor, the desire to isolate is common for grieving people. I suspect the degree of isolation and the desire to isolate are somewhat dependent on your personality though. I was relatively social before Reg died. I spent most of my time with him, and he usually accompanied me to most dinners or social gatherings. But, I was also content just being at home with him. My personality was a combination of introvert and extrovert. Now, I'm

111

much more introverted. I've observed that my widow friends who were more introverted before the deaths have become even more introverted and isolated themselves more.

On the other hand, my extroverted widow friends have not isolated themselves as much, even immediately after their partners' deaths. They've still attended gatherings, sought interactions with friends, and had the desire to be out in the world. Depending on your personality, therefore, you may or may not relate to this chapter.

The Grocery Store Is Hell

My friend Meg told me she read an article written by a widow that talked about how hard the grocery store is after your spouse dies. I couldn't agree more, which is why I've devoted a whole chapter to the grocery store, buying food, and the changes in my eating habits.

I can distinctly remember going to the grocery store one of the first times after Reg passed away. Meg accompanied me. It was right before Reg's memorial service, and people all around me were getting sick. I didn't want to be sick for his memorial, so I headed to the grocery store to buy supplements to boost the immune system. I stood in the supplement section, where I had purchased many supplements for him, and just stared and shook my head back and forth.

Meg needed to get an item, so she walked away and said she'd be right back. I became panicked and started sobbing when she left. Her walking away and going across the store was too much for me to bear. In my past, I had gone to this store multiple times per month and often alone (Reg and I often went together). But this time, I could not handle it. I was all alone in the store! I didn't know what to do and felt totally and completely out of my league surrounded by "normal" people. It felt truly too much! Meg came back, saw me sobbing, and said, "I forgot what your world is like now." Understandably, she assumed it would be safe to leave me alone in my own grocery store. But it nearly brought me to my knees.

My first time at the grocery store wasn't the only tough time. The grocery store became difficult for me because I didn't know what to purchase for myself. For as long as I can remember, I've hated to cook and have always just made a big salad with fresh vegetables. But after Reg passed away, I couldn't do that. That was something the "old me" did. Salad was something the "old me" ate, but the "new me" couldn't even stand the idea. I couldn't just go about life as if everything was the same. Everything had changed, so how could I eat what I had eaten in my past?

Plus, I no longer had any desire to live. Salad is healthy, and these healthy and fresh vegetables made me feel like I would just extend my life longer. I didn't want to do that. So, what was I supposed to purchase when I went to the grocery store? I can distinctly remember standing in the store completely lost. I froze, as I didn't know what to buy and didn't know where to go. In fact, I often went to the grocery store and didn't know where to go or what to do.

I often just went directly to the section with the cookies and purchased cookies, which became my main food staple after Reg passed away. I had never purchased Girl Scout cookies in my life but now, seeing the girls selling their cookies at the table was—and still is—exciting for me. Skittles candy also became a main staple for me. I don't think I'd ever eaten Skittles before Reg passed away, but I practically lived on them after he died. I don't know if all the sugar was something I needed to comfort myself or if it was a way for me to try to shorten my life, or both. I know I no longer gave a shit, so why not enjoy the food I was eating?

For a long time, I avoided the produce section altogether, the section where the "old me" had purchased most of my groceries. The "new me" couldn't even go into the produce section without feeling angry, sad, or resentful. At the grocery store where

I've always shopped the most, the produce section is at the front of the store. Therefore, I would walk in, see it, and feel absolute betrayal when I saw the produce. The mushrooms in particular were distressing for me to see. In the research I'd done, I'd discovered mushrooms are supposed to be helpful in combating cancer, so I often fixed Reg food with mushrooms. When I went to the grocery store after he died and saw the mushrooms on the shelf, I almost felt hatred for them. They let me down! That whole produce section let me down! So rather than browsing in the produce section, I generally hurried through it and proceeded to other parts of the store.

I remember another time going to the grocery store and attempting to buy some prepackaged food. In my past, I had noticed the prepackaged food at Whole Foods was pretty expensive. But with Reg, we had financial stability, and I could afford to buy those things. This time, I saw the price and burst into tears. I felt an overwhelming fear that the financial security I had once known had now disappeared.

I was lucky because my friend worked at Whole Foods that day. We had become friends when one day I purchased mushroom supplements, and she was my cashier. We discovered our husbands both had cancer, and we discussed supplements to give them and different ways to treat cancer holistically. Our shared experiences resulted in our becoming friends. Her husband passed away eight months before Reg died. She still worked at my Whole Foods, so on this occasion when I was sobbing in the store about how expensive groceries are, she was there. I wheeled my cart up to her counter and lost it. I felt lucky because I had someone—an ally—there who understood what I was going through. She could give me a big hug. I don't know how I would've gotten through the grocery store that day without her.

One woman in my young widows group told me that in order to handle the grocery store, she would listen to a podcast or her music via her headphones. That way she couldn't hear anyone. She kept her head down and just got through the grocery store as quickly as she could. Jessica switched grocery stores after her husband passed away. When I heard that (long before Reg died), I found that strategy perplexing and didn't understand. Now, I understand.

As I stated in an earlier chapter, my widow friend Tara said she found the music at the grocery store difficult. In her past, she had never noticed that the store played music. But after her husband passed away, she went to the grocery store and heard songs about heartbreak, missing your spouse, or being alone. Hearing the songs made her panic. She had to get away from the songs, so she would leave her cart right where she was and leave the store.

In addition to the grocery store, the pharmacy was also a challenge for me. Toward the end of my husband's life, he had a lot of prescriptions. I had to go to the pharmacy frequently, and the pharmacy clerk knew me by name and would ask me how my husband was doing. After he passed away, I could not go near the pharmacy. In fact, if I needed any prescriptions, my mom had to go to the pharmacy for me. I think it was almost a year before I could go to the pharmacy by myself. Granted, I don't have many prescriptions, so my mom didn't have to go frequently for me, but I just couldn't handle it. The first time I went to the pharmacy by myself, I cried the whole time. My mom had told the pharmacy clerk that Reg had died, so she didn't ask me how he was doing. But, it still felt hard to see her.

It wasn't only the grocery store and pharmacy that were difficult; I also struggled with the farmers' market. During the summer, I used to shop at the farmers' market twice per month or sometimes weekly. I loved purchasing the fresh produce, especially for Reg. Frequently, I purchased vegetables and small potatoes that I later cut up and prepared; Reg grilled them on our outside grill. At the same time, I would buy ears of corn that were piled high into the back of a pickup truck at the market. Reg always did a great job grilling those. We would sit on our outside patio, eat our grilled food, and enjoy the summer evening together.

The first time I went to the farmers' market after he passed away, it was almost too much to bear. The farmers' market is in a straight line with booths on either side of a wide aisle. I walked down the center of the aisle crying pretty hard. I had on sunglasses, so I just let the tears flow. Nothing had changed; the same booths that had been there the prior year and for years before that were still there. How could those booths still be there while Reg was gone? There was a man who worked at one of the booths who always wore a Hawaiian shirt. When I went to the farmers' market for the first time, he still wore a Hawaiian shirt. How could the same man be wearing the same shirt as if nothing had changed while my whole world had changed?

The same pickup truck that held the ears of corn was in the same spot. I saw people at the truck choosing which ears of corn they wanted to purchase. I just stared and felt dumbfounded that other people got to purchase their corn while I'll probably never grill corn again. The grill was Reg's domain, not mine. Therefore, seeing these fresh vegetables, the small potatoes, and the corn showed me what I no longer have. That life has ended. The farmers' market just shoved that right in my face.

Plus, as I indicated earlier, I had no desire to live and certainly not to extend my life. So I didn't know what to purchase at the farmers' market. I didn't want fresh berries, which combat cancer. I couldn't buy the veggies I used to buy, so what was I supposed to purchase? Thankfully, Denver has a vegan bakery, and it had a booth at this farmers' market. So I purchased a vegan pastry. Perfect—sugar and nothing healthy. Welcome to your new life, Kim!

I can now go into my grocery store and that farmers' market

without crying. But honestly, it still bugs me every time, and I don't enjoy it. It reminds me of the life I used to have. I used to buy groceries for him. Now, I only buy groceries for myself. I hate that!

I realize not every widow and widower dreads the grocery store. Gina didn't mind the store and didn't understand why it was so difficult for me. However, she struggled with the pharmacy and found it uncomfortable to go there. So, perhaps you can't relate to this chapter. But if you've found it challenging to shop at your supermarket, pharmacy, famers' market, or local stores, know that you're not alone.

Loss of Empathy & Tolerance

Since Reg's death, I seemed to have lost my empathy, patience, and tolerance. I had always considered myself a caring person, and when my friends told me about their troubles, I truly cared. I couldn't always relate, but I had empathy and would listen with a loving heart. After my husband died, however, I lost my ability to feel empathy. I felt no matter what my friends grumbled about, it just didn't matter. Compared with the pain of losing a spouse, I felt whatever they moaned about was trivial and probably short lasting. In some part of my brain, I felt mildly bad for them, but I could not feel true empathy.

This was especially true immediately after Reg died. It was hard for me to even have a conversation after he died. As people talked, I just kept thinking, "Reg is dead" or "He should be here." If the people with whom I conversed were suffering—such as from a death—I could engage in conversation and was interested in what they said. Otherwise, I could not pay attention and didn't care about whatever people were saying. As they talked, what I heard was, "Blah blah blah."

Even as time went by, I didn't care. For example, one of my friends had a car accident, probably one year after Reg died. It wasn't serious, and she wasn't injured. In my past, I would have felt sorry that she had an accident. But not now. When she arrived at a group gathering and told all of us about her accident, I think I outwardly said, "I'm sorry. That stinks." But in my head,

I was thinking, "At least you have your husband. At least you have your house (this was after my house caught on fire too)." I felt sort of glad that at least someone else besides me experienced unfairness.

The summer after Reg passed away, one of my friends had her house robbed while she was at work. No doubt, this was an awful violation. But, as she told me about what the thieves stole, I thought, "I would give everything I have if I could only have Reg back." She told me how her husband had been out of town and how scared she had felt. She felt so relieved when he returned home and installed a new, stronger front door. I kept thinking, "Reg will never return home. He will never keep me safe again. He will never install a new door. I will never again know what it's like to have the safety of him sleeping beside me." I just could not have the true, full empathy for her that I would have had in my past.

Similarly, I read an article in a magazine about the cleanup one woman—with her husband—faced after Hurricane Sandy flooded her home. I imagine it would be awful to have a hurricane wipe out your house and no fun at all to clean it up afterward. But as I read the article, I could not feel much empathy. At some level I knew I should feel sorry for these people. Instead, I thought, "I would give up everything—my house and everything in it—if Reg could come back. You and your husband will do the cleanup together. You can rebuild your life together; I can't."

A little over four months after Reg passed away, I attended a gathering where I saw a couple I had not seen for many years. During the previous year, the man had experienced a heart attack and had died briefly. The woman told me it was so awful to watch her husband die. Had she told the story to anyone else at the party, she would have received full sympathy. But, I had no sympathy for her, as her husband is now fine and at a party with her. I can't remember if I actually said it or if I just thought it, but in my mind I was thinking, "Yes, I saw my husband die too. But he didn't come back alive." Rather than feeling sympathy, I felt angry her husband, who was much older than mine, got to survive while mine didn't.

Another one of my friends complained about how lonely she felt because her husband was working long hours. She often didn't see him until late at night. She told me she understood how I felt having lost Reg and that we are all the same. I wanted to scream, "It's not the same! You get to see him. You get to talk to him even if it's late. I will never see or talk to Reg again! Stop bitching and be thankful your husband is still alive." It made me mad, and I couldn't feel sorry for her. In my past, I would have felt sad this couple was struggling and would have offered a full ear. But not now. Now, I had no tolerance or empathy.

Similarly, I went to the gym one day, and two women exercised on the machines next to me. One complained her husband was working so much that he was never home. She said, "I never get to see him." I wanted to scream, "Yes you do! *I* will never, ever be able to see my husband again! You don't know what it means to never see your husband, so shut up." Of course, I said nothing. I didn't need to be the psycho lady at the gym. But, I felt annoyed with these women.

Seeing cancer survivors also challenges my ability to empathize and tolerate people. One night, I turned on the TV and watched a program called *Stand Up To Cancer*. It was a one-hour show to raise money for cancer that featured survivors and occasionally people who had passed away. Survivors held up signs that said things like, "I got married" or "I went on vacation." Sadness and grief overcame me as I watched this show. Why did these people get to survive? Why didn't Reg survive? In my past, I would have had empathy for the stress and struggles of going through cancer. I would have felt happy for these people. Instead, I felt bitter and angry.

121

I know I'm not the only widow/widower to feel this way. My widow friend Dawn says she has no tolerance for people any more. She is just stomaching her life now but has no tolerance for others. Gina also says she has no patience or empathy for people. These were loving, kind women. But not anymore. Now, they find people annoying.

Tara gets angry when the media reports on someone's death. She gets particularly angry if the media talks about a bank account or some other way to donate to the deceased person's family. When the broadcasters say the person was wonderful, Tara gets angry and has to turn off the news. She feels her husband was as great and wonderful as the deceased person featured on TV. So why doesn't the news talk about her husband? Why don't they set up a donation account for him? Why can't the media show how much he is missed? Like me, she also gets upset when the news talks about people who have survived cancer or some terrible disease or accident, and are now all better. Why did they get to survive and her husband didn't?

Along the same lines as not having tolerance or empathy, I've found it amusing to make people uncomfortable. For example, two weeks after Reg passed away, I went to the dentist. I had made my appointment six months earlier, so I kept it. The appointment was right after Thanksgiving, so my dentist asked me how my Thanksgiving was. I ignored his question and asked how his was. He kept asking me, so I finally said, "My husband died nine days before Thanksgiving, so it was truly awful." His mouth dropped opened, and he had no idea what to say. He started stuttering, "I'm so sorry." For some reason, I found this amusing. I guess if I had to be in pain, I might as well make other people uncomfortable.

I did this a few different times. A couple of my widow friends also engaged in this behavior. They told strangers and acquaintances that their husbands had passed and enjoyed watching as people struggled with what to say. Again, they were in pain but felt entertained watching people trip over their words. They couldn't tolerate people; but they enjoyed making them squirm.

During one session with my grief counselor, I asked her if I was a bitch for being so impatient and lacking empathy. She told me grieving takes a lot of energy, so grieving people get tired easily. According to her, it's common to have a lower tolerance for dealing with people and situations. She said the grief causes so much exhaustion that I didn't have the reserves to be patient and tolerant; I wasn't a bitch. Even now—years later—I still get easily annoyed with people and don't have the patience I would like to have.

Interestingly enough, I have not lost empathy all together. I have empathy for people who have lost their spouse or a child. I have empathy for people who have suffered tremendously or if life has treated them unfairly. If someone suffers a loss, I unconsciously evaluate whether to be empathetic based on how old the deceased person was at death. If someone loses a parent or spouse who was older, I don't have as much empathy as I would have if the person died younger. I feel sad for them, as I know any loss is painful. But I don't have as much empathy if the deceased person was older. My widow friend Gina does the same thing. She asks how old the deceased person was, compares the age to her husband's age when he passed away, and feels empathy only if they were young.

I also have a greater capacity for empathy when individuals have been helpful to me. For example, one of Reg's best friends was freaking out that he was turning 50. I initially felt no empathy. After all, Reg died before he got the chance to turn 50, so I couldn't feel sorry for this man. But this man had been extremely helpful to us when Reg became paralyzed. He had also helped me with getting things ready for Reg's memorial service. He had spoken and cried at the memorial service. Today, he continues to be a connection and link to Reg. I feel thankful to him, so I can have empathy for him. I felt bad he was aghast at turning 50. I could put myself in his shoes and realize that would be shocking. I actually felt empathy.

If people have suffered an unfair loss, especially of a young spouse or a child, or if they've been kind and helpful to me in my grief journey, I feel empathy for them. I want them to be happy. I don't give a shit if anyone else is happy. I don't even really care if they are unhappy or suffering. I just don't have the capacity to sincerely care about other people's lives all that much.

Have you noticed a decrease in your empathy or tolerance? Some of my widowed friends did not have this experience and still cared deeply about others. But if you've noticed a decrease in empathy, don't worry; you aren't an awful person. As I stated above, grieving takes so much energy that you likely don't have the extra reserves to tolerate people. As time moves forward, I suspect empathy will come back, and you'll have a greater capacity to care. For now, don't fret if you find that you're lacking in empathy or are easily annoyed with people.

Please Honor & Remember Him

When Reg first died, I felt fearful I would forget him. My sister died 11 years before Reg, and I felt like I couldn't (and still can't) remember her well. I don't remember our conversations or even many of the things we did together. Granted, I didn't live with her, and she wasn't part of my daily life. But I was fearful that, like my sister, I also would forget Reg. So, I wrote a list of as many memories as I could remember.

While I wrote the list of memories and can still remember them all, I hate that I can't remember our conversations now. Reg and I talked daily and shared a lot. But I can't clearly remember our conversations with much detail. I have a hard time even picturing us talking. Similarly, I hate that I can't remember his voice. Thankfully, I live in the digital age, so I have movies that have his voice in the background or even all of him. I can listen to his voice. I don't know what I would do if I lived back in the age when I couldn't do that.

In addition to fearing I will forget him, I have this fear that other people will forget about him. We didn't have children, and most of Reg's friends, as well as his entire family, live in another state. So I often feel as if I'm the only one who remembers him or who notices he is gone. I have this huge fear he will be—or he already is—forgotten.

Around six months after he passed away, the main water line between the street and our house broke. I called the plumber we had used in the past to see if he could help. I gave him Reg's name, as all documentation contained his name and not mine. I told the plumber Reg had died. The plumber told me his wife had passed away ten years earlier and his biggest fear was always that his wife would be forgotten. He had a son, yet he still felt that way. He said to me, "I remember Reg, and I will never forget him." I burst into tears. I was so thrilled to think someone understood my fear, and he was kind enough to say he would always remember my husband.

In 2016, the Denver Broncos won the Super Bowl. A man named Pat Bowlen, who has Alzheimer's disease, owns the Denver Broncos. He is still alive but can no longer manage the Broncos. When the Broncos won the Super Bowl, John Elway, the Broncos' former quarterback and now the Broncos' president of football operations, held up the Lombardi trophy and said, "This one's for Pat!" I immediately burst into tears. Similarly, the next day I drove down the highway and saw a digital sign for a plumbing company. The sign said, "This one's for Pat!" Again, I burst into tears. Why? I desperately wanted—and still want—people to do something or hold something up and say, "This one's for Reg!"

Some of my friends have done things to honor Reg. Because Reg was a vegan and animal advocate, my friend Meg honors him every week by eating vegan for one day. I can't tell you how touched and thrilled I am that she does that. Similarly, my widow friend Gina participated in a relay for cancer. Luminary bags with the names of both survivors and those who died lined the course. Gina created a bag for Reg. She sent me a photo of it, and I immediately burst into tears. I felt so thankful someone remembered him and wanted to honor him.

There is a farm sanctuary called Peaceful Prairie Farm Sanctuary about an hour away from Denver. Reg and I had done volunteer work there and donated. So after he passed away, they named the first male animal they received after him. A rooster named Reg now lives at the sanctuary. I'm so thrilled someone was willing to honor him, and I'm enthralled with this rooster. Reg was blonde and devoted to just one woman. It makes me laugh to think of his namesake, this handsome, black rooster, strutting around with a harem of hens around him.

My mom's cousin, Trisha O'Keefe, wrote a book called *Poseidon's Eye*. On the first page, her dedication reads, "To Reg and all those gentle people who loved the earth, but left it too soon, this one's for you." I'd never told her I wanted someone to say, "This one's for Reg." So when I read this dedication, I felt so touched and relieved. I actually burst into tears. If I could make the book a bestseller so everyone would see that dedication and for just a second think of my Reg, I would.

About a year after Reg died, one of his coworkers sent me an email about a comment Reg had written into his code (he was a software developer). Apparently someone at work had seen that comment and told his coworker, "[Reg] can still make me smile." That made me feel happy to know people hadn't forgotten about him. Another coworker emailed me around the same time and said Reg still occasionally came up in conversation. But I doubt that is still true. It's been a long time since anyone, besides my mom and his sister, has told me they still think about him or care.

I wish I had the finances to build a building or a memorial, or to offer a scholarship in Reg's name. Queen Victoria decided to have "numberless" memorials devoted to Albert, including a 180-foot memorial built for her beloved Albert in London. The memorial cost £120,000, which today equates to roughly £13,000,000 ($16,000,000). She also memorialized him by naming the arts and sciences building constructed in 1867 the Royal Albert Hall. Such notables as Eric Clapton, Elton John, Sting, and Paul McCartney have performed at the Royal Albert Hall. Victoria's husband can never be forgotten!

Queen Victoria also gave instructions that the public mourning for Prince Albert would be "for the longest term in modern times." Staff at the royal household couldn't appear in public out of mourning for a year. If Victoria's signature was required, the paper had to be mourning paper with the proper amount of black around the edges. She commissioned busts and statuettes of Albert to give as gifts to family and members of the household. Mourning photographs of her and her children were manufactured and sold to the public. She even framed and gave some of these photographs to friends, family, and politicians. That way, people could see and understand her grief and keep Albert alive. She didn't allow Albert to be forgotten, and she required others to mourn him as well.

Perhaps one of the world's most famous memorials to love and bereavement is the Taj Mahal, a mausoleum built for the wife of Mughal emperor Shah Jahan. After his wife died after giving birth in 1631, he commissioned the construction of the mausoleum. Constructed of white marble inlaid with precious and semi-precious stones, including jade, amethyst, and turquoise, it took two decades, 20,000 workers, and 1,000 elephants to build this memorial. Every year, roughly three million people visit India's Taj Mahal, which is one of the Seven Wonders of the World. This masterpiece demonstrates Shah Jahan's love for his wife and even to this day—400 years later—she is still remembered.

Unfortunately, I don't have the resources or power that Queen Victoria or Shah Jahan had. So even though a few people have honored or remembered Reg, I usually feel as if I'm the only one who still deeply cares about him. I don't think people realize how much I want to know that they remember him. It torments me to think maybe people no longer care or remember.

I don't know about you, but I continue as much as I can to honor and remember him, and to make sure his life mattered.

For example, one of Reg's unfulfilled wishes was to race his bicycle in a ride called the BStrong ride. It's a 70-mile bike ride to raise money for alternative treatments for cancer patients at the Boulder Community Hospital. Reg never got to do it, so I rode it in his honor. I created a jersey with his photos on the front and back. On the back, I printed "I ride for you." On the sleeve, I wrote "I love you." A photo of him riding his bike adorns the shirt's front. I was only able to ride the 24-mile ride (the race has both a 70-mile and a 24-mile ride), so my goal is still to honor him by getting in good enough shape to ride the 70-mile ride. I've also honored Reg by purchasing a tile in memory of him that is displayed at Lambeau Field, where the Green Bay Packers play their home games.

I know I'm not the only widow/widower who wants her/his spouse remembered and honored. Dakota has her husband's name tattooed across her wrist. Desiree has a huge tattoo covering the whole inside of her forearm that is a dedication to her husband and includes both of their initials inside a heart. My widower friend Brad purchased a park bench and placed it in a beautiful spot where he can sit on it and remember his wife.

I only wish I could do more. And of course, I want friends, family, and the world to remember him too!

Staying Connected to Him

I try as much as I can to stay connected to Reg, which means staying connected to the things he loved, his family, his remains, and his friends. For example, I often use his shampoo, conditioner, and soap when I take a shower. All three of them have a distinct smell and when I smell them, I can immediately see him getting out of the shower all clean. Using them makes me feel closer to him, so I especially like to use them on important days, such as our anniversary, my birthday, or his birthday.

I divided Reg's ashes into small jewelry bags. I always carry at least one or two of the bags in my hiking backpack. Sometimes when I hike in a place where he and I had hiked, I spread a little bit of his ashes in honor and memory of him. I also have a bag by my bed, a bag in my purse, and a bag in my car. If it's an important day, such as his birthday or my birthday, I carry a bag in my pocket. Basically, I take his ashes with me almost everywhere I go, so I can pretend he is by my side.

In another attempt to connect with him, I've taken up some of his hobbies and even some of his tastes. For example, I started to ride his bike after he passed away. I've donned his bike shorts, bike jerseys, bike gloves, and helmet. Unfortunately, I had to lower the bike seat because I'm much shorter. This traumatized me, as it symbolized it was no longer his bike. But riding his bike feels like a way to connect with him. I've even attempted to do a difficult ride he had enjoyed.

I also have taken up his hobby of gardening. Granted, I had helped him in the past. I helped pick out the seeds and arrange the water lines as he directed. But mostly, it was his hobby. Prior to meeting him, I never would have thought about gardening. Now, I make sure to have a garden even though I'm not the best gardener and don't truly like it all that much. I've even received gardening tools for Christmas presents because it has become such an important part of my life. Gardening makes me feel connected to him and to the life I used to have.

When Reg was alive, I was a Denver Broncos football fan. As a Denver native, I grew up watching the Broncos, suffered through their Super Bowl losses, and cheered for them. Having grown up 45 minutes from Green Bay, Reg was a lifelong, hardcore Green Bay Packers fan. The two teams rarely met since they played in different conferences. But on the rare occasion when they did, I cheered for the Broncos. He cheered for the Packers.

Now, I've become a hard-core Green Bay fan. I've even become a member of the official fan club. I don't know if Reg was a member, but now I proudly am. As I've explained elsewhere in this book, every year Reg traveled with his buddies, Dean and Dave, to a different city to see the Packers play an away game. In the summer after he passed away, I traveled to Lambeau Field, where the team plays their home games, and met Dean and his wife. We spread some of Reg's ashes on the field and had lunch in the stadium restaurant where Reg and I had eaten lunch in the past. As a side note, for one and a half seasons after we spread the ashes, the Packers didn't lose a single home game. Dean and I like to think Reg's ashes helped them to win!

Not long ago, the Packers played the Denver Broncos, so Dean and Dave traveled to Denver, and I got us tickets. Had he been alive, Reg would have gone with them. Instead, I went. I wore Reg's Green Bay sweatshirt and traveled to the stadium—where I had cheered for the Broncos many times—as an opposing fan.

I cheered for the Packers and became upset when they lost to the Broncos. A good friend of mine, who is a diehard Broncos fan, also joined us. When I yelled at a referee for what I thought was a missed call against the Broncos, she good-naturedly yelled at me. Yes, I cheered for the opposing team even in my home stadium. But that's okay, because I felt connected to Reg. I did start crying in the stadium because I felt it should have been him there instead of me.

Even now—years later—I text with Dean, who lives in Minnesota, during the games. He has always been thoughtful and consistent about texting with me although he was Reg's friend and not mine. I also often text with Reg's sister, who still lives in Wisconsin. Sometimes, I watch the Green Bay games at Reg's friends' house in Denver. These friends both knew Reg before I ever met him and can share stories about him, which I always love. So, the Packers give me an excuse to stay in contact with many of his friends and, therefore, with him.

Also, quite a lot of Green Bay fans live in Denver. Therefore, whenever I wear my Packers clothing, inevitably I pass someone who says, "Go Pack!" During the Packers home games, fans in the stadium frequently yell, "Go Pack Go!" At our house, Reg always encouraged me to join and repeat this. So when I wear my Packers clothing and hear people say "Go Pack" to me, it makes me feel connected to Reg and all those games we watched together.

I get excited when I'm able to feel connected with Reg via not only Green Bay fans, but other strangers as well. For example, one day I went to the running store to buy new tennis shoes. For some reason, the store clerk and I started talking about Wisconsin, which is where the clerk's dad lived. I asked where his dad lived, and he said, "Do you know La Crosse?" Reg went to college in La Crosse, and I had actually visited there. I got so excited to talk with someone about La Crosse! It gave me a chance to talk about Reg and the town where he and I had visited together, which made me happy.

Similarly, a month after Reg died, I bought a barbecue spatula with the Green Bay Packers logo on it for my brother. Another woman shopping at that same booth was from Wisconsin. I felt ecstatic to talk to her and bond over Wisconsin.

In addition to watching football, Reg also loved to watch bike racing, especially the Tour de France. Although I wouldn't watch every race with him, I watched most of them. If I happened to be outside or in the other room while he watched, and a horrific crash occurred, he would call me into the room to see it. I always enjoyed watching the races, but he was much more into bike racing than I was.

Now, however, I watch almost all of the races. The interesting thing is I can't even tell you at this point if I like bike racing or not. I think I do, but it's so intrinsically linked to Reg that I wouldn't even know how to figure out if I like it myself. Do I like bike racing, or do I just watch it because we always did? To me, it has become a blur between him and me. It definitely brings some consistency to my life though.

I even subscribe to *Bicycling* magazine. When I read the magazine, I think of all the bike rides he enjoyed and how he had once been a part of the cycling community. When an article discusses demanding rides with hill climbs, I have flashbacks to our discussions of his epic rides. I can see him sitting in the chair wearing his yellow jersey and black bike shorts, with his legs spread open feeling elated and completely exhausted from the ride. As I read the magazine, I remember all of this and more, and I feel connected to him. In fact, just today, I read an article about a man who rode from Oregon to Massachusetts as a tribute to his father, who had passed away two years earlier. He called that ride Leave It On The Road. As I read the article and saw the ride's name, I immediately heard Reg say, "Leave it all on the road

Kim," which are the words he repeatedly used to describe his belief in giving a ride (or any athletic endeavor) all his strength and energy.

Another way I stay connected with him is by staying connected with his family. I call his parents on their birthdays, Mother's Day, Father's Day, Reg's birthday, Christmas, New Year's, and the anniversary of his passing. He was pretty good about calling his parents on important days and since he is not here to do it, I do it. I always appreciate talking with them because it feels as if Reg is just in the other room, and I'm having a conversation with them like normal. Also, I can talk about Reg all I want. They lost a son, so I know they don't mind hearing about him, while I don't know if other people always appreciate hearing about him. Reg wasn't close to his sister, so I had actually only seen her a few times while he was alive. But she and I have become close now, and she is someone who lets me talk all about him. She visited me on my first Valentine's Day without him and again on his first birthday. So, staying connected to his family has remained critically important to me.

Similarly, I always appreciate receiving Christmas cards from his cousin and his aunt. They had always sent cards to him when he was alive, and I appreciate they have continued even after his death. It makes me feel as if I'm still part of the family, which I cherish.

Gina still travels to her in-laws' house every Thanksgiving. She and her husband had traveled there when he was alive, and the whole family would congregate. She and her son now go alone but in her mind, her in-laws are her family and always will be. It's important to her to stay connected to them, not only for her son but for herself.

Desiree is lucky because her father-in-law lives in Denver, where she lives. Therefore, she frequently talks to him and periodically has dinner with him. Despite the fact her husband is gone, her father-in-law is family, and she loves that man like her own dad. My widower friend Brad frequently has dinner with his wife's daughter and grandchildren and even spends holidays with them. I know, therefore, I'm not alone in desiring to stay connected to my spouse's family.

In addition to connecting with his friends and family, I also try to stay connected with Reg through his tastes. When Reg was alive, he constantly tried to get me to listen to his music. I told him it was boring and refused. As I explained in another chapter, he created a funeral playlist on his iPod. I told him that was stupid because by the time he died in old age, no one would even know what an iPod was. Little did I know! This playlist consists of roughly four hours of his favorite songs. Though I refused to listen to his music before he died, I frequently listen to it now. Some of the songs have become my favorite tunes. Three of the artists on the list have come to Denver since Reg passed away, and I've gone to their concerts. This is just another way for me to stay connected to him.

Besides his musical tastes, I've found I also have tried to connect with him by picking up his beverage tastes. Reg rarely drank, but when he had beer, he drank Hefeweizen. I almost never drink, but on the few occasions where I've had a beer since he died, I've drunk Hefeweizen. That is the beer he drank, so that is what I drink. At this point, I wouldn't even know what I would like. But I feel I understand him more and am more connected to him if I drink what he drank.

Similarly, I've always been someone who counts calories and worries about what I eat. After Reg passed away, however, I tried to do what he would do, which was to eat and enjoy in moderation. For example, I went to an Oktoberfest with Gina and had a Bavarian pretzel because I figured he would've gotten one. Maybe I would've had a bite of his in the past, but I likely wouldn't have gotten my own. This time, I did.

My widow friend Dakota says it's important to her to stay connected to her husband. According to her, her husband does not love her if they become disconnected. Therefore, she wants to stay connected to him until she gets there (meaning the other side or heaven). She even signs birthday cards from her and her husband, and she was touched when her daughter gave her a family photo and inscribed it to both her and her husband.

I realize some widowed people don't have this instinct to stay connected. For some, staying connected may cause the grief to linger longer. Our society often frowns upon staying connected. But for me, staying connected is one way I've survived and been able to handle the grief. Whatever you decide—to stay connected or not—remember that it's your choice; friends, family, and society do not know what is best for your grieving process.

Trying to Be Like Him

Since Reg passed away, it's almost as if I want to become him. I often desire to do things like he did and adopt his likes, dislikes, and standards (which were generally higher than mine). If I don't do this, I feel as though he will disappear completely. But, it's stressful trying to be him. We had different skill sets, so trying to stand in for him has proved tricky.

For example, I started obsessing about the weeds in the garden, which didn't bother me in the past. They always bothered him though. I know Jessica has felt the same way. For example, her husband made sure the grass looked pristine and mowed it frequently. After he died, she continued to mow the lawn as much as he did, even though she had never cared about the lawn before. She felt that keeping this standard had been important to him, so she had to maintain it. Otherwise, who would uphold those principles? If she didn't uphold them, it felt as though he would disappear completely. She couldn't stand the thought of that happening, so she worked hard to do the things he did, such as mowing the grass frequently.

In addition to fixating on weeds during the summer, Reg also would open the windows at night and run the attic fan. This way, we could cool the house down and minimize electricity needed to run the air conditioning. As an environmentalist, he was obsessed with this, whereas I paid no attention. But now, I do everything I can to cool the house down before I go to bed, so I can minimize the use of electricity—just like him. Similarly, he kept the heat down in the winter, and we always piled under a blanket. I hated having the house so cold, though as an environmentalist I appreciated it. Now, I also keep the house cold in the winter and try to use blankets to stay warm.

I started saying words I'd never used in the past but that he used, such as the British word "wanker." ("Wanker" is a word some British use for "jerk" or a contemptible person.) I crack jokes that I would have never spoken in my past. Sometimes I'm amazed at the words that come out of my mouth and know it is his influence on me. I think my sense of humor has turned a little more dark and dry—just like his. Yes, sometimes it feels as if I've turned into him or have at least tried. Somehow, I think if I turn into him, he will still be here. If I turn into him, I can validate him and show his opinions, thoughts, and tastes were important. It gives me a way to understand him more and to show his life mattered. I'm sure you've heard the phrase "What would Jesus do?" To a certain extent, my phrase has become "What would Reg do?"

Queen Victoria seemed to think the same way. Before she signed official documents, people often observed her looking at Albert's marble bust and asking him if he approved. She often talked aloud to him on an issue or tried to remember what Albert had said on a particular subject to get insight.[iv] In a letter to her uncle, she declared:

> "I'm also anxious to repeat one thing, and *that one* is *my firm* resolve, my *irrevocable decision*, viz. that *his* wishes—*his* plans—about everything, *his* views about *every* thing are to be *my* law! And *no human power* will make me swerve from *what he* decided and wished . . . I live *on* with him, for him; in fact, I'm only *outwardly* separated from him, and *only* for a *time*."

My friend Gina said she often uses words and quotes her husband had used. Like me, Gina and Jessica both want a way to connect with their husbands, make what was important to them matter, and ensure they are not forgotten.

I don't know about my friends, but as I stated earlier, sometimes it almost feels as if I have to consciously *choose* to be myself. But as I stated earlier, I think if I turn into him, maybe he will still be here. My grief counselor assured me I wasn't alone; that is part of the grief process. However, don't worry if you haven't felt this way—as if you want to turn into your spouse. Many of my widowed friends haven't had this experience.

I Miss the Little Things

I saw a magnet after Reg died that said, "I'd rather do nothing with you than anything with someone else." That is so true! Even nothing with him meant conversation, companionship, love, and not being alone. That magnet is exactly how I feel. I miss hanging out with him. I desperately miss the little things, the things I thought nothing of and took for granted.

I would kill to just sit with him and watch football. I didn't always do that when he was alive. Now, I watch football religiously to feel connected to him. I wish he were sitting on the couch enjoying games with me, which is true for the television in general. We often would settle next to each other on the couch and watch TV (usually with the cats). As Reg would say, we would "let the cable wash over us." I miss this activity with him. I miss discussing the shows with him. Many people would say watching TV is a waste of time, but I miss doing this with him terribly.

Another little thing I miss is going to the grocery store with Reg. Our house is located a few blocks from a Whole Foods store. We used to walk to the store two to three times per week. One of us would need an item, so we would both go to the store. We had a little canvas bag that fit in the pocket. He always carried it, and we would head off to the store talking the whole way. It was such a banal experience. Neither one of us ever thought anything of it. It's just what we did. Now, it is still hard for me to even enter that store, let alone walk by myself to it. The store is still only a few blocks away, but somehow walking there is not the same. It now feels lonely.

Similarly, I miss going to Home Depot with him. That was a humdrum activity we occasionally did. I would go to be with him and had no idea what I was doing at the store. I would just follow him. Now, I've gone to Home Depot so many times without him, and every time I miss having him there. I feel out of my element there; it was acceptable for me to be clueless when I accompanied Reg. Now, I'm tasked with figuring out where to go and what to purchase. Plus, my Home Depot typically is filled with men, and seeing all of them reminds me of what I've lost.

I miss going to free concerts in the park. In Denver, the Denver Municipal Band plays free concerts in the local park on summer nights. We would pack up our picnic dinners and walk to the park almost every Sunday. It was sort of a dull thing to do, and it wasn't necessarily music I liked, but boy do I miss it.

Similarly, since Reg passed away, many rock bands have come to town that I wanted to see. In my past, he would always go to concerts with me. There was never any question, as we understood that if one of us wanted to do something, we were each other's automatic date. Now, I rarely go to concerts because it feels as if I have no one to go with me. Most of my friends have young kids or busy lives. My automatic date is gone.

Although we didn't do it often, a few times we sat on the couch and worked on a crossword puzzle together. I rarely knew many answers and largely depended on Reg to solve them. After he passed away, I found an old newspaper with a crossword puzzle, so I decided to sit outside and pretend he was with me doing it. It was depressing. I couldn't depend on him for the answers, and I was 100 percent responsible for it. Mostly, what I missed was the comfortable relaxation of hanging out and doing an activity together. Every winter, we also did a big (500- or 1000-piece) jigsaw puzzle together. To feel connected to him, I've continued to complete one every winter, but I dislike doing it alone!

After our spouses passed away, my widower friend Laurence and I went to IKEA and coincidentally saw two of his friends there eating ice cream cones. IKEA is not where I would want to go for dessert, but I felt so jealous seeing this couple sitting there together eating their cones. It wasn't an extravagant date or a big deal. It was only ice cream at IKEA. But that's the kind of activity Reg and I would have done together. I miss being with him, just hanging out with him like that.

I miss sleeping with the windows open in summer. When Reg was alive, we had the windows open every night to cool down the house. Although the bedroom is on the first floor, I always felt secure with the windows open when he was here. I took that for granted. Now, I don't feel safe leaving the windows open, so I'm no longer able to cool the house naturally.

Another seemingly small thing I miss is being able to talk with him. Before, I could ask Reg's opinion on anything. I could share my successes with him. I could share my stresses with him. I could gossip with him. I took for granted I could talk to him whenever I wanted. Now, I cannot talk to him. I cannot ask his opinions. I cannot share my fears and angers or my successes. I cannot gossip with him. So many times I've thought, "Wait until I tell Reg." My widow friend Rachel said when something good happens, she finds herself turning to tell her husband. Sadly, she then realizes he isn't there.

After Reg passed away, his friend's ex-wife remarried. I wanted so desperately to ask Reg's opinion about it. I knew he would have an opinion and hated I couldn't ask him. Plus, none of my friends knew his friend or the ex-wife, so I had no one to talk to about it. Yes, I know gossip is bad, but I certainly miss being able to gossip with him. It often feels as if my opinions are stuck in my head. He was an outlet for them before, and now they just float around in my head with nowhere to go.

I miss hearing his jokes and his making me laugh. Reg was a funny guy and made me laugh all the time. I loved his sense of humor. Sometimes, I rolled my eyes at his jokes and thought they were stupid. What I wouldn't do to hear him joke again and have him make me laugh. Though I often used to roll my eyes, I would kill to hear him just one more time.

I also miss the inside jokes we had. I miss the things only he and I knew. For example, we had this quirky habit where we took our index fingers and pulled down on the skin under our eyes. I don't know how we started doing that or why. But it became a secret symbol or greeting between us. For example, we would be at a party across the room from each other. One of us would pull on the eye, secretly saying "hi," or secretly saying "I love you." It was something only we knew. It was ours. Now, there is no one who remembers that but me.

It's the same with our memories. I am the only one who remembers them. If I can't recollect something (for example, how or why we started our secret eye-pull), I can't ask him. My memory isn't always that great. He would have remembered. So, I often feel as if half of my brain and half of my memory died when he died. I hate that I can't ask him for clarification on our memories. Why did we do that? How did we end up there? When were we there? Those are questions he can no longer answer or help me recall. I hate that I am the only one holding the key to the vault of our shared memories. I miss being able to ask him about them or sharing them with him.

I miss the random kisses and hugs. We often leaned over and gave each other a quick kiss. It was no big deal, just a little kiss. But I miss those tremendously. I also used to sit in his lap frequently, especially in his office chair, as we chatted. I even got to the point where I did not worry whether my weight was hurting his lap. I enjoyed sitting in his lap, and I miss that terribly.

The most mundane thing I miss is knowing he is there. I'm a pretty chatty person, so there weren't often long stretches of time when we didn't talk. But I miss having him there even when we weren't talking or doing something. I miss his companionship. I miss his physical presence near me. After he passed away, I had a dream where we were reading together. We didn't talk but were sitting there as companions engrossed in our books. I miss those days when that experience was real! I just miss him!

Institutions Just Want to Erase Him

In our society, institutions don't care that you have lost your spouse or have an attachment to your spouse. They care about efficiency, clarity, and up-to-date databases. A long time ago, I worked for a database marketing company. We sold lists of names to companies for direct marketing purposes, such as catalogs. Every quarter, we obtained a list of people who had died, so we could ensure they no longer received catalogs. I distinctly remember thinking that was a brilliant idea. A company wouldn't want to purchase names of deceased people since they no longer make purchases. It made absolute sense to me to have up-to-date databases. But, that was before my husband died. When he passed away, it distressed me that companies wiped him out of databases and that institutions just wanted to erase him.

Reg and I had a joint bank account but also separate bank accounts. We had all the paperwork set up so that if he passed away, his bank account would transfer automatically to me. A couple of months after he died, I went to the bank to transfer his account into my name. The banker assisting me said he had to close the account, give me a check, and then I could deposit the money in my bank account. I panicked and said, "No no! It's supposed to just transfer into my name. His account is not supposed to be closed." He told me by law, he had to close my husband's account. He couldn't just transfer the amount to me.

I immediately burst into tears and said that would erase Reg. That would be like saying he never had an account, as if he didn't exist. It felt like another way the door on his life was closing, and he would just cease to exist. Soon there won't be any legal proof he ever existed. Closing his account felt so final to me. I didn't want him erased!

I was lucky because the banker could see my distress. He handed Reg's death certificate back to me and said, "I'm going to pretend like I never saw this because I would have to close his account. When you're ready, you come back in and we'll close the account." I didn't end up closing it until April 15, the day I filed our taxes. I worried the IRS would somehow inform the bank that Reg had passed away. I didn't want the IRS or the bank closing the account on me. I wanted to do that myself. So ultimately I did close it, but that was five months after my husband passed away. It was still extremely difficult for me, and I hated that I had to erase that account as if it never existed.

My widower friend Laurence said when he closed his wife's bank account five months after she passed away, it was harder than he thought it would be. He also became overwhelmed with tremendous sadness and grief when he tore up his wife's checks seven months after she died. There was something so final—and therefore so painful—about closing the bank account and ripping up the checks.

My friend Tara had an awful experience with her bank, which just wanted to erase her husband and seemed to have no compassion for her. When she told the bank her husband had died, the bank representative assured her she could keep their joint account. With that assurance, Tara arranged to have her husband's pension and Social Security checks deposited in that account.

But then the bank closed it. In the meantime, Tara had written out checks and paid her bills with that account. Although it was supposed to receive electronic deposits, the bank was no longer willing to honor those transactions, and it froze the money. Of course, the checks she had written bounced since the account could not receive the deposits. Poor Tara became distraught. She called and yelled, but the bank—an institution—refused to help or change anything. This would be a stressful situation under normal circumstances. But dealing with this after losing her spouse made Tara despondent, traumatized, and stressed. The bank just wanted to erase him; there was no consideration for the pain and suffering it caused her.

For me, filing taxes was another blow. The first year, I filed our taxes jointly, as Reg was alive for most of the year. However, the next year, I had to file as a single person. To the IRS, Reg no longer existed, and I was no longer married. Reg hated having to do taxes and would complain about it. But the thought that he would never file taxes again upset me tremendously.

Similarly, I felt sad the first time I received election information in the mail. Colorado mails election information to provide details on amendment proposals and other issues up for a vote. Previously, the information packet was addressed to both of us. Now, it's addressed only to me. Here in Colorado, we do our elections via mail-in ballot. It was disturbing when I got my ballot, and none arrived for him. Again, I know it's efficient and necessary to have databases up-to-date, but I still hated to see he was no longer in the database or that he was filed somewhere in an archive of dead people.

Although things have changed with the bank, the IRS, and the elections, I've kept many things still in his name (basically the things I can control). A lawyer told me I should take his name off the title of the house. But, I cannot bear to do that. He purchased the house, not me. I know logically I'm now the sole owner of this house. But emotionally, I can't stand the thought of only my name on the title. I want to feel as if he still takes care of me. We are still a couple that way. Kim Murdock living alone is just a sad, single widow whom no one loves and who is alone. (I know the reality is I have friends and family who love me deeply, but emotionally, this is how I feel). With both our names on the title, we are a couple who love each other. I'm not alone.

Plus, with the internet these days, anyone can look up a street address to see who lives in the house. While I doubt there are deranged people, especially men, looking up addresses and targeting single women in their houses, I still feel safer having Reg's name on the title. That way, it looks as if a man lives here versus a single woman. This makes me feel physically safer; it makes me feel less likely to be robbed or attacked.

I've also kept the utilities in his name. My grandmother had my grandfather's name on her telephone for almost 30 years after he died. So I can too! Sometimes it gets a little complicated, as the companies (such as the cable provider or utility company) insist on talking to the person on the account, who is clearly male. I've called up and said I'm him or had my brother call and pretend to be my husband. Again, I can't stand the idea of taking Reg's name off everything and putting mine on there, as if he never existed. Institutions may want to wipe him out, but I cannot.

Dakota has done the same thing. All the utilities and the mortgage are still in her husband's name. She has even asked her son to call the public service company and pretend to be her husband, so he could authorize her on the account. For some reason, unlike my bank, her bank didn't insist on taking her husband's name off the accounts. So, she ordered checks with her husband's name on them—more than two years after he died.

I read a blog by a woman whose mother had died. She lived in England and described how English citizens have to bring their deceased loved one's driver's license into a government office, and it's destroyed right in front of them. I understand why the law would want that, as that way no one can steal that identity. But, I can't imagine how traumatic it would be to watch someone cut up Reg's driver's license. I'm thankful we don't do that here. But even though we don't do that in the United States (or at least in Colorado), it still feels as if institutions are systematically erasing Reg from the earth. If I had it my way, his name would stay on everything and in all databases. I hate that he is being erased!

I realize not every widow or widower feels this way. Some of my friends took their spouses' names off the mortgage, utilities, and accounts. Some, like me, have not. Again, we're all different.

The Dreaded Paperwork

After her husband died, my friend Gina wanted to start a nonprofit to help widows and widowers deal with the mountains of paperwork and financial issues that need to be handled after a spouse's death. My friend Tara became massively overwhelmed and almost despondent trying to deal with the financial necessities and paperwork after her husband died. Because of these two women, I realized this book needed to include a chapter on the headaches and nightmares of dealing with all the paperwork and financial matters. No, not because I know how to help you or can offer any advice. Rather, so you know once again you're not alone.

The amount of paperwork surviving spouses need to handle depends on their age, assets, whether they had arranged things before the death, whether they have children, or any number of other things. One form every widowed person I know had to deal with, regardless of assets or age, was filling out the paperwork for the death certificate. As I explained in another chapter, that was a heartbreaking and surreal experience for me. I remember trying to guess how many copies of the certificate I would need because the state charged per certificate. What would happen if I ran out? Could I get more? It wasn't high math, but it overwhelmed me.

As I explained in the previous chapter, Reg had filled out paperwork to transfer his bank account to me upon death. He also had a will, though I've discovered since his passing that having a will isn't always enough. Because I was only 42 years old and we didn't have children, I didn't think I qualified for his Social Security. So in many respects, my experience with paperwork and all the legal matters wasn't that bad, at least compared with a few of my widow friends. But even for me, it was still a crushing experience.

Social Security offers all widows and widowers a lump sum of money, which I believe was $250 when Reg passed away. Not wanting to pass on any money, I decided to fill out the paperwork to obtain it. Then I had to wait at least a month or two until I could get an appointment at the Social Security office. When I arrived there, I expected to see a room full of 80-year-old women. But I didn't. I saw a wide variety of people. I handed the paperwork to the woman with whom I met and told her my husband passed away. Then, of course, the tears began to flow.

She told me that because Reg had become paralyzed and unable to work, I could receive retroactive Social Security for the time he became disabled until the time he passed away. I was so relieved by this, as I felt concerned about money. Then she called me about a week later and told me she was wrong; I needed to fill out that paperwork within three months of his death. Three months! I was just trying to survive at three months. How in the world did Social Security expect me to fill out an application? I had no desire to live, let alone fill out an application. But that's the thing about these institutions, Social Security included; they don't care you're grieving and in tremendous pain. They have a job to do and want you to fill out the paperwork immediately.

Needless to say, I didn't get that retroactive money, which was disappointing. I was told that when I turn 60, I could receive Reg's Social Security. Until then, I was out of luck.

My experience with Social Security was nothing compared to Tara's experience. She is old enough to receive her husband's

Social Security and, like Reg, her husband had become disabled and qualified for Social Security disability. The Social Security office told her she had to fill out the information online. She filled out the application on the website's first page, but when she tried to go to the second page, the computer wouldn't let her proceed. She tried for a whole week and finally called Social Security out of desperation. It turns out she needed a different website to finish the application process. Thankfully, she finally figured it out and completed the paperwork, but she cried for a full week about it.

Because I didn't have to fill out this paperwork, I don't have a similar experience. But I do know grieving people, including me, get overwhelmed easily. I would only attempt to complete or even start one thing per day. Any more than that, and I couldn't handle it. Honestly, I could hardly handle one small thing. Unfortunately, though, banks, Social Security, and other institutions don't understand or care how difficult filling out paperwork is; they don't care or understand it needs to be simple for grieving people.

Tara's husband was competent and comfortable with computers, while she is not. So this experience was overwhelming and frustrating, and it also once again showed how her husband could no longer assist her. Also, this paperwork, like all the other paperwork surviving spouses have to fill out, is symbolic that our spouses are truly gone; every little reminder of that is extremely painful. Every time I had to fill out paperwork, it brought home the reality that Reg was truly gone. I'm sure Tara felt the same way.

Many of the widows I know not only had to deal with Social Security but also with their spouses' companies. Gina had to call the company to transfer her husband's pension to her. Of course, she had to fill out forms. The company sent her the incorrect forms the first time. The second time she received the forms, she forgot to write her name on one form. So while she was already overwhelmed, she had to fill out the paperwork yet again. I'm sure if she hadn't been in the midst of grief, she would have completed the paperwork properly. But, I'm not surprised she messed it up, as paperwork after you lose your spouse is overwhelming.

Tara also had to call her husband's company to arrange benefits from the company's human resources (HR) department. I also had to interact with Reg's company to transfer his 401(k) to me. Thankfully, the HR representative had known Reg personally and was kind to me, but I still felt uncomfortable having to call, especially because I knew I would likely cry. She treated me with compassion and said to call her anytime if I needed more help. As uncomfortable as that was, I can only imagine how it feels to deal with an HR department that doesn't know the person who died, which is what Tara encountered.

Of course, for me, receiving the 401(k) was heartbreaking. Reg had socked money away so that someday he could retire. I hate that he never got to retire! While at some level I feel thankful I'll have that money when I retire, I wish we'd just taken that money and traveled and enjoyed life more when he was alive. I wish we had "retired" for a few years and played.

Thankfully, Reg had already listed me as a beneficiary on his 401(k). So transferring it was relatively easy. I could not keep it where it was, though, because that was for company employees only. Therefore, I had to move it and open a new account. When I set up the new account, the representative asked me if I wanted the same setup Reg had. I remember feeling overwhelmed trying to figure that out. Should I keep it all the same? Reg hadn't looked at it for years, so maybe things had changed. It ultimately became too much for me to handle, so I made no changes and chose the same kind of account he had.

Gina's husband had forgotten to put her name as the beneficiary, and one of her husband's 401(k) advisors told her she had to go to probate court. She started that process, which ended up being unnecessary because she didn't need probate after all. But in her grief, she blindly followed the advice given to her even though it was wrong. Subsequently, she had to make numerous phone calls to get the correct information. Like Tara, who had to call frequently for her husband's pension forms, having to call many times on her husband's 401(k) devastated Gina. Each time she had to call, it exhausted her. Also, her brain was in such a fog—a grief fog—that she could not comprehend the paperwork she had to complete. She said in the midst of filling out the paperwork, she exclaimed, "What do they want from me!?" Then someone explained she just needed to fill out her name and sign the paperwork. No, not much was technically needed from her, but she became massively overwhelmed.

A few of my friends received life insurance. While they all felt grateful to receive the money, it wasn't without pain. Somehow it felt like blood money, or as if something decent came out of the death, which is an awful way to feel. Since their husbands had passed anyway, would they rather have received the money than not received the money? Of course! But it wasn't without guilt or ugly feelings. They have said they would give up the life insurance in a second if they could just have their husbands back. Plus, I know for at least two of my friends, figuring out what to do with the money was challenging. They were not in the right state of mind to interview or even find financial advisors. Yet, that was one more thing they had to do. I realize if you received no life insurance, you can't relate to this and may not feel sorry for these widows. But, it was extremely trying for them.

I had a conversation with my widower friend Laurence about life insurance. He assured me that as a man, he would want his spouse to have the insurance; he would want to know he took care of her or at least helped her even in death. I don't know any widowers who received life insurance, so I don't know if these same feelings (especially guilt) apply to them. But I was glad to hear Laurence's opinion on life insurance.

A couple of my friends were able to pay off their houses after receiving life insurance. However, I know at least one still has a mortgage. When she changed the deed of her house to her name only, she feared the bank would call in the mortgage note. So far, the bank has not called in the note, but in the back of her brain, she has lived with that fear for a while. In the midst of grief, having that fear just compounds the exhaustion and overwhelm. I, too, have worried about the bank calling in the note on the mortgage, since Reg was on the mortgage, and I'm not.

Most of my friends didn't have to go to probate court. Dawn, however, did. It took her over a year to finally receive her husband's assets and cost her $10,000. Yikes! In the meantime, she had the ongoing pain of dealing with the legal system and paying a lawyer to receive what she and her husband had shared before his death. My heart broke for her.

The most difficult part of all the paperwork (life insurance, 401(k), Social Security, pensions, and more) is that we had to handle it alone. Each time we had to make a call, meet with someone, or fill out paperwork, we had to tell the person on the other end of the telephone or meeting that our spouses had died, which was agonizing to do over and over again. We had to get the proper paperwork and proof—marriage licenses, death certificates, wills, trusts, etcetera—and present them to complete strangers.

As Gina said, she had a successful career, and she knew she was capable of doing this, but she just couldn't wrap her head around it. It was just too much. She had a note on her kitchen counter reminding herself to brush her teeth every day. Her brain and emotions were so overwhelmed and grieving that she could not even remember to do that. She couldn't handle the day-to-day activities she had done her whole life. So how was she supposed to do anything as difficult as filling out paperwork?

Tara said it made her angry she had to do so much paperwork. She hated that when she should be grieving, she had to interact with strangers and "act normal." She had tremendous anxiety over the paperwork and just wanted her husband there to help her. She still resents that she had to handle so much paperwork when she just wanted to be left alone!

Perhaps by now you've already handled all of the paperwork. If so, congratulations. I know dealing with it is challenging. Maybe you actually didn't have much paperwork. If, on the other hand, you're still in the middle of the paperwork, know that you're not alone. As I stated at the start of the chapter, Gina wanted to start a nonprofit to help widows and widowers because she knows how challenging and distressing the paperwork is.

Loss of Future Together

In addition to all the other losses, I hate that I lost our future together. I realize plenty of couples get married and think they'll stay together forever, yet divorce happens even after 30 or 40 years. So, I guess I could not have guaranteed Reg and I would have grown old together. But we talked about it, and I counted on it.

We discussed what we would do on future vacations. We planned to journey around the country—maybe in an RV—and take road trips, especially to the national parks. We had even discussed a trip to Utah to hike Utah's national parks: Bryce Canyon, Arches, Zion, Capitol Reef, and Canyonlands. Unfortunately, this trip was supposed to happen in the fall when Reg's cancer returned. He wanted to bank his vacation time for chemotherapy rather than the trip. We figured we would just travel the following fall. By the following fall, however, he was paralyzed and close to death. Every time I see an advertisement for Utah's parks or hear people discuss their travel to these places, I feel bitter and sad that we never got there.

We had also planned to travel to Disneyland in Anaheim. We aimed to spend more time in Colorado's mountains and even talked about possibly retiring in the mountains. Every year, Reg's parents traveled to Florida and rented a house for April and May in a retirement community. Every April for five years, we visited for a week. We would watch the older couples dancing in the square, eating dinner at the restaurants, playing golf, and just enjoying life together. We would say, "Do you think we will ever spend a winter down here like these people?" We didn't know, but we knew we would be together.

Even before he met me, Reg diligently socked away money into his 401(k), so he could enjoy life in his mature age. That future and those plans are now gone! I will not grow old with him. I will not enjoy the fun of traveling with him or enjoying life without having to worry about work. I regret we didn't just take the funds from his 401(k) and take time off work, so we could travel and play.

Last Thanksgiving, I saw a commercial on TV with a young couple holding pilgrim salt-and-pepper shakers. The ad showed the same couple over many generations and zoomed in on them as an old couple. It made me cry. I wanted to grow old with Reg! I thought I wouldn't need to worry as I started to get wrinkles and look older. Our society doesn't look fondly on aging and especially on wrinkles. I never worried about looking old when I was married; someone loved me anyway. Now, every new wrinkle feels like another torment.

When I see older men, I often stare at them and wonder what Reg would have looked like as he aged. Would he have needed a cane? Would he have become bald? Would he have become even thinner? Or would he have gained weight? I often wonder, but I will never know.

Queen Victoria also became upset that she wouldn't age with her husband. In a letter to her uncle, she declared, "But oh! To be cut off in the prime of life—to see our pure, happy, quiet, domestic life, which *alone* enabled me to bear my *much* disliked position, cut off at forty-two—when I *had* hoped with such instinctive certainty that God never *would* part us, and would let us grow old together . . . is *too awful*, too cruel."[v]

Jessica also resents the loss of her future with her spouse. She has multiple kids. Like most parents, she and her husband had sacrificed time together to raise their children. They had not minded the sacrifice, knowing someday they could focus again on each other, go for nightly walks together, vacation alone, and reconnect as a couple. Before that time came, however, he died. Their kids were just getting to the age where they could be left alone. The future she looked forward to died when her husband died.

Now, my future just feels so bleak and sad to me. During the first Christmas after Reg passed away, I volunteered to assemble baskets with food and grooming items for the elderly. As I compiled these baskets, I wondered if I were looking at my future—being alone, having no money, and depending on strangers to bring me a gift. It felt depressing.

Who knows? Maybe I won't live that long. Maybe I'll meet someone else. I don't know, but I do know it's not the future I wanted. In an episode of a TV show I watched, a woman said to her husband, "There is no one I'd rather spend my life with." That made me cry. I chose to spend my life and future with Reg, and now I won't get that chance!

I'm sorry that you, too, lost the future with your spouse.

Alone As I Age

As I explained in the previous chapter, I grieve the loss of the future I thought I would have with Reg. In addition to the future fun times we might have had, his death robbed me of the ability to have him there to assist me as I grow old. I've had some joint issues and have seen a doctor who specializes in joint and tendon problems. Because these problems tend to happen to older people, most of the doctor's patients are older. Inevitably, I see couples at her office together. One is getting the treatment, and the other is there to drive and support the person getting treated. It makes me sad every time I go. Thankfully, because my mom is retired, she drives me and supports me. But, it's not the same as having Reg there, and what will happen when my mom dies? Then, who will drive me and who will hold my hand? It should have been Reg!

Many years ago, I had a pretty bad car accident and totaled my car. My blood sugar had dropped (I have Type 1 diabetes), and I had driven right into two signs and hit an oncoming truck—not my finest moment. Though I was almost unconscious, I called Reg. While I sat in the back of the ambulance getting sugar intravenously, I distinctly remember looking up and seeing Reg walking toward the ambulance. My hero was there to rescue me, to help me deal with the aftermath of the accident, and to take me home. I felt so incredibly relieved to see him and so happy. After he died, I realized he will never rescue me again!

The summer after his death, I misjudged a corner while riding his bike and flew off the bike, injuring myself and slashing the tire. I could not ride the bike home, but unlike the last time I needed rescuing, Reg wasn't here to assist me. It made me so sad. Thankfully, my mom came to get me, so I wasn't stranded. But when I arrived home and tried to remove my bike jersey (which was actually Reg's jersey), my arm was so banged up I could barely move it. I struggled to remove my jersey and started sobbing. Reg should've been there to help me get out of my jersey and get into the shower to clean away the debris from my skinned-up knee, arm, and face.

One day, I was at the gym and watched as an older woman on crutches and her husband entered the room. He opened the door for her and helped her on and off the bike. For me, it felt like a slap in the face because Reg can never assist me if I'm ever on crutches or in a wheelchair. In other words, I'll have to manage myself without him there helping me. I felt depressed and sad watching this couple.

Even at my current, young age, I've felt the loss of Reg's care. As a long-term Type 1 diabetic, I can't always feel when my blood sugar drops (hence the car crash described above). Reg, on the other hand, was excellent at knowing when I needed to eat. Often, he would tell me to eat; I would adamantly tell him he was incorrect and that I was fine. Sure enough, he was almost always correct. I would test my blood sugar, and I would discover my blood sugar had fallen; as he predicted, I needed to eat before I got in danger. As he was dying, I remember feeling panicked that he would no longer be here to tell me to eat. How will I know when I'm supposed to eat? In fact, the day before he died, I asked him to please continue to take care of me. I said, "Wherever you go, I assume you'll still want to take care of me." He whispered, "I will." Those were the last words he ever said to me.

In case you're wondering, I used (and still use) a medical device that alerts me to low blood sugar. Therefore, I've been fine and haven't had dangerous moments. But even though I knew this device could alert me as well as Reg could, I still felt frightened he'd no longer be here to help me. I hate that I have to deal with my medical issues alone.

Because we didn't have children, Reg would often say, "Who will take care of us in our old age?" Because he was so healthy, and I have diabetes, I was absolutely confident he would outlive me. I was sure he would care for me as I aged. Now, I ask the same question he had asked, "Who will take care of me in my old age?" One day, I assisted my nephew in purchasing an air conditioner from Home Depot. He planned to pay me back, and I told him he didn't have to do that. Instead, I jokingly (only half joking) told him to remember this generosity when I'm old and need someone to change my diapers. I was jesting, but I do worry I'll be alone some day in a nursing home withering away without my spouse.

I fear the future. I fear I'll be all alone as I deal with physical ailments, aging skin, and mental decline. As I stated in the last chapter, who knows if I will even live long enough to worry about mental decline or living in a nursing home. Maybe I will meet someone. But for now, I dread the future and am just hoping I'll be gone before my decline becomes too much to handle on my own.

I realize not every widow and widower worries about aging without their spouse. In fact, many are already older when they become widowed. Some—maybe you—have children who will care for you as you age, or you're sure you'll marry again and won't be alone. I, therefore, recognize that you may not relate to this chapter. But if you're like me and dread your future and aging without your spouse, I understand.

Don't Tell Me How I Should Feel & What I Should Do

Throughout my widowhood experience, I've found that people keep trying to tell me how I should feel, how Reg would feel, and how I should move on with my life. Nothing makes me angrier than when people who've never been a widow or widower tell me how I should feel and what I should do. I know people only care about me and think they're doing the right thing. But, it really makes me angry. Let me give you examples.

I told one of my friends (who has no experience with loss) that I don't think I'll ever be truly happy again. I may have jovial moments. Maybe I will even be happy. But I don't think I will ever be *truly* happy or joyful again. I'm at peace with that. When I told her this, she said I should use the words "may not be happy again." She said we can get stuck in negativity, and that keeps us depressed. I told her, "No. That sets up expectations that I will be happy again. I'm open to being happy again but don't expect to be." Having that acceptance is easier for me.

What I actually wanted to say was, "You don't know what this is like and can't understand, so don't tell me what to do or try to minimize this!" I know she doesn't understand, and I wouldn't have understood before Reg died either. But since she gets to go home to her husband, and her life wasn't turned upside down, she has no right to tell me how to feel. It makes me irate when she tries.

Similarly, a massage therapist asked me, "How can you bring joy into your life?" This question made me furious. How dare she tell me to bring joy in my life. I told her I can bring fun and some days of happiness, but "living joyously" is ridiculous, unattainable, and sets me up for disappointment. She said, "He wouldn't want you to not have joy." That made me angry. After our massage, she got to go home to her husband; I didn't. I know she just wanted to help, so I didn't lash out, but I felt angry.

I told another friend that one of my cats kept pooping outside the litter box. She said the cat was bored, and the energy in the house was stagnant and not moving forward. This comment, just months after Reg died, infuriated me. I wanted to say, "Fuck you. You try losing your husband and see how you do. See if your energy moves forward."

One of Reg's friends sent me an email on the anniversary of Reg's death that said, "We owe it to him to move on and to ourselves to remember him." That just pissed me off! Don't tell me to move on. I wanted to say, "When you lose your spouse, then you can tell me to move on. You try losing your spouse and see how you feel!" These types of statements enrage me!

I have another friend who told me I still have a nice life and should count my blessings. Yes, it could be a lot worse. I could have lost my home or my whole family. But in my circle of friends, who live in comfortable homes and still have their spouses by their sides, my life stinks and is painful. I wanted to say, "You sit in my place and see if you can count your blessings." My widow friend Rachel told me when people tell her to count her blessings, she visualizes herself smashing them in the throat.

I have multiple friends who told me I *choose* how I feel and how I respond. I know they just wanted to help, and I know they said it out of love. This might be something I would've said in my past. But, I'm not *choosing* to be sad. My heart feels truly broken. I've wanted to respond with, "Fuck you. You and your husband will have a nice evening in your home tonight. Until you've walked in my shoes, don't tell me I get to *choose* how I perceive things and how I feel." I had someone else tell me I was choosing to be stuck. Although I didn't do it, I wanted to smash her in the throat, just like Rachel said.

My widow friend Dawn says she hates when people say you get to choose how you perceive the loss. Really? Like me, she didn't *choose* to wake up one day and feel immense sorrow. To suggest we *choose* how we perceive the loss is unrealistic. I understand why people say that; in my past, I might have said that too. But, it's unrealistic to perceive the loss of your spouse as anything but painful and extremely sad. Maybe people like Jesus or the Dalai Lama could perceive the loss as something beneficial or okay. But for us mere mortals, that's just not realistic.

Dawn also hates when people tell her, "Everything happens for a reason." In fact, while I've wanted to tell people to fuck off upon hearing this, she has actually done it. That is awesome! She makes me proud.

Tara has a friend that tells her she should get out more often and be more social. When Tara went to a party that had many couples, she felt understandably sad and left. Her friend told her she needed to stay at the party. This non-widowed woman has her husband at home and has a nice life. So how does she know what's best for Tara? Although the woman just wanted to help, until she becomes a widow, I believe she has no right to tell Tara what Tara should do.

Dakota lies to people and tells them she is okay even though she still feels sad and despondent. She doesn't want to hear them telling her she is being negative and that she should be okay now. It hurts her when people judge her grief and make her feel as if she is wrong in grieving. Her family lectures her that she

165

is taking too long to mourn, and they often ask, "Why are you sad?" One day she asked me, "Why do people feel they can tell me to be happy and to put a time limit on my grief?" I agree! She says if her husband were here, people wouldn't treat her this way. But since he is gone, they judge her and try to make her feel wrong. Rather than deal with that, she just lies or isolates herself at home to protect herself.

In addition to telling me how I should feel, I also hate when people tell me what Reg would want. For example, the same friend who told me I can choose how to respond also told me, "Reg would not want you to suffer just because he is no longer physically here." Another woman told me life is precious, and Reg would want me to be happy and live. Another friend suggested Reg wouldn't want me to continue to be sad. I wanted to say to all of them, "Fuck you. You don't know how Reg feels. You don't know what it's like to have your whole world turned upside down."

When people try to tell me what Reg would desire and how Reg would want me to feel, I get mad. How dare people presume what he would want me to do and what he would wish for me? How dare they assume he'd want me to be happy? In truth, I know he would hate to see me suffering so much and would want me to be happy. But, I know he would understand why I'm in pain, and it angers me when other people use him to tell me what to do.

Rather than using Reg to share their feelings, I wish people would just say, "I think you should be happy and enjoy life." It seems as if they transfer their feelings onto Reg and make statements for him when he cannot defend himself or say his opinion. I want to smack people for saying what he would want. Shut the fuck up! *That's* what I want to say.

The final thing that annoys me is when people tell me I should and will date again. In fact, I've devoted a whole chapter earlier in this book to this idea. For some reason, people think it's appropriate and fine to tell me I should get into another romantic relationship. As I stated in the earlier chapter, it's possible I may date again. I just can't imagine doing it now, and I hate when people tell me I should or that Reg would want me to date again.

So why do I become livid when people tell me how to feel, that I should move on, and that Reg would want me to be okay and date? When someone says these things, I feel as if they are minimizing how I feel and undermining my emotions. I feel as if they are trying to make me wrong. I feel they are judging me. I desire to be heard and understood, not minimized and judged.

I want to tell people it feels as if I had my chest cut open, my heart yanked out and crushed into many pieces, then put back into my chest. If I had had that physical experience, would they expect me to be okay and to not be upset? Would they expect me to choose how I feel about this experience? Maybe they would. Who knows? All I know is I want to tell them if they haven't walked in my shoes, don't tell me my feelings are wrong. Don't tell me how I should feel. I will be okay when I'm damn well ready to be okay. Maybe someday I will move on. But not today. Maybe someday I will take off my wedding ring. But not today. Maybe someday I will get rid of his possessions. But not today. So leave me alone!

Perhaps you've felt the same way. Or perhaps you've had an experience similar to that of my mom's friend, whose husband recently passed away. Her husband was 95 when he died, and his wife had cared for him for many years. Though they were married for over 60 years and she loved him very much, the caregiving had become a burden. When he died, my mom's friend felt lighter and happier. Her children and grandchildren struggled with this. They wanted her to cry and show her grief. They thought her grief wasn't long enough or painful enough.

Again, each of us grieves in our own way and in our own time. I wish that society, friends, and family would honor whatever approach we take and leave us alone. I wish they wouldn't tell us how we should feel or what we should do.

Getting Rid of Belongings

As widowed people, we all face the task of getting rid of our spouses' material things, or choosing to not get rid of them. In this area, I think there is a lot of variation among widows/ widowers. For example, Tara moved her husband's clothes out of their bedroom roughly a week after he passed away. Jessica lost her husband eight years ago, and she still has not given his clothes away. So, I think this is one of those areas where probably every widow/widower is different. However, I think for all of us, it's an upsetting process regardless of when we do it.

I'm a sentimental person, so for me, getting rid of anything has been grueling. Every time I let something go, it feels like a loss all over again. Plus, getting rid of Reg's possessions makes me feel as if he is getting further and further away, and that is too much for me to bear. People tell me nothing can take the memories and material "things" don't matter. But, the "things" remind me of the memories.

The first thing I had to release was his body. He died in our bed, and the mortuary people came to get him. The hospice nurse and chaplain wanted me to release the body immediately, but I fought them and held on for a few hours. I knew when the mortuary took away his body, I would never see him again. So even though the hospice nurse called the home office and said I was going to be "difficult," I hung onto the body as long as I could. When I finally released the body, the mortuary people put

Reg on a stretcher, zipped the bag leaving only his head exposed, and placed a red rose next to his head. They wheeled the stretcher close to the front door, so I could say my final goodbye. I kissed him on the forehead and said, "Goodbye sweetie." Then I followed them out the front door and watched them wheel him to the van. I truly didn't know it was possible to feel that much pain. Letting him go brought pain I can't even begin to describe. I stood on my front porch sobbing while the hospice chaplain played a wood flute as two men rolled the stretcher along the sidewalk to take Reg away forever. In retrospect, I don't know how I was even standing.

Tara agrees that letting go of her husband's body was the most dramatic and awful experience she had. Like me, she found it impossible to say goodbye. Also, she felt protective of him and didn't know where the hospice people took him. She looked online and read a rumor that the place where they took her husband mutilated bodies. She didn't know if that was true (I doubt it was), but she completely freaked out and started looking for alternative places to transfer him. She paid $150 to transfer him and was upset the mortuary wouldn't allow her to pick him up herself. Needless to say, letting go of her husband's body traumatized her and was a huge ordeal.

The funeral flowers were the next items I had to discard. I remember this from my sister's death as well. People send flowers, but then like your loved one, those flowers die. I had dead flowers in my house for quite a long time after Reg passed away and finally made a potpourri bowl with some of the prettiest flowers. Letting go of those flowers was hard for me because they felt like a symbol of honoring him and remembering him. But then they, too, died.

Many months later, I donated Reg's dress shoes, ties, and some sweaters he never wore to a drug treatment facility for low-income people. I figured the people getting out of treatment could use some nice clothing to find a job. Although I cried, I felt okay about giving those away. Reg called ties a "noose," so I figured it would thrill him to have those ties out of his closet.

At the same time, I got rid of his Carl Sagan books and his *Dune* books. I never saw him read those, so getting rid of them didn't mess with any of my memories, but made me feel as if I was making progress. (It seems ridiculous I felt I needed to make progress.) I gave the books to one of Reg's friends, so that felt okay to me. I also got rid of his Bundt cake pans because I never saw him using those. I donated his childhood blanket to an animal organization that needs linens for newly spayed and neutered feral cats. Reg had been a big believer in helping the animal overpopulation problem and had donated to this charity. That blanket had been tucked away in the closet, and I had never even seen it, so it felt okay to give it to one of his favorite charities.

Over a year after his death, I had a quilt made from his favorite T-shirts. That's not the same as getting rid of them, but it was still tough for me to let them go into a quilt. Thankfully, the quilt looks beautiful, and I love it. One snowy, spring night, the weight of the snow on the trees made my neighbor's tree fall into my yard. It was late at night, and it caused an incredibly loud noise. It pulled the electricity box off my house and made me frightened about yet another fire. I was so freaked out that I was glad I had that quilt to crawl under and feel as if he was comforting me.

After that, I gave away a pair of bowling shoes he rarely wore. In fact, I'm not sure I ever saw him in those shoes. Letting go of those, therefore, let me feel I was doing something helpful for a good cause but without letting go of him or my memories.

Not long ago, Goodwill called my house to see if I had anything to donate. I had debated about giving away Reg's underwear, as I could use his drawer for my gym tank tops. I asked the person calling if the Goodwill accepted used underwear. She said they did and asked me if I had any to donate. I sat there for a second debating about it and then said, "No, not right now. Maybe next time." I guess for me, nothing says he is never coming home like packing up his clothes and getting rid of them. So, I've held onto anything he still wore before he died and held memories for me (other than his T-shirts).

Getting rid of Reg's car felt excruciating for me. His car was a manual, and I had never learned how to drive a stick shift. However, I couldn't bear to get rid of the car, so I tried to learn to drive it. My widower friend Laurence gave me lessons numerous times, and I actually got to the point where I could drive on the highway. But, I hated to drive it and felt scared every time. One day, I was only a couple blocks from my house when I stalled out. Traffic built up behind me, and I panicked and flooded the car. I sat in the car sobbing while all the traffic went around me. Feeling distraught, I knew I couldn't call Reg to rescue me. I had to get the damn thing started.

Ultimately, I did get it started and was able to drive home. But, I was so scared to drive it that I rarely did. I finally let practicality take over. I was paying for insurance and registration on this car while it just sat in the garage losing value with each passing day. So, I finally sold it.

When I sold it, I put it online and received at least five or six inquiries. Therefore, I had anyone who was interested meet me in the nearby high school parking lot on a Sunday morning. One of the men who showed up made a comment about how the car at least had the right license plate holder. The license plate holder said Green Bay Packers. This man was from a town in Wisconsin where one of Reg's best friends grew up and got married. I had actually been to that town!

There were enough people interested in the car that I decided to let them bid on it. The whole time, I hoped it would go to this man from Wisconsin. He wanted the car for his daughter who lived in one of the ski towns here in Colorado and loved to snowboard. Reg absolutely loved to snowboard, and he had wanted to live in the mountains at some point. So, I loved the idea of the car going to a snowboarder in the mountains. I figured Reg would love the idea too. Thankfully, that man won the bidding war.

The next day, I met him at the bank to exchange the car for the money. He wore a Green Bay Packers hat and said he told his daughter—also a Packers fan—that she must keep the license plate holder as part of the car. He arrived at the bank with his sister, who was a widow and understood how difficult this was for me. I couldn't have asked for a better scenario! It made it just a little easier to let go of the car. However, when they drove the car away, I was wracked with tears. I had so many happy memories in that car. We took that car on road trips, to visits in the mountains, to restaurants, and more. Reg was always the one to drive anytime we went anywhere, so being in that car with him had been such a big part of my life. Watching it drive away was heart-wrenching.

Other than these items, I believe I still have everything else of his. One of my friends told me she read an article about a widow who would go into her husband's closet to smell his smell and feel closer to him. Reg didn't have a smell, so I've not done that. But I periodically look at his clothes, see him wearing them, and just remember all the memories that go along with them.

Reg and I were roughly the same size. He was, of course, much taller but he was physically fit. Therefore, I can wear his clothes. In fact, for probably the first six months after he passed away, I only wore his clothes. I wore my underwear and bra but otherwise dressed in his shirts and jeans. Now, I wear his clothes on days such as my birthday, his birthday, our anniversary, or any day where I feel he absolutely needs to be there.

Before Reg passed away, he commented on how I could take

over his side of the dresser (we shared a dresser with my clothes on the left and his on the right). I think in his mind he was trying to assuage his guilt over dying. But now, although my drawers often overflow and I can use the space, I refuse to move his clothes from his side of the dresser and use it for my clothes. It feels wrong to me. I can't prove him right or make any part of his death beneficial. Similarly, his closet is in our bedroom, whereas mine is in the spare bedroom/office. His closet has a light, and mine doesn't. But I cannot get myself to switch my clothes into the better closet.

About a year after Reg died, I talked with someone who tried to get me to move my clothes into Reg's closet. He told me I needed to let go. He said he understood my hesitation, as his dad and brother had both died, and he had to release their things. Are you kidding me? I'm sure letting go of their belongings was challenging, but it's not the same as a husband's things, especially a husband who died young. This man also tried to pressure me into cashing in all the coins in Reg's change bottle. Reg kept an old milk bottle on our dresser and emptied his change into it every night. This man was convinced I should cash it all in. I almost gave into the pressure but ultimately didn't. I'm thankful I held off his pressure, as I love seeing that change bottle on the dresser.

Not only have I kept most of Reg's possessions but I also have kept them where he left them. For example, when he rode his bike to work, he had a backpack with a change of clothes and grooming items for when he arrived. I've left his backpack in his closet exactly the way he had it packed. I have a few of his shoes still by the front door. I honestly don't even notice them anymore and don't necessarily take comfort in them. But when I think about moving them, it feels like a sucker punch in my gut. So, I've just left them there. I've also kept his old report cards and

ACT scores. I just don't feel I should be the one to throw them away; that would feel as if I were throwing away his childhood.

I've also kept the food Reg grew in our garden and canned, especially the pickles and pumpkins. I periodically eat a pickle, so it still feels as if he is feeding me. At Christmas or family gatherings, I make a relish dish using his pickles and canned peppers. When we had parties in the past, Reg usually cooked all the food. By making a relish dish from food he made, I feel he is still contributing to the party. Plus, everyone loves the taste of the pickles and peppers.

In my mind, although I technically now own all of Reg's things as well as my own, I still label them as his. For example, it's still "Reg's computer" or "Reg's bike" or "Reg's desk" or anything else that was once his. For his memorial service, one of my friends helped me create a memorial video for him. She needed me to download software on his computer, and I said I couldn't. It was his computer, and I wasn't supposed to alter it. She said, "Well, it is your computer now." Wow! That was a sucker punch that hurt so much. I told her that may be true, but I wasn't ready to think of it as mine.

I know I'm not alone in struggling with getting rid of possessions or in calling items mine. Like me, Dakota still calls her husband's car "[my husband's] car." She doesn't call it her car. In fact, she still labels all of his things as "his…" and not hers. She also still has all of her husband's clothes in his drawers. Though he rarely used his tools, she has kept them. She can't stand to get rid of anything of his. Her husband even kept a glove on his car's dashboard. She has kept the glove there and will not let anyone touch it.

Not long after her husband died, Gina accidentally gave her husband's ski boots to a charity. She had thought they were her boots so felt good about donating them. After they were gone, she realized they were her husband's. She was distraught when she realized she had given away the wrong pair. Like me, she also has her husband's shoes by the door. She has packed up some of her husband's clothes because she needs the closet space. But she has not gotten rid of them. She also had a quilt made of her husband's favorite T-shirts, and she often cuddles under it.

My friend Tara had what I consider a classic widow reaction to giving away her husband's clothes. Because having her husband's clothes in the closet made her so sad, she decided she would donate them. He had many suits and dress shirts, so she wanted them to go to someone who could use them. After six months of looking for the perfect place, she found a donation center that said they would love to have the clothes. The center's address happened to be on Hooker Boulevard and was over an hour's drive from her house. When she arrived, she looked at the neighborhood, which wasn't in good shape. The donation center had a six-foot wire fence around it. She decided she could not leave these beautiful clothes at a place like that: a rundown place on Hooker Boulevard! To her, it felt as if she would be leaving her husband in a bad part of town. So, she turned around and drove home with all the clothes in her car.

The next day, she went to the Salvation Army donation center. Two nice men gently removed the clothes from her car. She told them her husband had passed away, and she wanted the clothes to have a good home. They asked her name and told her they would pray for her. She was comforted by them and left feeling sad but comfortable with her decision. She took another six months to donate more of his clothes. She still has his favorite clothes in a different closet.

Tara also has kept her husband's papers. She said he will never write anything on paper again, so she has kept those. After Jessica's husband died, she dug through the trash to get any papers with his handwriting. I've kept all of Reg's papers with his handwriting as well. I even have his work "to do" lists and a note he wrote with his order from our favorite Chinese restaurant.

On the other hand, my widower friend Laurence got rid of his wife's possessions eight months after she passed away. He decided he could no longer live in the house where they had lived, as it felt too painful. So before he moved, he gave away all of her things, and he sold their furniture. However, he kept her car. He said getting rid of the car would just be too much. In fact, I think I'm the only widowed person I know who hasn't kept the spouse's car.

In summary, what I've observed is that we widows and widowers are all different when it comes to our spouses' belongings, especially the timing and the recipients. It seems for most of us, when we decide to give something away, it is important that it goes to places that feel right, such as to our spouses' favorite charities, their friends, or places that will respect their things. Every time I've given anything away, I could only release it to a friend of his or to a charity Reg believed in or cared about.

Also, for me, if it doesn't feel 100 percent right to give a possession away, then it isn't time. Once an item is gone, I can never get it back. Reg will never wear new clothes to replace the ones I donate. I cannot create new memories with him, and many of his possessions represent old memories. So once they are gone, there is no turning back. Therefore, if I don't feel 100 percent certain I'm ready to let something go, I don't let it go no matter what anyone says to me. They may think they know what's best for me, but only I know what's best for me. And for now, keeping his things is best for me. Maybe for you, it's best to let your spouse's belongings go, and that's okay too.

People Have Disappointed & Surprised Me

Pretty much every widow I know has had the experience of feeling disappointed and saddened by their friends and family. I'm no exception. I was incredibly hurt by what I perceived as a lack of caring. As I stated in a previous chapter, the world does go on, and people do forget about you. Logically I understand other people need to move forward or they have a busy life, but it's still heart-wrenching to me how people just disappeared after Reg passed away.

It's interesting to me that the individuals who specifically went out of their way to assure me they'd be there are the ones who truly haven't been. One person actually spoke at Reg's memorial service, looked me in the eye, and said he would be there for me. I thought that meant he would check in on me. Maybe he would call; maybe he'd make sure I didn't need any help around the house. Maybe he'd invite me to dinner or invite me over to watch a lacrosse or football game. I thought I would receive some sort of communication to show me he cared. But after about a month, he never once reached out to me.

Roughly eight months later, I called him out on it and told him how much his lack of communication hurt me. He said he was sorry and said he'd just been busy. He had intended to be there for me, but life got in the way. I realize his life was jam-packed with a full-time job and family, but in the midst of my overwhelming grief, I didn't care. I felt his absence and felt tremendous pain that he said he'd be there for me but instead ignored or seemingly forgot about me. It's not that he was withdrawing due to emotional pain or sadness; he didn't withdraw because he didn't know how to handle my grief. Rather, his life was too busy while my life was shattered! This didn't sit well with me.

One of Reg's friends actually stated in an email that she was somebody who'd be there for me. She said that when everyone else went away, she'd be there. I saw her one time after Reg's memorial service and have never heard from her or seen her again.

Another person told me I could call him with questions about Reg's computer anytime. This man works with computer hardware and software and had helped me with the computer shortly after Reg passed away. But four months later, the hard drive on the computer died, and I needed advice on how to replace it. I emailed the guy and left two voicemails, but I never heard from him. I guess when he said "anytime," he meant anytime within the first month or two and not after that.

One day, a friend advised me not to reach out and request help from a mutual colleague, because the colleague was too busy and had a lot going on in her life. Are you kidding me!? I wanted to scream, "At least she still has her husband!" I didn't scream; instead, I sobbed.

For the one-year anniversary of Reg's passing, I decided to hold a commemoration party for him. I wanted everyone to be there, or at least as many people as possible, so I sent an email asking people if Saturday, November 22 would work for them. Twenty-two people said that day would work, so I set the date for November 22. Only twelve people came. Three of those people didn't even know Reg and attended just to support me or their date. Nine people actually bailed on the day of the party. I know I should be thankful for the twelve people who attended, but I was crushed by the ten who said they'd come but then didn't. I felt as if they didn't care anymore. I realize their plans changed after they said they'd attend the party. Some had relatives visit from out of town; some had family activities that day; some just said they couldn't make it but didn't give a reason. Regardless, it felt to me that their lives had gone on without Reg. They had no consideration for how much this would hurt me. All I wanted to do was honor my husband and remember him. But, their lives were too busy. I felt devastated.

I talked with a widow the other night who told me how upset she is with what she perceives as a lack of caring from the people around her. She said it feels as if they don't care about her anymore (two and a half years after her husband's death). No one ever checks on her to make sure she's okay, or they just tell her it's time to move forward. She feels wounded by this. I understand.

I think people believe if they tell us they are there for us, then that is enough. They expect us to reach out and tell them what we need or to let them know we're still here. My experience, however, is that I couldn't handle reaching out to people. I couldn't handle the possible rejection. All I wanted to do was isolate myself, so I couldn't reach out to people. I needed them to reach out to me. I don't think people understand that for widows/widowers, it's hard to reach out and say we're still in pain, we need assistance, or we just want people to say they care.

To me, all of these examples show how people become self-involved and don't give a shit. Maybe it's not fair for me to think this way, but that's how I feel. It feels as if they had— and still have—no consideration for Reg or for me. After he passed away, I unconsciously started evaluating my friends based on who helped or who cared. If they didn't reach out to me or seem to care, I pretty much took them off my friends list. I couldn't take up space in my brain for them anymore. I know at least two of my widow friends have felt the same way and done the same thing.

Other people are amazing . . .

While many people have disappointed me, other people have stepped up and been wonderful. My friend Meg has lost no one in her life. Her grandparents are dead, but she wasn't close to them. Her family dog passed away, but I think she was at college so wasn't affected that deeply. She has no experience with death. But she has been amazing. After Reg passed away, she called me every couple of days to see how I was doing. She would just listen to me talk and cry. Though she had a full-time job and two young kids, she took the time to talk with me for hours. She never told me I needed to move forward or that it was time to stop grieving. She just listened—and still does listen—to me.

My neighbor Dave has also stepped up to be a helpful friend. He is an older man who has worked in construction his whole life. Anytime I need help with my house, he helps me. He tells me what I should do and tries to teach me, so I can do things myself, such as change the filter on the furnace. He shovels my walk in the winter and mows my lawn in the summer. I know I can call him if I have an emergency.

As I said before, one day I received an email telling me not to bother someone else. I was in the car sobbing about this when I drove up to my house. My neighbor Dave was there painting my house. I had hired him to paint my house, but I forgot he would be there that day. He was meticulous and made sure to paint the house to the highest standard. It made me feel good to know someone cared. I felt such relief to know I wasn't all alone at this moment, especially after receiving that email! Someone wanted to help me and cared.

Reg's hairdresser, Nicole, also showed me great compassion after he passed away. She owns a hair salon and sent me a packet of gift certificates for manicures and pedicures. Her father had passed away in a car crash when she was young, and her mom was in her forties. Therefore, she understood my devastation. She said I needed pampering so gave me these gift certificates. I greatly appreciated this gesture and was touched!

Another woman who was exceptionally kind to me was Tami, a woman who volunteered at the animal shelter where I had volunteered. She and I trained new volunteers together, and I had been to her house once for a volunteer party. But, we weren't close or even friends. However, she made a lot of food for me after Reg passed away. This wasn't immediately after he passed away, as people tended to do. This was months later when I actually started eating again but still found the grocery store or cooking too upsetting. This is when I needed food. She also knew Reg was a Green Bay Packers fan and that I had become one as well. So, she sent me a Green Bay Packers teddy bear. When I lived in a hotel after my house fire, she brought me bags of frozen foods and other snacks I could easily eat at the hotel. I told her the fire had destroyed the poor Packers teddy bear, so she got me a new one.

About two years after Reg passed away, she also made me a Green Bay Packers fleece blanket. By two years out, I felt as if most people didn't care about me anymore. Their lives had moved on, or they assumed I was okay. But this woman still cared. She is a perfect example of compassion, kindness, and what is right in this world.

I also had a stranger show great compassion. When my house caught on fire, the firefighters released asbestos from my ceiling. My house became a hazmat zone, and I had to have asbestos abatement in my whole house. One day, I put on a hazmat suit as I was required to do, and I went into my house while the asbestos removal people were there. There was a young man who was cleaning my house. I told him my husband had passed away. A few weeks later, I once again showed up at my house, and a card in an envelope waited for me. He and his girlfriend left me a beautiful note saying how sorry they were for everything I was going through. Inside, there was a gift certificate for a massage. His girlfriend was a hairdresser so also told me I could come in to get my hair colored or cut. These are two young people who couldn't be earning much money, yet they showed me great kindness. Of course, I sobbed when I opened the card because I was so touched that people cared. I hope they have a special place in heaven someday.

My widow friend Gina said one of her friends once just casually handed her a lipstick and told her the lipstick was to make her feel pretty. Gina felt so touched by this. It was a small gesture but showed someone cared about her. She appreciated it. Gina recently told me she feels as if people think she and her child should be okay now—almost four years after her husband's death—and she's not. She said she feels people just don't care anymore, and that hurts her.

I guess all I can say to sum up this chapter is that people surprised me. I found some people disappointing and hurtful, but there were others who were angels. I hope you've had some angels; but if your friends or family have disappointed you, you aren't alone.

Wishing to Die

After Reg passed away, I lost my desire to live. The pain was so intense and all-consuming, and the future looked so bleak. Plus, I believe in life after death, so I just wanted to be reunited with Reg.

I had a doctor's appointment six weeks after Reg passed, and because I'd made that appointment six months earlier, I kept it. While I was there, the nurse took my blood pressure. It was 98/60. When I saw that, I immediately burst into tears. In my past, I was eager to tell Reg how good my blood pressure was, as he and I often competed on who was healthier. But this time when I saw my low and healthy blood pressure, all I could think was, "I'm never going to die." It was a painful realization for me.

At that same appointment, the nurse asked me what he could do for me. I said, "You can tell me how to give myself a heart attack, but that probably goes against your job description." I thought it was funny, though I was only half kidding, but he became concerned. At that same appointment, I passed on the yearly vascular tests I normally receive. I told my doctor I was declining the tests because I'd just gotten new insurance three days before that. But the truth is I didn't want to pay for any tests designed to keep me alive. During that appointment, my doctor told me I would live another 50 years, which would probably make most people happy, but it was depressing and disappointing to me.

Before Reg died, his mom and I had discussed microwaves and whether they damage your health. She said she wondered if they could cause damage if you routinely stood next to them while they worked. So for a while, I stood in front of my micro-wave while it was in use just in case it could harm my heart and cause me to die sooner.

Six months after he died, I had another appointment with my doctor. At this appointment, the doctor wanted blood work, including cholesterol. I told my doctor there was no point because if any results came back negative, I wouldn't do anything to treat it. What's the point in putting my body through blood draws or paying for lab work when I wouldn't do anything to change it? My doctor became concerned and suggested maybe I should go on antidepressants. I told him I couldn't medicate away my grief and that losing the desire to live was a common feeling for widows or anyone who's experienced a big loss. I told him this was normal, to which he replied that I should be dating.

Almost every widow and widower I've met since Reg passed away has indicated they no longer wish to live. My widow friend Dakota said she just wants to go be with her husband. As Laurence put it, he was "no longer attached to being here." I think that is a great way to put it. Neither one of us was suicidal. Neither one of us would've considered taking our lives. We just were no longer attached to being here. Sadly for me, either on his way to go or just returning home from jogging, Laurence had a massive heart attack and died. While I felt sad, angry, and shocked (and I miss him), I was also happy for him, as I knew he was ready to go.

Although she lived another 40 years after Prince Albert passed away, Queen Victoria also expressed her desire to die. In fact, soon after he died, she expected she would soon die, so she composed her will and arranged guardians for her children. She apparently wrote a letter to her daughter stating she "wanted to join what was the sunshine of her existence, the light of her life."[vi] In a condolence letter to a recent widower (written on mourning paper with thick, black edges), Victoria wrote:

> "Irreparable as his loss is how blessed to have lived together until the evening of their lives with the comfort and hope of the separation being a short one.

> "To the poor Queen this blessing so needful to her has been denied and she can only hope never to live to old age but be allowed to rejoin her beloved great and loyal husband before many years elapse."[vii]

I watched a TV show not long ago with a dad who lost his son. He said, "It's easier to die than it is to be left behind." I couldn't agree more. In fact, a few months after Reg passed away, there were widows in Russia who became suicide bombers. Don't get me wrong; I can't imagine killing innocent people or dying in a suicide bomb, nor do I approve. But for the first time, I understood why a widow would do that or at least have the desire. Becoming a widow has made almost every widow I know wish to die. These Russian women may have felt they had nothing to live for anymore; therefore, they might as well die for what they believe in and to revenge their husbands' deaths.

I do have one widow friend, Tara, who still desires to live. Her husband worked hard to ensure they could retire and enjoy life. She often wonders if all the stress he endured at work led to an earlier death. She doesn't want all of that effort—and even his death—to be for nothing, so she desires to live. Similarly, she doesn't want his Social Security to go unused because he worked so hard; she's not going to let Social Security get away with not paying anything. Although I've not felt this way, this makes a lot of sense to me.

In some ways, not caring whether I live or die has created

some freedoms in my life. For example, I've not had the dreaded PAP test or mammogram. I still wear sunscreen but don't freak out if I accidentally forget to apply it to my skin. Please understand that I'm *not* telling you to not have tests or take care of yourself; I'm just telling you what I've done. When my house caught on fire eleven months after Reg died, the firefighters released asbestos from my ceiling. Asbestos covered one of my favorite blankets. I joked that I was going to rub my face in the blanket. Surely that would take me out, right? Needless to say, I didn't do that. However, I didn't worry about walking through my house immediately after the fire, when there was asbestos and smoke all throughout the air. I did nothing to hasten my passing, but I didn't worry about the exposure.

Similarly, I went for a hike with a group of women in the fall after Reg passed away. A lightning storm was approaching, so most of the women turned around. I, however, wasn't afraid. In fact, I often joked I couldn't die if I tried, so I felt confident lightning wouldn't hit me. I even convinced two of the women to join me because I said there was no way lightning would strike me. In my past, I might have turned around and missed this beautiful hike. But with this new freedom, I wasn't concerned.

I was in the park one day when another storm happened. I stood under a huge tree with a man who exclaimed this was the worst place to stand and was a death trap. I desired to respond, "Lightning will not strike here. You're safe with me, as I know I will not die no matter how much I desire to."

During the summer after Reg died, I had an interesting experience when my friend's dog bit my face. My face became infected to the point where I couldn't move my head fully, and half of my neck turned red. I went to the doctor, who dug the abscess out of my face and administered antibiotics. It was nice to move my head again; but later that day, I sobbed because I felt

I missed my opportunity to peacefully pass away, and another opportunity wouldn't come for a long time.

My non-widowed friends become worried about me when I make these comments. But, I assure them I'm not suicidal. I have Type I diabetes, so every day I make the decision to stay alive and take my insulin. As Laurence would say, however, I'm no longer attached to being here, and I often say, "Come get me Reg. I'm ready." I would miss and worry about my cats and my family though.

Maybe I will change my mind in the future and have a desire to live fully again. But for now, I'm just plodding along and would be fine going to the other side.

Let me pause here and make sure you understand that a lack of desiring to live is not the same as actually taking my life. Based on talking with other widowed people, I believe the desire to escape the pain and join our loved ones is normal. However, my normalizing this feeling is not intended to give you permission to stop living. Please seek immediate professional help if you feel suicidal or clinically depressed.

Why Don't We Honor Grief?

As I demonstrate throughout this book, Queen Victoria mourned the loss of her husband, Prince Albert, for the remainder of her life. Her grief set an example for the British; in fact, during Victorian times (the 1800s) there was a strict mourning etiquette that dictated how long mourning should continue, what grieving people should wear, and how they should behave. It prescribed that widows should remain in deep mourning for two years. There were even manuals published to outline the guidelines. During "full mourning" (a year and a day), widows were supposed to wear only black and a weeping veil. Widowers were supposed to wear plain dark suits with black gloves and hatbands. Stationery, envelopes, and cards had to have a black border around them. Widows had to curtail their social interactions.

After the first year of deep mourning, widows entered "half mourning." During this time, they could wear jewelry, including pearls. Often, the jewelry contained hair from the deceased. After a year of "half mourning," widows' clothing could include other colors. Like Victoria, some widows remained in black for the rest of their lives.

Unlike the Victorians, I don't believe we should dictate how long a widow or widower should grieve. As I've suggested throughout this book, each of us grieves differently and takes a different amount of time. In my opinion, having formal or informal grieving etiquette is unreasonable. However, we seem to have gone to the opposite extreme. Victorian widows were allowed, and even expected, to grieve for at least two years. Victorians didn't tell each other the grief had gone on long enough. They didn't expect a widow to be social or "over the death." They didn't try to rush grieving people and tell them they should be happy again. They didn't change the subject if a grieving person discussed their deceased loved one. Instead, they were open to talking about death. They didn't pretend death doesn't exist or ignore it.

In contrast to the Victorians, I felt that people expected me to be okay after just a few months. People seemed surprised that years later, I still cried and still wanted to talk about Reg. They seemed surprised that I still missed him. As I discussed in another chapter, many friends expected me to date again and even nega-tively judged me for not dating.

The Torajan people of Indonesia serve as another example of a society that honors grief. In their culture, families keep the mummified remains of the deceased loved ones in their homes, sometimes for years. They believe the spirit is still alive in the body after death; they bring food to the deceased and talk to the bodies as if they are still alive. They discuss their deceased loved ones in the present tense (for example, "How are you today?"). Eventually, they bury the remains and have an elaborate funeral. Every few years, they have a "ceremony of cleansing corpses" or *ma'nene*. During this ceremony, they honor and love their deceased family members. They even remove the bodies from the grave to have a reunion with them. The Torajan groom the corpses, offer them cigarettes and food, change them into fresh clothes, give them access to the sun, and pose for photos with them. Essentially, the Torajan maintain a connection between the living and the dead; they still honor the deceased for decades after the deaths.

I realize this culture's rituals and beliefs are shocking to those of us in the West. But, these rituals and beliefs allow the Torajan the chance to get used to life without their loved ones. These customs lessen the grief. Society doesn't force these people to get rid of the body or "get over the death" quickly. In contrast, I was forced to allow the mortuary to take Reg away within just hours of his death. Within two hours of his death, the hospice nurse tried to bully me into releasing the body by proclaiming bugs would start eating away at Reg's body. The hospice chaplain rudely asked me if I understood Reg was dead when all I wanted to do was spend a little time with Reg's body, knowing that once they took him away, I would never see him again. Or another example is my friend Jessica. Her husband died in an accident and within four days, his funeral was over, and he was buried. He was gone before she could even process his death. The Torajan give mourners time to get used to the idea that their loved ones are dead; we don't.

In Mexico, people celebrate Día de los Muertos, or the "Day of the Dead," on November 1 and 2. During these celebrations, people honor and reconnect with deceased family members by building altars to welcome spirits back from the spirit world to the living. The altars contain offerings, including flowers, photographs of the deceased, candles, and the deceased's favorite foods and drinks. These foods and beverages help with the hunger and thirst that result from traveling from heaven back to the realm of the living. The festivities, which celebrate the lives of the deceased, feature dancing and social activities, and many people dress up as skeletons. In essence, these celebrations honor the dead and occur every year, regardless of how long the person has been dead.

In the late 1790s, a group of women in the United States organized the Society for the Relief of Poor Widows with Small Children. The organization gave support to hundreds of widows and sought work for them. I recognize that a society such as this one needed to exist in the 1790s; women didn't have opportunities to support themselves and had limited rights. Therefore, the death of a husband could leave the widow and family destitute. Today, widows can work and maybe were the breadwinners before their husbands died. Therefore, we don't need an organization specifically dedicated to widows. I mention it, however, because I believe the society shows an awareness of widowhood. It demonstrates that people cared about widows; widows weren't just left on their own. Today, despite the financial hardship that many encounter after losing a spouse, there isn't recognition of the difficulty that losing a spouse can bring—both financially and emotionally.

Unlike these other cultures, or even the United States in the 1700s, our culture seems to want to limit the bereavement period. After Reg died, I became aware of how uncomfortable our society is with death and grief. I'm not suggesting that we should have a society for widows or that we keep the bodies in our house for years. Rather, I'm questioning why we don't honor death, grief, and grieving people. Why don't we give people the space they need to mourn? Why don't we acknowledge how painful it is to lose a spouse and to keep moving forward after their death? We honor and celebrate the people who march on, who date and remarry again, and who act like they're okay. But we don't honor people who are sad, who are struggling, and who are grieving. In our society, we celebrate resiliency. On the other hand, we seem to have disdain for people who struggle.

I don't know if you have felt this way. Perhaps you're reading this chapter and thinking I'm crazy. Perhaps your inner circle and community have gathered around you and made sure you're okay. Perhaps you believe we should quickly close that chapter of our lives and move into the next. I know my friend Laurence felt that way. I completely understand. I respect that. While that hasn't been my experience, I appreciate this approach. But I also wish we would honor the grieving process and the dead.

Doing Everything & Making All Decisions Alone

I hate that I now have to do things all by myself and make all decisions by myself. Decision-making has honestly never been my strong suit. Reg, however, was skilled at it. He had the ability to foresee circumstances of decisions and feel confident in his decisions. He made almost all decisions regarding our house and took care of issues, so I never had to worry. But now, I'm entirely responsible, have to make all decisions, and take care of everything by myself, which I despise.

Some of the decisions are not even that big of a deal. For example, the light in my back patio broke, so I had to go to Home Depot to purchase a new one. If Reg were here, we would have gone together, or he would have just handled it. It would be no sweat off my back. However, this time I stood in the aisle staring at the lights in the middle of Home Depot and cried. I felt I shouldn't be at Home Depot alone doing this. I was paralyzed trying to figure out which was the best light, which would be the most environmental, which I could afford, etcetera. I felt I shouldn't have to make this decision—he should!

Other decisions are larger. For example, after my fire I had many decisions to make, such as which cleanup and storage, asbestos abatement, and contracting companies to use. Which companies would do the best job? Which companies would treat me fairly? Who would treat my house with respect? It felt so overwhelming for me that I wanted to bury my head in the sand. Also, not only was I overwhelmed with trying to decide which companies, but I was fearful they'd take advantage of me as a woman. I even asked my widower friend Laurence to be my stand-in man in dealing with the contractors. Of course, I wouldn't have needed that or even worried about being taking advantage of if Reg were here.

Even once I made those decisions and chose the companies, I then had other big decisions to make. What lights should I install? Which shower door should I choose? You have no idea how many shower doors exist in this world! It felt overwhelming to decide by myself. Also, should I add sun tunnels or skylights to the house? Reg and I had discussed adding sun tunnels to our house in the past, as our house is old and gets pretty dark. But which would be better, sun tunnels or skylights? We hadn't discussed skylights, but now I had to rebuild my ceiling, so I had the opportunity to install them if I wanted. I felt almost paralyzed trying to make this decision. I needed him to bounce the ideas off of and for him to foresee the consequences of either decision.

Of course, either decision would change the house, which would alter how it looked from when we lived in it together. This caused me angst. Thankfully, I knew he would at least approve of the sun tunnels, so that made my decision a little easier. In case you're interested, I ultimately decided to put a skylight in the living room and sun tunnels in the office. Luckily, that decision pleases me.

After her husband passed away, my friend Gina remodeled some of her house. Even though she chose to do the remodel (unlike me), she often felt overwhelmed. It pained her to make all the decisions. She desperately wanted her husband there to discuss the project and to help her with the decisions. She felt angry he wasn't there to assist her, and she kept telling me her husband should be there.

The house is not the only thing I have complete responsibility for now. I'm now entirely responsible for all decisions regarding our cats. Seven months after Reg passed away, I found a lump on my cat Rita, who was extremely close to Reg. When I found out Rita might have cancer, I was almost numb to the pain after everything I'd been through already. But then, I was brought to my knees in pain and crying.

The thing is, Reg and I had always dealt with bad news together. We had many animals who had experienced medical conditions or died, but we faced those together. When I found out Rita had a lump, all I wanted to do was turn to him, call him, hug him, or somehow have him there to comfort me and to help me. Instead, I had to take the blow myself. Reg had been in Washington DC on one of his Green Bay Packers trips when I found out one of our cats was dying of bad kidneys. I was alone when I took that blow, but then I immediately called him for comfort because he was the only other person who could share that pain with me. But this time with Rita, I was all alone with the pain.

After doing a biopsy on the lump, the vet told me she thought the lump was probably not cancer, but she couldn't be sure. Reg had two biopsies on his lump, and neither showed cancer; yet he is dead. Therefore, I decided to give Rita surgery to remove the lump. Sure enough, it was cancer. But the vet assured me she got it all, and the prognosis looked good.

Six months later, we found yet another lump and once again had it removed. It, too, was cancer. So, I was faced with the decision of what to do. Another vet—an oncology specialist—suggested I remove Rita's entire mammary chain, which is a grueling surgery. Reg had had numerous surgeries to remove his cancer, and yet it didn't work. Would it work for Rita? I alone had this huge decision to make. The consequences could be fatal to my cat if I made the incorrect decision. I felt tormented trying to decide what was best for her and for me. I couldn't stand the thought of losing her, but given what I'd learned with Reg, I wasn't convinced that putting her through a life-changing surgery would ensure the cancer never returned. I needed Reg to help me with this decision and to bounce the ideas off of, but instead I had to make it entirely alone. It felt like so much responsibility with such huge consequences—life and death consequences! Ultimately, I opted not to give her the surgery and instead put her on high-quality food and supplements targeting cancer. Knock on wood, it seemed to work, as she is still alive and healthy.

My widow friend Gina just faced this same torment. Her cat ingested a foreign object, which negatively affected his intestines. The vet told her the cat needed emergency surgery, which would cost quite a lot of money. Of course, she felt extremely upset. But it was made even worse by the fact that she could not discuss it with her husband. She was entirely responsible for the decision for her sweet cat. Also, it wouldn't have been quite as difficult with her husband here because he was the main breadwinner, so the financial consequences wouldn't have been so much. Ultimately, she decided on the surgery, and her cat now runs around the house, plays with toys, and makes her laugh. She is glad she made the decision to give her cat the surgery. But, it was hard for her to do on her own.

Jessica has told me she's tired of having to make all the decisions for not only her pets but also for her children. In the past, she and her husband made the decisions together. Now, she is entirely responsible. She said she has decision fatigue and is worn-out from having to decide everything herself, whether it's choices for the kids, the house, the animals, vacations, or just life. Gina has also expressed how she hates that she has to make all the decisions, especially for her child. Her child should have his father as a role model and instead has to grow up without his dad. Gina will now be the one who has to decide—all alone—on punishments, rewards, activities, vacations, and more. Her husband should be here to help! Tara says she hates that she cannot call her husband at work to ask him what to do. Instead, she often asks aloud, "Is this a good idea?"

And it's not just the decisions that are hard to make alone, at least for me. It's also all the *things* I now have to do alone. In my past, Reg was always here to help me. In fact, one way he showed love was to just take care of hassles for me, so I didn't have to stress. For example, if I had a problem with my computer, he immediately came to the rescue and took care of it. He set up the networking in the house and handled it if it went down or became slow. I had my own little geek squad in the house. If I could not open a jar, he opened it. If a drain got clogged, he took care of it. Basically, he did everything.

Now, the buck stops with me, and no one will rescue me. If the drain becomes clogged, I have to deal with it. When the Wi-Fi goes down, which I don't remember ever happening when Reg was alive but has happened numerous times since he died, I have to fix it. Sometimes I avoid doing something—such as fixing the Wi-Fi or putting dishes away—and then realize if I don't handle it, it won't get done. So, I begrudgingly do it.

One day I went to a friend's house to receive help with a software issue I had. Her husband is competent with computers and set up their network. I watched as he maneuvered around the network. It felt like watching Reg. It felt so nice to be at their house and watch him with the computers. I didn't need to know all the answers. I could just sit back and let someone else figure things out. Of course, it made me miss my old life so much. I used to be able to sit back and let someone else—a.k.a. Reg—figure things out; but now I can't.

Yet another example of my having to do everything was hooking up the garden hoses for the first time. Our house is old, so hooking up hoses to the outside spout can be challenging. I had never hooked up the hoses in the past, and the first time I tried to do it, I couldn't. I didn't have the strength. But again, there was no one else who could do it. I felt so powerless, helpless, and frustrated. I was determined to keep the house looking nice, however, so I kept trying until I finally accomplished the task. While this probably seems like a silly example, it represented once again how much he had done that now I have to do alone. I hate it!

Another example was my first trip to Costco. We used to have a membership, but I didn't think it made sense for me to have a membership alone. So I went to Costco with a friend one day and stocked up, filling the whole back of my car. Normally, Reg and I went together, and then he would unload all the big boxes and carry the heavy items. This time, as I drove up to my house, I knew he wouldn't be there to help me unload. I'm not suggesting that unloading boxes from Costco is that big of a deal, and I'm certainly capable of doing it myself. But knowing he wouldn't be there to help when I arrived made me sob uncontrollably. This was just one more thing I had to do alone!

Tara's husband traveled frequently for work. So unlike me, she was accustomed to making decisions and doing household tasks by herself. However, she could still call him for his input. Now, she can't. She also told me she hates driving in Colorado's mountains. Until her husband died, she'd never driven in our mountains by herself. The first time she had to do it, she didn't trust herself and became panicked and upset. I used to live in the mountains so think nothing of driving in them, unless the roads are icy. Tara didn't feel comfortable but wouldn't think anything of unloading from Costco alone or choosing new lights or any of the other responsibilities that upset me.

While the things we widows and widowers hate having to do alone are different for each of us, the emotion and pain are the same. We became used to having our spouses and now are on our own, and that hurts!

Weekends Suck

Need I say more?

Pretty much every widowed person I know doesn't like the weekends. Work, kids, or normal day-to-day living occupy the time during the week. But the weekends don't provide distractions. While I miss Reg every day, whether it's a weekday or weekend, the weekends do feel more painful. That is when we should be going out to dinner, running errands together, hiking together, gardening together, or doing any number of things. That is when we should just be hanging out together without worrying about work.

Also, I frequently see my neighbors head out on a Friday or Saturday night, which causes me enormous pain. I can't begrudge my neighbors for having fun, but their lives are such a contrast to mine that it hurts. When I sit home alone on a weeknight, I don't see other people going out to have fun. Sitting home alone on Friday or Saturday nights, however, feels more lonely and pathetic. I see couples riding their bicycles down the street on weekends and just enjoying each other's company. People are happy on weekends, and their happiness is such a contrast to my state of mind. So, I see how different I am from the rest of the world on the weekends.

Perhaps you don't feel this way. Perhaps you enjoy weekends, which definitely makes sense after a long week at work. But if you do despise weekends, you're not alone. There are millions of us in the world who loathe them.

Why? Why? Why?

Why? Why? Why? I've asked this question incessantly since Reg died. How can he be dead? We did everything right, or at least I thought we did. Reg ate a plant-based diet, which meant he ate lots of vegetables, fruits, nuts, and beans—basically the foods health experts tell you to eat. Plus, I would estimate that roughly 70 or 80 percent of the food was organic, as we didn't want to eat pesticides that could harm our health. He did eat dessert occasionally, but not all that often, so he didn't consume much sugar. In his younger years, he ate sugar. But for many years, he rarely ate sugar, which the health experts say feeds cancer.

We spent our free time hiking and walking. On his days off, Reg's favorite activities were snowboarding or going for a bicycle ride. And it wasn't an easy bike ride, as he would ride 70 miles with a 3,000-foot elevation gain. He would always tell me about the ride when he returned home, but I had never seen it myself. After he died, I drove my car up the mountain that he would ride. My car struggled due to the steepness of this mountain. I just kept thinking, "How can a man who can ride his bike up a hill that my car struggles with be dead?" I cannot understand it!

Reg probably drank a few beers per year, but otherwise he pretty much never drank. At one point, he heard red wine was healthy because of the resveratrol, so he would drink a daily glass. Even that was pretty short lived though. He didn't consume soda or drinks with sugar in them, except Gatorade on his long bike rides in order to refuel. He lived on water and green tea because green tea is supposed to be good for cancer and your health.

We used natural dishwashing soap and laundry detergent. I cleaned with white vinegar rather than the cleaning supplies that are chock-full of chemicals and can harm your health. We even purchased an organic mattress, so we would sleep on a mattress free of chemicals. We didn't use pesticides in our garden or expose ourselves to products such as Roundup or bug sprays.

Yet, he still got an aggressive cancer and died. How is this possible? I'm not suggesting that people who eat poorly or expose themselves to chemicals deserve to die or that their deaths are explainable. But I couldn't understand—and still can't—how we followed medical wisdom by living a healthy lifestyle, and yet he died. Why? Why? Why?

I asked numerous spiritual people why he died. But, no one could give me a specific reason for his death, at least one I could accept. None of them could explain why he was dead. Since I couldn't find the answer in our lifestyle or from spiritual people, I tried looking elsewhere for the answer. I read the book *When Bad Things Happen to Good People*. I was sure it would give me an answer, but it didn't. I read other books on death but still could not find my answer, which disappointed me. Maybe there is no answer, but I still want to know why.

A few months after Reg died, I drove my grandmother to the hairdresser. My grandmother was 96 years old and had dementia. She repeatedly asked me how I liked school (I hadn't attended school for almost 20 years) and kept commenting on how far we had to drive to the hairdresser. Now, I'm not suggesting I wanted my grandmother to die. But, I kept thinking, "Why does she get to live and Reg didn't?" She had expressed that she was "ready to go." Reg had expressed that he wasn't ready; yet, she got to live and he didn't. Reg's grandmother smoked her whole life and was far from the model of health. Yet, she died at 88. Why did she get lucky and he didn't?

Similarly, five days after Reg passed away, I went to a football game at the University of Colorado. My mom and I have had season tickets for almost 20 years, and while I had missed the rest of the season, I figured I might as well go to this game to try to distract myself. I remember seeing an obese man. I turned to my mom and said, "Why does that man get to live and Reg didn't?" Again, I'm not suggesting I wanted that man to die or that he didn't have a right to live. I just couldn't understand how someone who didn't appear to take care of his health got to live while Reg seemingly did everything right and had to die.

For that matter, I have Type 1 diabetes. When I was diagnosed at the age of nine, the doctors didn't think I would live a long life. Reg, on the other hand, was exceptionally healthy. He had his thyroid removed because of the cancer and had to take thyroid medication. That was the first time he'd ever taken medication. He didn't even know how to refill his prescription at the store. The first time he attempted to refill it himself, my mom coincidentally was at the store and discovered him in the incorrect line. He'd been so healthy that he was clueless. Because of his almost-perfect health and my long duration with diabetes, I absolutely knew I'd die first. I never thought I'd outlive him! Why did I live, and he didn't?

Reg was far from perfect and was definitely no saint, especially as he cussed at other drivers on the road, cursed like crazy while doing his taxes, and was sometimes judgmental; however, he was a good man. I felt as if it was a loss not only for me but also for the world, especially animals. We did hospice for dying cats, and he poured compassion and love onto those animals, so they would die feeling loved. If we went for a walk after a rainstorm and saw worms on the sidewalk who needed help, Reg picked them up and put them back in the grass. Why did this good man have to die? I thought of all the animals who would now not be saved because he died. My heart felt crushed knowing those animals no longer had him as a savior and advocate. Reg was an environmentalist, and people listened to him. In fact, that is why he became a vegan. So, I felt the earth also lost when Reg died. I kept thinking, "Why? Why? Why would you take this man away from the animals and the earth? Why?!"

It wasn't just the earth and animals that lost someone special. He was never mean to anyone. When we had elderly neighbors, he shoveled their sidewalk. He often solved complicated issues at work and was an asset for his coworkers. He was the guy coworkers turned to when they needed help. Even though assisting others took Reg away from his own work or caused him to work later, he helped his coworkers. I felt his death was a loss for them too. The day after he died, one of his coworkers emailed me and said the world had suffered a tremendous loss when he died. I couldn't agree more!

Meanwhile, there are evil people in the world who rape women, slaughter animals in inhumane ways, treat people poorly, and focus only on themselves. Why do they get to live while Reg had to die? Why? Why? Why? I want an answer! I've repeatedly wondered how Reg's death could have happened. How could we be so happy and then he was gone? Why? Why? Why?

I know I'm not the only widow who feels this way. I think almost every widow and widower I know has asked why. Dakota told me she constantly asks why. I've had many conversations with Gina and Jessica just asking, "Why? Why? Why?" One friend's husband was 11 years younger than she was. Although men typically die younger than their wives, her husband was young enough that she was sure she would die first. Like me, she never thought she would become a widow, and she also asks why. Another friend's husband died in an accident. While I don't understand why Reg got cancer, I at least understand that cancer can kill you. This woman went on vacation and came home without her husband. Why did that have to happen? How can this be explained?

I think none of us will ever get answers that satisfy us. We will likely continue to ask why. Maybe someday when we die, we will understand. But until that time, we will likely continue to be confused and question why this had to happen to our spouses and to us. If you don't question why and have learned to accept it and understand it, I commend you. I have not.

His Death Has Changed Me

Reg's death has changed me. I'm no longer the person I used to be. One day, I went for a walk with my widow friend Desiree. We talked about the ways we are different from before our husbands passed away. She said, "We will never be the same again. We can't be." Boy is that true! Below, I will try to explain the different ways I've changed since Reg passed away.

There is an underlying sadness to me now

As I've stated elsewhere in this book, I enjoyed watching a television show called *Downton Abbey*, which is a British television show popular in the United States. In the show, one of the main characters became a widow. Her dad, Lord Grantham, said a quote I love and that fits me:

> "The price of great love is great misery when one of you dies."

In my past, I definitely felt sadness. Volunteering at an animal shelter made me sad. But, I wouldn't say that sadness was part of who I was; it was just a transient emotion I felt. Now, I feel sadness is just a part of who I am and that I carry with me everywhere I go. Similarly, in my past I definitely cried. It was rare, however, and only when something was truly upsetting or sad (usually relating to animals). But now, I cry constantly. For probably at least a year and a half, I cried every single day. Now, I still cry probably two or three times per week.

Silence and spiritual music are especially prone to make me cry. When there is silence, I get emotional. For example, when I ran the Turkey Trot 4-mile race for the second time after Reg died, I felt bored and ready for the race to start as I waited at the start line. As I stood by myself and looked around at all the people, I felt okay. Then, it became quiet for the national anthem. At that point, I could feel the tears. All the chatter and energy had distracted me, but when the noise stopped, I could feel emotion.

My widower friend Bill told me he cried every single day for three years after his wife passed away. I'm clearly not alone in crying. However, I know not every widow and widower cries. Gina tells me she feels envious of how easily I cry because she has a harder time. So you may not relate to this, but for me, crying has become a part of my life. In my past, if I cried, I was likely having a bad day. Or if it had been a good day and then I cried, it probably would've turned into a rotten day. Now, crying occurs so frequently and feels like a part of me—almost like a new appendage or a new best friend—that if you asked me at the end of any given day if I had a good day, I might tell you I did. But, I still might have cried—and likely did cry—that day. It's just a part of me now. Sometimes the cries happen for only a couple of minutes, and sometimes they are snotty, full-blown sobbing fests.

The crazy thing is sometimes I don't even cry about Reg. I often cry at something on the TV or something someone says. I can't tell you the number of times I've cried during the TV show *Hawaii Five-O*. This show often has violent gunfights, so this isn't a sad program by any stretch of the imagination. But it has made me cry a few times. Why? I guess because crying and underlying sadness are just a part of who I am now. My heart has broken wide open, so I now cry at the drop of a hat.

I no longer expect to feel true joy

Recently, I talked with a man I've known for about ten years. He is a caring man and told me he wants me to be happy. I immediately felt the tears and thought, "That ship has sailed." In my past, I absolutely expected and wanted a joyous life. But now, I no longer believe my life will be truly happy again.

I know I'm not the only widow to feel this way. When Prince Albert passed away, Queen Victoria said her happy life was over. Sharon Sandberg, chief operating officer of Facebook, wrote a post thirty days after her husband's death. It was a letter on grief. She said she will feel happiness again, but she will never feel joy. That's how I feel. I have cheerful moments and won't be surprised if one day I'm happy again. But, I doubt I'll ever feel true joy again. I don't even want to feel joy. How can I without Reg? How can I when I know it can be taken away from me in a heartbeat?

I don't know what happiness even feels like anymore. I have days where I feel reasonably content. Some days that includes crying. Some days it doesn't. I no longer know what true happiness feels like.

When I reconcile myself with the idea that I won't ever be absolutely happy again, I'm at peace. I know I'll have delightful moments and enjoy myself tremendously at times. However, I no longer expect to ever be truly, truly happy again. Joy definitely feels unattainable. Recently, I listened to an interview with someone talking about how we should do things daily that bring us joy. I struggled just coming up with anything that brings me joy. I thought of things that used to bring me joy—dancing, riding the rides at Disney World, going to concerts—but I engaged in those activities with Reg. I'll never be able to participate in those activities with him again. Now, interacting with my cats or with dogs in the park brings me pleasure; but other than that, the thought of living a joyful life and spending my days doing blissful activities definitely feels unattainable. I'm not closed to the idea; I just don't see how it's possible.

I listened to another interview with a woman who said when her husband passed away, it felt as if three-fourths of her also died. She was no longer truly living; she was just existing and surviving. About a year after her husband passed away, Gina told me her life was over. I understand both women. I feel I'm in this waiting period until I reunite with Reg again (in other words, I'm waiting to die so I can join him in heaven or "the other side"). In the meantime, I just exist.

People get upset with me when I tell them I never expect to feel happy again. I understand that. People love me and want me to be joyful. But, it feels like too much pressure to try to be jovial. I've told my grief counselor I feel best when I just tell myself I'll probably never be happy again. It lets go of expectations and is easier for me than feeling the pressure to be jolly or okay.

Besides, I don't know how I could be truly joyful without Reg. I don't want to set myself up just to be heartbroken again. When I think about trying to be truly happy again, I get anxious. I feel peaceful when I think I probably won't. At this point, I need peace and not anxiety, so I'm okay with the thought that I'll never feel true, absolute happiness again.

My belief system has changed

In my early twenties, I made a list of the goals I wanted for my life, and I believed goals were always achievable. In fact, I achieved all those goals. In my late twenties and early thirties, I entered the life coaching profession. As a coach, I taught people to say affirmations, create compelling goals, and change their belief system, so they could have the life they desired. I taught that with the proper belief system, enough hard work, and persistence, you could truly have the life you wanted. I thought if you're a good person, life would treat you fairly. I thought if you treat people with kindness and care for the environment and animals, bad things wouldn't happen to you. Logically, I knew bad things could happen but thought if you're an honorable person, life would treat you fairly. I also thought prayers work, and miracles could happen.

Then Reg died. Everything I had believed went right out the window. What I had thought and taught people didn't work. Reg said daily affirmations or at least looked at them. We worked on changing his belief system, so he believed he could cure himself of cancer. He had shoveled snow for the elderly neighbors. He was the guy at work whom everyone asked for assistance, and he always helped them. He had treated people with fairness and respect. We volunteered at the animal shelter, and we did hospice for dying cats. We once had a cat with advanced kidney disease who could no longer use the litter box. Reg allowed her to sit on towels piled in his lap. She would pee on the towel, and he would lift her up. He would change out the towel and put her back in his lap. He was that caring, compassionate, and loving.

Yet, he died. He was a good person. He worked hard. He treated people with respect. He was an advocate for the environment and animals. Yet, he died! So how could I trust anything I used to believe? Instead, I changed my belief to "life shits on you." You never know when you will die, and it doesn't matter whether you're a good person. The thought of setting goals, saying affirmations, or changing your belief system seems pointless now.

I used to enjoy inspiring quotes, and I believed them. Now, I find those quotes annoying. There is a car dealership right on the highway between my house and the gym, so I drive by it multiple times per week. It has a huge sign that displays quotes. While I'd been a fan of quotes in my past, I feel angry every time I drive by this dealership and see the sign. The quotes say things such as, "You can never succeed if you don't try" or other "inspirational" sayings. Yesterday, I drove by, and the sign read, "Be good and good will come to you." I wanted to scream, "My husband was good! And look what happened to him! He treated people well. He never harmed anyone in his life. He was good, and now he is dead!" or "Don't you think my husband tried?" I want to tell the dealership to stop displaying those stupid quotes because none of it matters! You can do everything right and still die! Those quotes aren't the real world!

Another quote on the sign that has angered me is "Think positive. Good things tend to happen." I used to think that too. In fact, I was absolutely sure that even though Reg had an aggressive cancer, he would survive. But look what happened! I recently saw an interview with a famous, retired NFL player who had cancer and a small chance of survival. But, he survived. He said a positive attitude was the most important reason he lived and just as importantly, he survived because his family and wife also kept a positive attitude. I wanted to throw something at the TV because I was furious. I wanted to scream, "That is not enough! I had a positive attitude, and my husband is dead!"

I like to be alone more

In my past, I wasn't a fan of being alone. I wasn't afraid to be alone and didn't avoid it, but I didn't seek it out. However, after Reg's death, I often wanted to be by myself. For example, I visited a yoga retreat center with a group of friends nine months after he passed away. I participated in one of the yoga classes and attempted to take part in the nightly event, which consisted of a fire ceremony to let go of whatever you no longer needed. But, I found I often wanted to be alone rather than participating in all the events. I preferred to sit by myself by the lake.

In my past, I wouldn't have wanted to sit by myself. I would've hated to feel left out of the activities everyone else was doing. I would've felt sorry for myself that the rest of the group was having fun without me. That was the "old me." The "new me" felt better alone—which is how I felt in the world anyway—than trying to make conversation with people. By being alone, I didn't have to pretend to care about people's happy lives or their measly problems.

Even now, I often wish to be by myself. I often feel as if I can't genuinely relate to others anymore, so it's easier to be alone. Alternatively, I prefer to be with my cats, who don't expect me to be jovial or demand anything of me except food and love. They comfort me by sitting in my lap or on the couch near me. They don't care that I'm home alone on a weekend (in fact, they're happiest when I'm home). They play with their toys and make me laugh. My cats loved Reg very much, so I feel they— and only they—can understand how life feels without him. They understand me and love me unconditionally.

Essentially, I understand why people become hermits after losing a spouse. When I'm alone, I don't have to hide my feelings or pretend things are okay. It's often just easier to be alone.

I am not as optimistic

I used to think life was for the taking. I believed if you thought positively, your life could be good. I went to a funeral for a friend's mom about one and a half years after Reg passed away. At the end of the funeral, a musician sang "I Hope You Dance" by Lee Ann Womack. I used to love that song and believed we should dance through life. When I heard it at the funeral, all I could think was how naïve I was in believing life is for your taking, and you should dance through it. Now, I often wonder if I will ever dance again, literally and figuratively. I didn't know life could be so painful and could do this to you. Now I do. Now, I have low expectations for life. I often expect the worst, which is a huge contrast to how I used to be.

One day, I went to a University of Colorado football game and watched as the players gathered in the end zone, bowed down, and prayed. I started to cry because I felt jealous of their naïveté in believing that God actually cares about them and would assist them. I wanted to scream out, "You're wasting your time. It doesn't help!" Since Reg died, I've had friends ask for prayers or I've received group emails asking for prayers for someone. In my past, I would have done my form of prayer. But now, I can't do that and tell them I'm sorry; I will send them love, but I don't believe prayer works anymore.

I know I have no control, so I don't try to decide where my life will take me or should take me. I certainly would never have chosen to watch my husband die and be a widow at 42 years old. I fought like hell to keep him alive. I tried with everything I had to control the outcome, but I failed. I believed we could heal ourselves from cancer and somehow, we could affect the cancer journey. But, I was wrong. He died anyway. So I now believe life will take me where it will.

Similarly, I won't say I no longer trust self-help books and seminars. However, after Reg passed away, I felt livid with the self-help industry. It had led me to conclude that we have control over our lives. It had led me to expect that life could have a happy ending. It had led me to trust that with the right tools and beliefs, we could do anything. But, I now understood firsthand that wasn't the case. We can have the rug pulled right out from under us even if we do the right things.

I felt especially angry with all the books and self-help authors and coaches who professed you can heal from cancer. They set me up to believe we could cure him and live happily ever after. For many years, we ate the foods they recommended. We never used toxic chemicals and instead cleaned with natural products. We exercised daily. He took supplements shown to kill cancer cells. We did what they recommended, but he died anyway, so I was extremely angry at these books and people.

I also became angry with the self-help world because I felt all the experts and gurus were telling me I should be okay. Even though his death shattered my whole world, I felt they were ordering me to rise up by my bootstraps and be okay or even great. But, the reality is my heart was broken, and I could not just *choose* to be happy, stronger, and better. Focusing on gratitude, as the self-help industry advises you to do, didn't take away my pain. In our society, especially the self-help industry, we celebrate the people who've had their whole family murdered, their arm cut off, and yet still manage to graduate summa cum laude from the country's top college. In other words, as I stated in an earlier chapter, we celebrate resiliency. After Reg passed away, I became acutely aware of how we don't honor people who are not okay, who feel sad, who are struggling, and who are grieving. I blamed the self-help industry for this and became incensed with the industry, which is an industry I had previously loved, supported, and applauded.

I don't engage as much with the world

I've always been an active and big advocate for animals and the environment. I called my senators and representatives when there was an issue I cared about or wanted to change. Online petitions to stop animal cruelty and abuse bombarded me daily, and I almost always signed them.

But after Reg died, I could not even open those emails. Grief consumed so much of my energy that I just couldn't expose myself to any more sadness, which is what the petitions brought me. I felt as though I was turning my back on animals and the issues I cared about, and this made me feel guilty. But I just could not do it. I had to disengage from the world. In fact, I changed my email address because I couldn't handle looking at my old life. Also, I used to use Outlook for my email, but I couldn't face all the old emails in my inbox—from the animal shelter, from causes, from Reg, from our old friends, etcetera—so I stopped using Outlook and instead now use the webmail application from my new email address.

Similarly, I used to be incredibly involved with a cat shelter. I wrote biographies for the cats up for adoption, I trained new volunteers and served as a volunteer mentor, I headed a marketing committee, I responded to adopters who needed help, and I visited with the cats at least one day per week. After Reg passed away, I couldn't get myself to engage with the shelter or even talk about it. I felt horribly guilty for not helping the cats anymore. But I also felt that if I engaged with the shelter, I would get swallowed in an abyss of sadness and never find my way out of it. I felt as if my spirit couldn't handle any more emotional angst. So sadly, I gave up on something that had been important to me and had been a proud part of my identity.

Volunteering is just one of the activities I no longer felt motivated to do after Reg passed away. Other than hiking, I felt unmotivated to do any of the activities I used to engage in and enjoy. For example, I used to love going to free summer concerts or movies in the park, but I stopped going after he died. I used to love to travel, but I no longer had the desire after Reg passed away. It felt like if I did travel, it would be bittersweet because he wouldn't be there. So why bother?

I did continue to go to University of Colorado football games, because my mom and I continued—and still continue—to have season tickets. In my past, I screamed and cheered, sometimes to the point where I practically hyperventilated. But after Reg died, even though I sat in the stands, I no longer cheered excessively

216

or tried to make noise to help the team. It seemed pointless. Why bother? So I just sat there and watched but wasn't engaged.

At the same time, I stopped going to professional lacrosse games. Reg and I had season tickets to the Colorado Mammoth, Colorado's National Lacrosse League team. I went once a few months after Reg passed away and sobbed throughout the game. As I walked down the aisle toward our seats, I felt I should be following him. I saw our same usher and the same people seated around me. Everything seemed the same, but I was different; my world had been shattered. I attempted to go to the game one other time and still felt too sad. So, I gave up our season tickets and stopped going. My mom still has season tickets and tries to get me to go with her. I suspect that with time, I will return to the games. But for now, I find it too emotional, so I've stopped engaging with that world.

My widow friend Jessica also disengaged from the world after her husband passed away. Her husband passed away in the summer of 2008, shortly before the stock market and economy crashed. Years later, she found out about the crash. She had disengaged from the world so much that she didn't even know the economy had been in trouble.

After Reg died, life became something to get through and not something to enjoy. Basically, I lost my hopes and dreams. I became somewhat disengaged with the world and felt as if I was just drifting.

I've become paranoid about other losses

My dad died in 1998, and my sister passed away in 2002. After their deaths, I didn't fret about other people dying. But since Reg's death, I've become panicked about people close to me dying. This is especially true with my mom. The summer after Reg passed away, she shredded her meniscus and could barely walk. She looked and acted old as she limped around. I was beside myself with grief thinking that she, too, was going to die on me.

Thankfully, her knee has healed and she can walk just fine. But, I've sobbed more times than I can even tell you just thinking about her death. At some level in my logical mind, I recognize my mom will likely die long before me. But emotionally, I cannot handle it. I'm brought to my knees just thinking about it. In my past, I would have felt upset to ponder my mom potentially dying, but now it sends me right over the edge.

I also worry about my friends dying. One of my friends has two young children and a stressful, full-time job. I often fear the stress will cause her to become sick and die. I expect most people my age don't worry about their companions dying. But I do, and I keep trying to encourage my friend to lessen her stress.

I agonize about my pets too. In my past, I didn't feel anxious when one of my animals had surgery, such as a dental procedure. But when my cat Rita had surgery to have a lump removed seven months after Reg died, I was beyond scared and beyond consolable. If Reg hadn't died, I wouldn't have felt scared. However, I felt paranoid she wouldn't wake up and one more loved one would be taken from me. I knew logically she would likely be okay, and the people around me tried to console me. But I was inconsolable and sobbing hysterically. Now, I know God can take what I love in a heartbeat and not care. I realize life can change for the worst in one minute, and it's hard to recover. So handing my cat over to the vet to operate on her made me paranoid, illogical, and despondent.

After Reg died, I read Agatha Christie's book *And Then There Were None*. In that novel, ten people are lured to an island and killed one by one until they're all dead. As I read the book, I kept thinking this would be my life. One by one, the people and animals closest to me will be picked off until I'm all alone. Before Reg died, I had not thought that way. Now I do.

I feel jealous

When Reg attended college, he had a serious girlfriend and was actually engaged to her. They parted as friends and still chatted occasionally or sent birthday and Christmas cards. I had felt no jealousy toward this woman. I had talked to her on the phone, as she lives in another state, and thought she was nice. Confident in my relationship, I had no need to feel jealous.

But after he died, I was envious of this woman. Why? Because she got to spend time with him. He was on this planet for such a short time that I felt jealous she had years with him I didn't have. I felt as if I needed to gather up all his time and hoard it. I even felt a little jealous of his family. They got to know him and be with him as a teenager and young adult. I think he and I were pretty different teenagers, so I might not have even liked him, and he probably wouldn't have liked me. But again, he was here for such a short period of time that if I couldn't have more time with him in the future, I wanted his years in the past.

At the same time, I've become protective of him. I feel angry with anyone who ever hurt him. For example, I saw a photo of him escorting a girl to prom. His high school had paired Reg with this girl because he was on varsity track. According to his friends, she didn't want to attend the prom with Reg. I feel angry with that girl every time I see the photo. How dare she reject him or cause him any pain. (I don't even know if she did; maybe he also didn't want to go with her. I've just assumed he felt rejected knowing she didn't want to go with him, and that infuriates me.) I also sob when I think about the anguish he experienced as an awkward teenager, and I want to fold his younger self in an embrace. It's as if I want to protect him from any pain he ever experienced.

For a while, I couldn't do many of the things I had done before

I've always been an avid reader. Before Reg died, I read at the gym, while lounging around, and to fall asleep. In fact, unless I was extremely tired, I always read to fall asleep. After Reg died, I couldn't read. It felt to me that I couldn't just continue my life as if nothing had happened. Because reading was part of my old life, I couldn't just move forward with it as though nothing had changed. I did still read at the gym, as I liked the distraction while exercising. But beyond that, I could not read. Instead, I watched TV to fall asleep. I needed the distraction and not only could I not read as if nothing had happened, but I needed something to hold my attention; a book couldn't do that. The "old me" read; the "new me" watched TV.

I know I'm not the only one who had this experience. Gina and Tara also stopped reading after their husbands passed away. Both had been avid readers before but were unable to read after the deaths. Tara didn't pick up a book for at least a year, and I believe it was almost two years for Gina. I asked my grief counselor about this. She said it's common for people to be unable to read books because reading takes concentration. When you're in the midst of grief, it's often impossible to concentrate. Jessica had watched TV before her husband died. But after he died, she stopped watching TV except for sports. She could not concentrate long enough to watch anything besides sports.

Besides reading, I also couldn't eat as I normally had. I've never liked to cook and have typically just made a salad for dinner for as long as I can remember. After Reg died, I could not eat salad. I couldn't just eat the same meal I had eaten all these years, as I no longer felt like the same person. I can't remember what I ate, but it wasn't salad. For a while, I lived on candy and cookies and often didn't eat dinner. At other times, I have no idea what

I ate, but it wasn't my staple food. After a year, I finally started eating salads again. The first time I reached for the spinach at the grocery store to put in my salads, I cried. It felt like a betrayal (I don't know to whom—maybe myself?) to eat salad again and to eat healthy.

Even once I started to eat salad again, I couldn't use the same knives or the same cutting boards I had used to chop the vegetables. Instead, I used a smaller knife and cut directly over the dish. Reg and I had once gone to a place where you paint the ceramics. He made me a huge salad bowl and painted it with carrots and cucumbers. That is the bowl I had used every night for my salads. After he died, I could not use that bowl. Even when I went back to eating salad, I had to use a different dish. I finally started to use the bowl he made for me a little over one and a half years after he passed away.

Similarly, in my past, I occasionally cooked stir-fry (the one thing I did enjoy cooking). Neither of us liked zucchini, so I rarely used zucchini in the stir-fry. When I made stir-fry after Reg died, I specifically added a zucchini so that it was a different meal. I couldn't just prepare the meal that the "old me" had cooked in my former, happy existence.

In summer, we often sat outside on the patio and enjoyed the evening. I loved eating dinner on the patio. After he died, it took me nine months to dine outside. It felt too sad before that. Also, during his last summer, we spent almost every night on the front porch watching the world go by, talking, and reading. Because he became weaker, he laid in a lounge chair. I took nine months to sit in that lounge chair. Even then, I only felt comfortable sitting in it because I was studying a course to connect with your loved one; therefore, it felt okay for me to sit there. In my mind, I wasn't sitting there alone.

After Prince Albert passed away, Queen Victoria sent out an injunction that she could never again join in the "frivolities of court." She would never again attend or give a ball, even though she had enjoyed dancing when she was younger. In fact, she discouraged enjoyment, laughter, and light-heartedness around her. She even forbade parties for her children. Those were things she had enjoyed in her happy life. Now, she didn't seem able to tolerate them.

I hate getting my hair cut

In my past, I liked to get my hair cut. I have thick, curly hair that tends to stick up and is often unmanageable. I always felt I looked pretty after getting my hair cut. Reg and I would make plans to "take my hair out" after I visited my hairdresser. It was as if we were showing me off, and I would apply makeup and dress in nice clothes.

Now, I hate getting my hair cut. I find it so depressing. I attempt to schedule my appointments now when I desperately need a haircut or when I have something planned already (such as his memorial service or going to dinner for his birthday). I think I've worn makeup only a few times since he died. Granted, I wasn't a woman who wore makeup regularly when Reg was alive. I've always been more natural. But, we usually had a date night at least once per week, so I would wear it weekly. Now, it just feels depressing to me, and I have no reason to look good.

After my fire, I had to purchase some new jeans. When I tried on the jeans, it made me sad. In the past, if I got new clothes, I wondered if Reg would like them. It was important to me that he liked them. Now, I have no one who cares. As I tried on jeans, there was no one to be proud of me. There was no one who wanted me to look pretty. So why bother?

Other than making sure her clothing showed her mourning, Queen Victoria stopped paying attention to fashion. With Albert gone, she no longer dressed to please anyone. Often, she even stopped wearing her corsets (apparently an important garment in the 1800s).

Two of my widow friends have felt the same way. Angela told me hair and makeup go out the window when you're a widow. On the other hand, some of my widow friends still wear makeup, style their hair, and look nice. I know they did this before their husbands passed away as well.

I no longer like happy movies or books

Before Reg died, I wasn't a person to seek out romantic movies. But, I didn't go out of my way to avoid them. In fact, I enjoyed a pleasant Hallmark Christmas movie, which usually included romance. For the most part, I just liked good films. I tended to gravitate more toward murder mystery and crime books and television shows, but I didn't get super annoyed if/when they had romance or coupling in them.

Now, I avoid romance altogether. I prefer movies, books, and television shows that have crime and mysteries. If they have romance or coupling, I avoid them like the plague. If films have happy endings, I tend to avoid them. Television programs usually catch the murderer at the end and have a happy ending, which is fine. But when they pair characters up as a couple, I get annoyed.

I strive to be a nicer person

I think I was a nice person before Reg died. I expect that if you asked people who knew me, they would say I was compassionate and kind. But after Reg passed away, I tried to be nicer to strangers. I read blogs by psychic mediums and read a lot about death. The theme I kept seeing is that as humans, we are here to love and to be loved. So I've strived to take that message to heart.

As I explained in an earlier chapter, I lost a lot of empathy and tolerance for people. But on the other hand, I've tried to be kinder. I try to be friendlier to random people at the store. I also attempt to encourage my friends to be more loving and kind. I do my best to remember to wish people a happy birthday or contact my widow friends on the anniversaries that are important, such as the passing date. As my grief counselor told me, there are a lot of walking-wounded people out there. So I do my best. I try to remember that at the end of the day, my mission as a soul is to love and to be loved.

Trust me, I'm far from perfect, but I've tried. I think about how I would feel if my life were coming to an end. Could I declare I was a good person? I'm doing my best to make sure I can answer affirmatively when it's my time to pass.

My friend Jessica told me that since her husband passed away, she has become a nicer, more patient mom with her kids. She hates that in some ways she has become a better person, as she wishes she had remained patient with her kids when her husband was alive. But she acknowledges that she is more patient with them now and realizes that some of the issues she stressed about in the past don't matter. According to her, when you lose your spouse and your kids lose their father, you realize most of the little things truly don't matter.

I must admit I still sweat the little things. In some ways, I feel I'm a worse person than I was before. I still stress if my house is messy, and I still get annoyed at small matters. I was like that before, but there were positive attitudes I used to believe in, and I was a fun, happy person. Now I feel like I'm a bitter, angry, sad person who still gets frustrated and triggered, and who still sweats the small things. Sadly, now I don't have the positive attributes to balance those out. Then again, it's hard for me to consider being a better person because that would mean something good came from Reg's death. How can his death result in anything beneficial? As I stated earlier, though, I've focused on trying to be a kinder and more loving person to others. I try to remember that there are walking-wounded people everywhere, and I do my best to be kind.

I feel broken

Recently, I read an article by a widow who said her husband's death made her stronger. I know the self-help industry and our society in general like to say the difficult situations we have to face in life make us stronger. Going through cancer treatment with Reg brought out a lot of strength in me. Dealing with the aftermath of my house fire brought out strength.

But his death definitely didn't make me stronger. Maybe this is because I already felt like a strong person. In some ways, I feel his death took some of that strength by turning me into a different person (as described throughout this chapter).

Overall, I feel as if his death just broke me.

The Challenges of Kids

I don't have children, so I have not had to figure out how to navigate my grief while still taking care of my kids. However, most of my widow friends have them, so I felt it was important to include information about children in this book.

My friends tell me that now that their spouses have died, they have to be both parents. They have to be strong when they don't want to be. They have to be responsible when they don't want to be and when they just prefer to bury their heads under the covers. They have to be the "good" parent and the "bad" parent. Previously, they made decisions with their spouses or could at least discuss their children with their spouses. Now, they are forced to make all the decisions on their own. My friend Gina tells me this is extremely stressful. What is best for her son? She is now entirely responsible with trying to figure this out.

I met a widow one day who had two young, active boys. Her husband had died six months before I met her. I'll never forget hearing her say, "I need to find my kids a new daddy." It was a reminder yet again how people with children sometimes have other worries, such as what is best for their children. This woman thought it would be best to find a new partner rather quickly. On the other hand, Gina started dating a little less than two years after her husband died; she's been pretty careful to keep her dating life separate from her son.

My friends now have the dread of having the sex talk, the

drug talk, and the other discussions parents are encouraged to have with their kids. According to them, their husbands probably would've been better and more comfortable having these talks. They have had to teach their children how to drive. For at least two of them, they felt their husbands should have been the ones to conduct the driving lessons because their husbands had a calmer personality and more patience. Sure, single people teach their kids to drive and have discussions, and they think little of it. My mom was a single mom and had to do all these tasks herself, so she doesn't understand why these are so difficult. But as I explained to her, when you think your spouse will help you, it makes doing these things exceedingly hard.

Almost every widow and widower I've met has lost the desire to live. But at the same time, the ones with children know they have to live, and they want to be here for their children. They have to keep moving forward and living even when they have no desire to live or even get out of bed. Queen Victoria declared, "My life as a happy one is ended! The world is gone for me! If I must live on . . . it is henceforth for our poor fatherless children—for my unhappy country, which has lost all in losing him."[viii]

The other difficulty people with children have is watching their children grieve the loss of their parent. I know it torments my friends to see their children grieving and so sad. They don't understand why they had to lose their spouse, but they have the added pain of knowing their children also experienced loss. This just adds even more to their grief.

My friend Jessica lost her dad when she was a teenager. She said her biggest hope and goal for her children was to not lose a parent. Yet, her husband died when her children were all under 14. It torments her that her children have had to grow up without out a parent as well. Further, she often wonders if she should have hidden her grief from her children or if it was okay to not hide her pain. I often felt guilty—and still feel guilty—that my poor cats have had to witness so much grief and have had to try to comfort me as I've sobbed my heart out. So, I can only imagine the difficulties of dealing with grief wondering how it's affecting your children.

Plus, there is no rule book that tells you how to parent a child going through grief. For example, Gina often wonders if it's okay to let her child stay home from school when he feels sad about losing his dad. She tries to walk the line between having her child go to school to receive a good education while not forcing him to face his peers on days when he just wants to cry. Is he better off going to school or staying home? Who knows? There is no rule book to help! Parenting is hard enough without navigating grief.

In Denver, we have an organization called Judi's House that helps children with loss. Here, parents can get advice on how to help their children and counseling for their own grief. At the same time, the kids join group counseling to help with grief. Gina took her son here and said that for the first time, her son didn't feel so alone when he joined other kids facing grief. As a 13-year-old living in the suburbs, his friends all had their parents and had never experienced this kind of grief and loss. So, he felt isolated. At Judi's House, he finally felt understood. Sadly, this kind of organization doesn't exist in most cities, and parents have to figure out how to counsel their children or get one-on-one counseling. My heart goes out to all of you trying to handle your children on top of your own grief.

Proud But Bittersweet

My widow friend Jessica told me she hates how competent she has become in fixing items around her house. Her husband used to take care of all the household problems and maintenance, and now she has to do it all. I totally understand. Reg used to take care of everything, and now I'm responsible. I didn't even know how to change the filter on our furnace or turn off the main water line; Reg did those. I had no need to know. But now I do, and I hate that!

After Reg died, my neighbor showed me how to change the furnace. Similarly, Reg's boss came to my house and showed me a number of practical tasks, including how to turn off my main water switch. Reg's boss told me if I need anything else, I could always watch YouTube videos, as there are videos now for everything. I burst into tears. I didn't—and still don't—want to watch videos! I want Reg to continue to manage things. While I'm proud of how I am now more competent, it feels bittersweet.

The first time I felt this way—proud but bittersweet—occurred a few weeks after Reg passed. We had installed a tiny sink in our bathroom, so his wheelchair could fit in the bathroom. After he died, Reg's boss helped me put our old sink and cabinet back into the bathroom. However, somehow the plug to the old sink got lost. I decided I could no longer depend on Reg to take care of household problems, so I had to learn to handle them. I installed the new plug, got under the sink, and tightened the bolts for the new plug. When Reg was alive, I would never have done that; he would have handled the sink. But this time, I did it! I remember thinking, "Look at me! I'm under the sink tightening the bolts. Good for me." At the same time, I was upset that I had to be the one to fix the sink. Simultaneously, I felt proud of myself but also bittersweet.

In another example, after my house fire, the walls and ceiling had to be rebuilt. The contractor and I had a big disagreement about the walls. I thought the drywall person had done a bad job and not connected the walls properly. The contractor tried to bully me into thinking I was wrong. Thankfully, two of my neighbors have done construction or built houses, and both told me I was correct. So, I held my ground and told my contractor I wouldn't compromise on this. It was difficult though. I felt so angry and felt as if the contractor was taking advantage of me because I'm a woman. Had Reg been here, would the contractor have tried to produce substandard work? I suspect not. While I felt proud of myself, I was bitter that I had to be the one to take control of this situation.

Similarly, our house was built in 1911, and over the past 100 years, people have added many layers of wallpaper. In 2010, Reg decided to peel the wallpaper off the walls in the hallway and bedroom. He discovered five layers of wallpaper under the paint. He planned on removing the wallpaper in every room at some point. But, of course, he died before he could complete this project. While my house sat empty after the fire, I decided to complete the task. Again, my contractor and I fought about this with him refusing to do it. Therefore, I hired my own crew of five men, rented equipment at Home Depot, and peeled the wallpaper off myself. The walls (which also had five layers of wallpaper) now look smooth and great. I felt so proud of myself for taking control and getting this done. I felt empowered. But again, it was bittersweet. Why hadn't I helped Reg with this task when he had worked on the walls in the bedroom and hallway? I had just let him do it himself. Clearly, I was competent, but I didn't bother to even try to help. So the pride I felt had a layer of guilt and bitterness underneath.

Also, had Reg been here, would the contractor have complied? As I stated above, I often wonder if people try to take advantage of me since I'm a woman. For example, I had my garage door greased one day just as a tune-up. The garage was working fine, and I had no reason to believe it wouldn't continue to function. But as a precaution, I hired a garage repair company to give the garage a tune-up. The garage guy said I needed a new bracket on the door. Really? Would he have suggested that to Reg? I didn't know enough to distinguish if this man was lying to me, but I knew that if Reg were here, Reg would have known. As an aside, I didn't purchase the bracket, and the garage has worked fine, once again making me wonder if someone was trying to take advantage of me. At least three other widow friends also worry that repair companies and contractors have tried and will try to take advantage of them; they did not have this worry before their husbands died.

Reg also handled all computer matters in our house. He was a computer genius, so I never had to do a thing. Plus, because his knowledge surpassed even people who manage hardware at companies, things were not set up simply. My basement has routers and many network cords and looks like the computer room of a small company—way beyond my knowledge! I had no idea how to connect to the Wi-Fi; because of the complexity, I feared it would go down, leaving me to figure out how to handle it. Sure enough, the Wi-Fi went down, and I figured out how to handle it. Again, I felt proud but mad that I had to handle it. I shouldn't have had to figure it out; Reg should have been here to do it!

Not long after Reg died, the calendar on my phone lost

everything. I hated that I could not turn to him and ask him to fix it. He either would have been able to fix it, or I would have known it could not be fixed. Unfortunately, I never figured out how to fix my calendar.

Tara's husband also took care of all things computer related. She still has no idea how to scan papers into her computer or even copy and paste. My friend Gina had an unusual amount of appliances and fixtures break within six months of her husband dying. In the past, he would have handled all of it. Now, she had to handle them. She got to the point where she just laughed with each new item she had to fix (it was either that or cry). She has a full list of her "accomplishments" that year because she was proud. But like me, she felt bitter she had to do it all.

Like many of my widow friends, I depended on Reg to handle not only inside household issues but also outside matters. Five months after he died, there was a man aerating the neighbors' lawns. I started to panic because I didn't know if I was supposed to do that. Reg always handled the lawn care, and I completely freaked out trying to figure out if I was supposed to aerate it. I didn't know if I should ask the guy to come over to aerate our yard. I started crying hysterically because I didn't know what to do and, of course, I couldn't ask Reg. Another neighbor was outside working on his lawn, which was depressing for me to see. My man used to mow the lawn. Now he never will.

The first time I went to my young widows group, one woman asked, "How do you mow the lawn?" Like me, she had no idea how to handle the outside jobs. Gina had her son mow the grass. But when the mower didn't work, she took it to Home Depot to get repaired. The repair person at Home Depot told her there was nothing wrong with her lawn mower. She just needed to clean it. Like me, she was clueless on lawn things. While she felt glad her mower was fine, she was upset her husband wasn't there to handle it; he would have known the mower just needed to be cleaned.

I distinctly remember trying to attach our garden hoses together in the past. I didn't have the strength and just gave up and handed them to Reg. The first time I put the hoses together for the garden by myself, one hose gushed water. In the past, Reg would have just fixed it. This time, every cell in my body wanted to give up and walk away when I didn't have the strength. But I couldn't. There was no one else now. The buck stops with me. So, I forced myself to figure it out, and I did. I was proud. But at the same time, I hated that I had to do it. It felt bittersweet.

I recognize that many women are experienced and knowledgeable about home repairs and stereotypical "men's work." We have a female friend who handles all repair work and maintenance at her house. When Reg used to upgrade items at our house or engage in household tasks, he frequently consulted this female friend. Her husband, on the other hand, is as clueless as I am. If you are knowledgeable like my friend, you may not relate to this chapter.

Likewise, my widower friend Laurence didn't face these situations. However, his wife had done the cooking. He had no idea how to cook. Within the first year of his wife's death, he lost quite a bit of weight. Yes, some of that was because of the grief. But some of the weight loss was because he didn't know how to take care of feeding himself. I know on some occasions, he just ate a bag of chips for dinner after attempting to cook a meal and ruining it. I know in the times when he did successfully cook a meal, he felt exceptionally satisfied. But like all of us, the pride was also bittersweet. I know another widower who didn't know how to even navigate the grocery store.

Again, I'm not suggesting that men don't know how to cook, shop at the grocery store, or engage in other stereotypical "female work." Reg was an amazing cook, whereas I hate every minute of cooking. Rather, I'm suggesting that for my widowed friends—and for myself—when our spouses handled one area of expertise and now we have full responsibility, it is difficult. We are forced to handle areas where we feel out of our element; while we may feel pride, there is sadness and bitterness mixed with it.

To sum up this chapter, I'll repeat what Jessica said at the start of the chapter: "I hate how competent I've gotten at fixing things." While I'm proud of myself, I hate that I have to do tasks and solve my own problems. For every proud moment, there's another sad or angry emotion right behind it. It's not just 100 percent pride. It's also bittersweet.

Pain Makes Me Feel Closer to Him

Pain makes me feel closer to Reg. I know that doesn't make logical sense, but that's how I feel emotionally. If I'd never lost my spouse and someone told me that at some level, he/she holds onto the pain, I'd think the person was crazy. Or, I might think he/she was too dramatic. But, though the grief hurts and has sometimes felt unbearable, the thought of giving it up is frightening to me.

My grief counselor attempted to tell me repeatedly that I don't need the pain to feel close to Reg. But in my mind, I often feel closer to him when I'm in tears. I don't know how to explain the feeling or why I feel this way.

I know many widows and widowers don't agree with me. They can't wait for the pain to lessen. My grief counselor told me her clients often ask her how long the grief will last, as they want it to end as quickly as possible. That, however, hasn't been my experience; the loss of pain torments me more. In fact, as time has progressed and the suffering has lessened, I look back at the first few months after Reg passed away and miss that time. Why? Because I felt closer to him. He hadn't been gone that long, and I felt like his spirit was still with me.

If you don't feel this way, don't worry. It is a little counter-intuitive. I suspect I may be unique. But if you do feel the same way, you're not crazy or dramatic.

People Say Stupid Things

I don't think a widow or widower exists who has not been the recipient of stupid comments. In fact, my friend Meg sent me a link to a website specifically listing absurd things people have expressed to widows and widowers. When I read the website, some of the comments absolutely amazed me.

They broke my heart, too, because these individuals were grieving the loss of their spouses and were subject to incredibly stupid, and often mean, comments. I recognize that other people don't realize how raw and sensitive you are as a widow/widower, but I'm baffled by the insensitivity of some people's comments.

As I explained in an earlier chapter, I believe that to a certain extent, talking to widows and widowers is like walking through a minefield. What will make one widow angry will comfort another one. For example, as I explained before, Jessica told me she has kept her husband's name as the official name on her telephone's caller ID. When she called her friend, her friend asked her to change the name because it was too difficult to see her spouse's name on the caller ID. This outraged Jessica. How dare that woman tell her to remove her husband's name from the caller ID! As she told me this story, I remember thinking that comment would have comforted me. I would have felt as if someone still cared and missed Reg. Jessica telling me this story made me realize for the first time that each of us has our own hot buttons and that the words that comfort one of us may infuriate another one of us.

Similarly, my widower friend Laurence detested when people asked him, "How are you?" He thought that was the most ridiculous question to ask. He wanted to say, "My wife died. How do you think I am?" That question, on the other hand, would've comforted me because it showed they cared. I felt people either avoided the subject or avoided me altogether.

With that said, I asked my widowed friends to share stupid comments people said to them. This chapter includes their responses. Some of these comments were so bad that I laughed, because I was amazed people actually verbalized these remarks.

Here are the stupid remarks people said to me:

- One day, a friend attempted to get me to reengage in an activity I used to enjoy. I informed him I wasn't ready yet; I was no longer the person he used to know. I told him when Reg died, that person died as well. My friend said I am "carrying around a corpse, and it's gross." Are you kidding me? I couldn't believe he said that!

- I mentioned to another friend how I felt sad and how much Reg's death hurt. He responded, "When you hit your thumb with a hammer, you recover." I was absolutely baffled he was comparing Reg's death with smashing my thumb! This same friend also would routinely ask me, "So you're okay?" When I indicated I wasn't okay, he would question, "Why are you upset?" Really? I wanted to ask him how he'd feel if his wife died. How could he be so clueless?

- A couple of months after Reg passed away, a friend

asked me what goals I had now. Goals?! I told her I would never make goals again. In my past, I had goals, including to find a loving man and have a wonderful relationship. I achieved that goal. I had the goal to keep Reg alive, and I did everything I could. Look where those goals got me! I could barely get through the day and was praying for death. Yet this woman wanted me to formulate new goals.

- A few people advised me to make new friends. I've always had good friends, but I spent most of my time with Reg. I didn't need too many other friends. Almost all of my friends are married with young children; therefore, after Reg died, I didn't have many people, other than my mom, with whom to do activities. I complained to a friend about this and informed her that I felt so alone. I told her I didn't even know any single people to attempt to befriend. She proceeded to tell me about three col-leagues at her work who were single. That made me so mad. I didn't want her to tell me to go out and make new friends. I just wanted compassion.

- One day, I was sobbing and explained to my mom that I wanted my old life back. She responded, "You'll have to make a new life now." I know my mom tried very hard to support me and be as compassionate as possible. But that comment just angered me. Although at some level I understood she was right, I didn't want her to tell me that. I told her to never say that to me again!

- Another stupid thing people frequently expressed was, "It is only his body that is gone, not his spirit."

Or another variation of that, which is, "Our loved ones are still alive." I believe his spirit does go on and is still alive; however, that doesn't help when I ache for him to hug me and want so desperately to pull his arms out of photos to wrap them around me! I can no longer snuggle with him. He cannot fix problems at the house or offer advice. He cannot protect me. He cannot help financially. He cannot make me laugh, like he always did in life. Maybe I can talk to him, but I can no longer hear him. So don't tell me it's just his body that's gone; that declaration doesn't help me.

- "You'll be okay. It will pass." How do they know I will be okay? It will pass? Reg wasn't gas that would eventually pass!

- "He would want you to be happy." I recognize that he would choose happiness for me. But Reg knew me better than anyone, and he would understand I'm sad. Therefore, I get mad at people who suggest it's wrong for me to be unhappy because Reg would want happiness for me.

- "He is at peace now. At least he is no longer suffering." I know I should be a nice person and say I'm glad he's at peace and no longer suffering. But, knowing he's at peace doesn't take away my pain. I don't care that he is at peace. I just want him back!

- "Be strong." In my opinion, that is one of the stupidest comments you can make to a widow or widower.

- When I say I want him back, people say he was in

pain; they believe it's not fair for me to want him here when his being here would mean intense physical pain for him. I recognize that. But it's so painful without him that I would take him back even with the pain and wheelchair.

I assume people make these types of comments believing they will help. But in some ways they dismiss the pain and sadness, and the absence of the person. They minimize the heartbreak of loss. For me, they don't take away the loss, and the comments certainly don't help. They usually just make me mad.

Here are some of the stupid comments people said to my friends:

- "It has been three months; have you gotten used to living by yourself?"

- "You're not eating on purpose."

- "I never do anything with my husband anyway." This person implied that it was no big deal that my friend's husband died. Or another variation was, "My husband and I never talk."

- "Divorce is worse than death."

- "Let him rest in peace." Dakota's sister said this to her when Dakota cried and got upset. Dakota's sister suggested that her grief wasn't allowing her husband to rest in peace. Her sister was actually attempting to guilt and shame Dakota into stopping her grieving. Unbelievable!

- "You're looking for someone to snap their fingers and you'll be over it."

- "God doesn't give you more than you can handle."

- "He's in a better place." Every time someone suggested this to my friend Gina, she wanted to declare, "No, his place is here with his son and me!"

- "Everything happens for a reason." As I explained in another chapter, many people expressed this one to quite a few of my friends. Maybe everything does happen for a reason, but widows/widowers don't want people to tell us that. Dawn felt angry enough that she desired to smash her friends in the face every time she heard this.

- "He was the lucky one."

- "Will he give you the dead wife discount?"

- Just days after her husband's death, someone told my friend Angela that she should write a goodbye letter.

- As happens to many widows and widowers, one widow lost weight after her spouse died. Her brother visited her five months after the loss. The brother asked the widow, "You look good. What's your secret?"

- Just days after her husband's memorial service, Gina's mother-in-law posted on Facebook, "Back from Denver. Life goes on." She didn't directly say this to Gina, so maybe this doesn't quite fit this chapter. But Gina thought it was a stupid and hurtful thing to declare. Similarly, I know another woman whose in-laws posted a photo of themselves having a great time at Sturgis just one week after her husband's memorial service. Ouch!

- Gina was sweeping snow off her driveway when someone yelled out, "Can't you get your husband to do that?" Granted, the person didn't know Gina's husband had died, so I guess it wasn't necessarily a stupid thing to say. But it was a dagger to Gina's heart.

Yes, every widow and widower has endured stupid comments. I realize friends, acquaintances, and family wish to help; they can't understand what we are going through. But sometimes I feel it would be better for people just to keep their mouths shut! If you've heard ludicrous comments, I'm sorry. You're definitely not alone!

"Heal" Is a Stupid Word

In the last chapter, I discussed stupid things people have said to me and to the widows/widowers I know. In my opinion, one of the stupidest words—and one I absolutely hate—is "heal," so I've devoted a whole chapter to it. I realize society, friends, and family want grieving people to heal. But, in my opinion, losing a spouse is not something I can be completely "healed" from. This isn't a broken bone that I hope will eventually mend back together and be the same. It feels as if someone took out my heart, stomped on it, shredded it to pieces, and put it back in my body. How can I heal that much damage? Losing my spouse is something I am learning to live with; I don't think I will ever fully heal.

I once ate dinner with my widower friend Laurence and his friends. His friends asked me what my definition of "heal" was. I replied that I hated that word and didn't wish to be healed. To me, if I were healed, that means I'm okay without Reg. How could I be okay without him? I said I assume I'll be okay at some point; I will live on. But I will never be healed.

Thankfully, though neither of his friends had experienced the loss of a spouse, they had lost their parents and realized you truthfully never heal fully. One said loss is similar to a wound that has left scars and a scab. It's healed, but there is a scar that will always be there. He suggested we need another word because "heal" is too loaded and doesn't connote what the emotion is or what it truly means. I agreed.

It annoys me that people assume I *want* to be healed. A woman approached me at Reg's memorial service and gave me a crystal she believed would help me heal. I appreciate that this was a kind and thoughtful gesture, and she wanted to help me. But I remember thinking, "Why do you think I want to heal, especially so soon after his death?" I think if she had given me the crystal and said it was to comfort me, that she thought it was pretty and thought I would like it, or that she didn't know what else to do and just wanted to be kind, I would've appreciated her gesture. But insinuating I wished to heal right after he died just astounded me.

Another friend gave me a book shortly after Reg died called *How to Heal a Grieving Heart*. Again, I appreciated the gesture and knew she gave it out of love. But it shocked me once again that people thought I should be ready to heal. Even now, while some suggestions in the book are helpful, I don't like the title. I have respect and admiration for the two authors who wrote the book, but it's obvious to me that neither has lost a spouse. Otherwise, I don't know how they could give the book that title.

Another woman sent me an email shortly after Reg died and told me to ask for help with the grief and healing. It's as if people think there should be a time limit on grief and that I should be healed and okay even though I didn't—and don't—feel okay. As I discussed in another chapter, in Victorian times mourning etiquette actually dictated that widows stay in mourning for years and that grieving people should not attend fun places, such as the theater. Grieving was to be public and not private. I'm not suggesting it's good to insist on public mourning for at least a year or two like the Victorians, because everyone grieves differently and in their own time. But now it feels to me as if friends just want me (and the widowers and widows I know) to be healed. I know many of my widow friends feel as if their mourning is offensive to others and they have to hide their grief.

For me, there is some guilt in even thinking I could be healed. It feels as if maybe I'm betraying Reg if I'm okay or if I'm good. Maybe someday I will not feel this way but for now, it's distressing for me to even ponder the idea of being fully healed. So, I ignored this woman's email suggestion.

One of my friends sent me an email with a photo of a wise saying. It said, "Anyone who says grief only takes so long to heal has never lost a piece of their heart." Amen!

As I explained in an earlier chapter, the pain makes me feel closer to Reg. Therefore, the idea of being fully healed also scares me, because then it feels as if Reg would be further away. Apparently, Queen Victoria felt the same way. She admitted to her daughter Alice that she was afraid to get too well. When *The Times* reported that Victoria looked better, Victoria "ordered it to be contradicted." A lord, Lord Clarendon, said Victoria was "anxious that all her hair should be grey," which would show her grief.[ix]

Along the same lines, people have asked me if I'm "better." Like "heal," I think that is a stupid thing to ask. I don't need to get "better." There is nothing wrong with me. It's not as if I have a virus. It's not as if I'm trying to get "better" at something such as running, painting, or some other activity. Again, there is nothing wrong with me. I'm grieving my husband and feel as if I lost part of my heart and soul. So I don't need to get *better*.

My grief counselor told me she has a client that says, "I'm okay. I'm not good." I admire that. I'm okay. But I'm not good for sure. The woman lets people sit in discomfort when she says that, since people generally want her to be okay or good. They expect her to "heal" or be "all better." I have a quote on my wall that says, "I'm not okay and that's okay." That brings me peace because that is the truth. I appreciate that friends and family want me to be "healed" and "all better," but it's important for me to just be at peace.

You may be ready to be healed and "all better." I certainly understand that. That is the prevailing attitude in our society, and many grief books specifically focus on the healing process.

This Shit Never Happened When He Was Alive

This chapter may not apply to every widow, and it probably won't apply to most of the widowers. But a good portion of the widows I know, including me, have had some bad luck since our spouses passed away. I had to deal with many issues that rarely happen to most people, and I had to handle most of them within the first year. Do you know the whack-a-mole game? That's how I felt—like every time I lifted my head up or came up for air, I got whacked in the head.

Around five months after Reg passed away, we had a windstorm in Denver. As luck would have it, it blew the roof right off my garage. In all the time that Reg and I lived in our house together, nothing like this had ever happened! Granted, this would've been stressful and annoying to deal with even if he were alive. But he was the one who handled the maintenance of the house and would have taken care of this. Instead, I had to find a roofer to repair my roof, and I had to pay for it when I was already worried about finances. I couldn't believe my bad luck.

As I was finishing the repairs to the garage roof, the main water line between the street and my house broke. My home was built in 1911 and apparently still had the same main water line that was originally installed. I realize a water line that old was bound to burst, but did it have to break just six months after

Reg passed away? It stood for over 100 years. It could have broken two years earlier, and Reg would have been there to help. It could have broken two years later, when I at least wasn't quite so raw and overwhelmed.

I had to hire plumbers to fix it. The plumber we had used in the past, and whom I knew was trustworthy, didn't do lines between the house and street. So I was tasked with finding someone who could. A neighbor, who is a builder, offered to help me with the plumbers. According to him, "People in construction often take advantage of a single woman." Great! Again, I couldn't believe Reg wasn't here to help!

The plumbers had to dig out my front yard to bury the new line, which upset me greatly. That caused changes to the house where Reg and I lived happily together. Plus, Denver doesn't pay to repair the line between the streets and houses. So when I was already feeling stressed about finances due to the loss of the breadwinner, I had to fork over $3,000 to repair it. I remember standing on my porch writing a check to the roof guy for $1,600 when a man from Denver Water arrived to tell me my line had broken. The roofer looked at me and said, "You're not having a good day." Ha! If only he knew.

A couple of months later, a baby raccoon somehow got trapped in my cat enclosure. Many years ago, we had a cat enclosure built so our cats could go outside and get fresh air but stay safe. A doggie door lets them in and out, and it's basically a large cage that theoretically should keep out other animals. But in the middle of the night, a young raccoon slipped in and got trapped inside; his mom stood on the top of the cage. I live in the city. It's not as if there is wildlife all over the place, and I was accustomed to dealing with this. I had no idea what to do!

This kind of shit never occurred when Reg was alive! If it had, he would have dealt with it. Instead, while half asleep, I had to figure out how to get this raccoon out of the cat cage.

It turned out just fine with no damage done to my cats or the raccoons. But I couldn't believe this happened and I once again had to handle an issue alone that had never happened when he was alive! Just last week there was a fox running across my roof. I was alarmed because the fox was right near my cat enclosure and cat. At the same time, all I could think was, "This shit never happened when Reg was alive."

A few months after the raccoon incident, my house caught on fire. Believe it or not, it happened on my wedding anniversary, the first one without Reg. Because our house was built so long ago, it had outdated wiring in the attic, which caught on fire. Like the main water line, I guess in some ways it's not surprising the electrical started a fire given how old it was. But waking up with my house on fire on my first wedding anniversary without Reg felt unbelievable to me. I truly couldn't wrap my brain around it.

On the morning of my first wedding anniversary alone, I stood out on my sidewalk in my pajamas as firefighters went through my house, and neighbors congregated. Thankfully, the fire remained in the wall and ceiling, so the house's foundation and most items inside it remained unharmed. But my cats and I had to live in a hotel room for over six months while the contractors—strangers—repaired my house.

The firefighters had to tear out the ceiling in two of the rooms, and they released asbestos into the house. In Denver, even a small amount of asbestos requires asbestos abatement, which means specially trained people have to wipe down and clean every item in the house that could've been exposed to asbestos. At one point, I had to go into the house to meet with the specialists. By this time, the dwelling had been declared a hazmat zone, so tarps and danger warning signs surrounded it. I had to put on a hazmat suit just to enter my residence. As I walked through my house, I remember thinking that not long ago, I had been living a happy life with my sweetie. Now, he was dead, and I had to wear a hazmat suit with breathing apparatus just to go into my house. How could this be?

Eventually, the cats and I got to move back into the house and were quite happy to be home. But I had one more this-shit-never-happened-when-he-was-alive experience. As I've explained earlier in this book, our neighbors' huge pine tree toppled over into my yard after a snowstorm that brought heavy, wet snow. It blocked my path to the garage and pulled the electricity box right off the side of my house, leaving the live wire across the ground. Reg hated that tree, as it shaded the garden and dropped pine needles all over our yard. He probably would have been glad it fell, but I was shocked this happened!

This kind of shit never occurred when Reg was alive. I became terrified that with an exposed wire, my home would once again catch on fire. Had Reg been here, I wouldn't have felt scared; he could have comforted me. Instead, I was once again left alone to deal with a random accident. Although it didn't cause a fire, the tree did cause damage. I also ended up fighting with the people who owned the dwelling (it's a rental property) because they declared they were not legally responsible for paying the damage.

Since I've moved back home, the fire alarms have gone off three times in the middle of the night. They are wired into the electrical system and are attached to the ceiling, where I cannot reach them. I wouldn't be thrilled to have the alarms screeching in the middle of the night even if Reg were alive. But I panic every time because I don't know what to do and I can't reach the alarms to turn them off, not to mention the PTSD from having my house already catch on fire. Each time, there was no warning the batteries were low or needed to be replaced; when I checked the batteries, they were fine and fully charged. These appear to just be this-shit-did-not-happen-when-he-was-alive incidents!

While most of my friends didn't have this degree of shit

happen to them after their husbands died, many had unusual situations they had to manage alone. My friend Gina had numerous fixtures and appliances break in her house in the first six months. As a homeowner, you can expect something could break at any given time that will need repairing. But she had an unusual number of things fail, including her water heater, garage door, washer, dryer, light fixture, and garbage disposal—all within the first six months. It became a joke after a while because there was so much she had to do, and now she had to do it alone. She and I often joked that we seemed to be trying to one-up each other; with each issue we had to deal with, the other person would say, "You've won."

Tara's refrigerator failed during Christmas week, which was her first Christmas without her husband. Again, as a homeowner you can expect that appliances will stop working. But her refrigerator was only a few years old and was still under warranty. It didn't break two years after her husband passed away, when she likely would have more energy to deal with it. It didn't break two years before, when her husband would've been there to commiserate and help. Instead, it broke during her first Christmas without him!

Tara hired a repair person who fixes refrigerators under warranty. This repair person had a car accident on the way to her house, and he couldn't return for another few weeks. Ultimately, she didn't get a new refrigerator until mid-February. In the interim, she kept her food in an ice chest. Because it was too warm in the house and too cold outside, for almost two months all of her food was either lukewarm or frozen solid. This kind of shit hadn't transpired when her husband was alive!

Tara also had someone get her IP (internet protocol) address and download movies from one of the movie studios. Her internet service provider shut down her internet, and she received a warning from the FBI that downloading is illegal. The FBI said it could charge her with a crime. She had to spend hours on the phone with her service provider trying to convince them she was innocent of the crime and had no idea how to download movies. I've known this older woman for over ten years. I know she is a sweet, rule-abiding woman, so I can't imagine anyone thinking she could do something illegal like this.

Needless to say, it took nearly three weeks before this mistake got straightened out. In the meantime, she had bills piling up that she needed to pay online but couldn't. She had things she needed to check but couldn't. Her husband was the computer whiz, not her. Had this happened when he was alive, he would have taken care of it. But no, this shit didn't happen when her husband was alive. Instead, while grieving the loss of her husband, she had to manage this scenario alone!

Finally, Tara's dog passed away. Having lost many pets, I know it hurts regardless. But to lose her dog so soon after her husband passed away was just cruel. My widow friend Rachel's cat died of a brain tumor, the same way her husband died, six weeks after his death. Gina's cat also passed away not too long after her husband died. One of my cats, Rita, got diagnosed with cancer seven months after Reg passed away.

In some ways, Rita's diagnosis and the deaths of my friends' pets don't surprise me. Our pets felt all the stress, worry, fear, and other emotions of taking care of our husbands before they died, combined with the absolute heartbreak after they died. Therefore, in some ways, these deaths probably are not random accidents or bad luck like the rest of the events in this chapter. But, it definitely seems unfair to have to grieve a pet's death or sickness on top of losing our spouses.

I hope you haven't had unusual things or bad luck happen to you since your spouse passed away. But if you have, know that you're not alone!

His Death Has Affected Me Physically

Apparently, doctors use a term called "the widowhood effect" to describe how, when a husband or wife dies, the surviving spouse faces a higher risk of death. In fact, in 2007 the University of Glasgow conducted a study of more than 4,000 married couples ages 45 to 64. The researchers found that widows/widowers were at least 30 percent more likely to die of any cause in the first six months following the death of a spouse versus those who hadn't lost a spouse. In another study, a professor at the University of St. Andrew's studied roughly 58,000 men and 58,000 women in Scotland dating back to the 1990s. The professor found that there was a 40 percent higher risk of death following widowhood than would otherwise be expected. Plus, it's not just the first six months that showed a higher mortality rate for surviving spouses. The research showed a higher mortality rate of the surviving spouse for a decade after losing a spouse.

Obviously, I have not died. But Reg's death has affected me not only emotionally but physically. For example, I've always been someone who turns to food in times of stress and for emotional comfort. I've often joked that I will be the person who still eats on her deathbed, when most people don't. But when Reg died, I could barely eat. My mom took me out to dinner every night to make sure I ate, and I would usually only eat half of my food at the most. Trust me, I've never been someone who had leftovers on her plate. I usually finished all of my food. But after he passed away, I could not eat. In a short period of time, I lost quite a bit of weight and could feel my ribs easily. It has always been challenging for me to lose weight, so this was definitely a new experience. I finally forced myself to start eating because my fingers were getting thin enough that my wedding ring was falling off. I didn't want to lose my wedding ring so decided eating was a better idea.

Another strange experience that happened to me after Reg passed away was that I passed out one night. I got up to use the restroom and the next thing I knew, I was on my butt on the bathroom floor. My grandmother was in hospice at the time, so my mom asked my grandmother's nurse if she had ever heard of this. The nurse said possibly I was dehydrated. I had drunk a lot of water, so I shouldn't have been dehydrated. But I cried for hours and hours every day, so could that have dehydrated me? I'm not a doctor and have no medical training. So, I won't even begin to try to figure out what happened. But, I'm sharing it because it's another example of physical manifestations from my grief.

Yet another physical manifestation for me was a change in body temperature. I've always gotten cold easily. But after Reg passed away, I could go for a walk when it was 10 degrees outside and not feel cold. I think my body was in such shock that extreme temperatures didn't affect me like they had in the past.

Gina told me that I looked ashen the first time I met her. Also, my eyes lacked sparkle. When I smiled for photos in my past, you could see the sparkle. After Reg's death, my eyes looked dull. Jessica believes her eyes still look dull, even after eight years.

Sleeping troubles are common for widows and widowers. I didn't have sleep issues. Then again, I took sleeping pills for a while to ensure I could sleep. Sleep was the only time when

I wasn't in pain and when I had the opportunity to maybe dream about Reg. So thankfully, sleep wasn't a big issue for me. Laurence, however, experienced sleep issues after his wife died. Eight months after her death, he went camping for the weekend and told me he had finally slept better than he had since his wife had died. My widow friend Angela told me she is still dealing with complications from not sleeping after her husband died, which was roughly 20 years ago.

The death of a spouse can also affect the brain. There is actually an expression called "widow brain" because many widows and widowers forget the whole time period around the death of their spouse and can't remember much. I didn't have this too much and remember most things from that time period. Jessica, however, has no memory of the first year after her husband passed away. When people tell her about events in that first year, she has no memory of them.

While I didn't seem to have memory issues or sleep problems, an area where I felt a physical manifestation was in my heart. According to the American Heart Association, there is such a thing as broken heart syndrome. The American Heart Association's website says:

> "Broken heart syndrome may be misdiagnosed as a heart attack because the symptoms and test results are similar. In fact, tests show dramatic changes in rhythm and blood substances that are typical of a heart attack. But unlike a heart attack, there's no evidence of blocked heart arteries in broken heart syndrome.
>
> In broken heart syndrome, a part of your heart temporarily enlarges and doesn't pump well, while the rest of your heart functions normally or with even more forceful contractions. Researchers are just starting to learn the causes, and how to diagnose and treat it."

The idea that you can die of a broken heart gained the lime-light when Debbie Reynolds died the day after her daughter, Carrie Fisher. After Reg's grandfather died, his grandmother died just six weeks later. Former pro-football player Doug Flutie's mom had a sudden heart attack and died just an hour after his dad died.

I have no doubt this is possible given how Reg's death affected me. I have a strong heart due to my vegan diet and my daily exercise regimen. But I distinctly remember running in a 4-mile race after Reg passed away and feeling as if I would have a heart attack. My heart was racing and felt as if it would explode. I obvi-ously don't know what a real heart attack feels like, but I had run numerous races in the past. This had never happened in my past. I guess the stress and the fact that my heart was so broken affected my heart physically. As I've explained in an earlier chapter of this book, my friend Laurence died suddenly from heart problems. He was physically active and seemed healthy, so I often wonder if he died of a broken heart.

A non-widowed friend told me that after her father-in-law passed away, her mother-in-law went to the doctor. The doctor found an actual hole in her heart and thought she would need open-heart surgery. However, the cardiologist wanted to watch the heart before proceeding with such a big operation. To the doctor's surprise, the heart spontaneously closed over the course of roughly a year and is now fully healed. My friend is certain the hole in her mother-in-law's heart was a physical manifestation of how she felt about losing her spouse. I'm not a doctor, and neither is my friend; I have no idea if holes in the heart often heal without medical intervention. Maybe it's a coincidence. But maybe not.

After Reg passed away, my heart felt exceedingly vulnerable. I felt I needed to physically protect it. Nine months after he passed away, I went to a yoga retreat center and took a yoga class. The instructor suggested we open our chests and open our hearts. When I thought about physically opening my chest and exposing my heart, I nearly doubled over in sadness and pain. I couldn't do the pose properly. I could not stand the idea of opening my chest and leaving my heart wide open and vulnerable. Even if I tried to imagine my chest open, I couldn't do it. I felt I needed to protect my heart any way I could. That included physically.

Tara has had challenges with regulating her blood pressure since her husband passed away. Maybe it's a big coincidence, but she often feels sick, which then makes it where she can't even leave the house. Also, she is often so tired that she doesn't want to go anywhere; she just wants to rest and be quiet or listen to soft music. Sometimes she walks her dog or does a simple chore around the house, as these are familiar activities; she feels comfort in doing something she is used to doing.

Tara also has experienced panic attacks since her husband passed away. Out of nowhere, her head throbs and hurts, and her pulse and blood pressure go up. Her ears ring, and her heart pounds. It gets so bad that sometimes she thinks maybe she is dying and should go to an urgent care center. Sometimes she trembles and paces because she can't decide what she should do. She will enter a room and forget what she wanted to do or why she entered. Sometimes she takes anti-anxiety medication to mitigate the physical symptoms. Sometimes she tells herself to calm down, breathe slower, and sit in a comfortable chair while she reads or plays games on her iPad. At the end of each anxiety episode, she feels exhausted.

Dawn got diagnosed with rheumatoid arthritis about a year after her husband passed away. Again, this could just be a coincidence. But her doctor told her, and she believes, the stress of losing her husband was a factor. She belongs to an online support group for rheumatoid arthritis patients. She told me a large percentage of the members got diagnosed with rheumatoid arthritis after their spouses died.

While not every widow/widower has physical manifestations or physical changes, I think one thing we all have experienced is getting tired. I can't even begin to tell you the number of times when I've just felt exhausted. My grief counselor told me grieving is tiring and takes a lot of energy. I definitely think that's true. On numerous occasions, I've gotten into bed early, which is not normal for me. I've never been someone to stay in bed all day or even get in bed before 10 o'clock at night. I've always gotten up immediately upon waking. But now, I'm often too tired and just get in bed early.

I hope you haven't had physical or medical issues since your loss. Not everyone does, and I don't want you to get scared thinking you will have problems. Most of my widowed friends have had no issues. If you've experienced health challenges, though, know that you're not alone.

He Balanced Out My Flaws & Weaknesses

Reg was logical while I'm more emotional. He was calm while I can get pretty worked up. He balanced me out, and I miss that (though sometimes that drove me crazy).

Let me give you an example. In my past, before I responded to an email that had upset me, Reg would read my response to ensure I didn't say anything too inflammatory, get myself into trouble, or risk alienating others. For example, I often held different opinions about how to handle some cats at the shelter where I volunteered. When corresponding with the shelter staff, I sometimes became enraged after reading their emails. I desired to fire off an emotional response and unleash my anger. This is where Reg assisted. I always had Reg read over my reply before I clicked send. Now, I don't have my "editor" to make sure I don't get myself in trouble. He can no longer keep me in check.

Not only do I not have him to keep me in check, but I feel I lost the person who balanced me out and made me seem normal. At Reg's memorial service, my friend Meg, who has known me since I was 15, said she never thought I'd find anyone who would tolerate my diabetic and vegan diet and lifestyle. She emphasized that not only did Reg put up with it, but he joined me in being vegan. Laughter exploded when she said this. I laughed too. But, her comment shows how perhaps my lifestyle isn't normal. Yet, I didn't feel abnormal with him.

Let me give you another example. As I've mentioned a few times already, we volunteered at an animal shelter for eight years. It was nearly impossible to volunteer at an animal shelter and not come home with cats. It was a no-kill shelter that often had older and sick cats. No one wanted to adopt these felines, so rather than let them languish at the shelter and die a slow death there, Reg and I did hospice for cats. Sometimes, the cats lived with us for only a short time before they passed. Sometimes, they lived for years. That meant we often had many cats. At one point, we even had five cats. Because I was married to an intelligent, masculine, logical man, I never wondered if we seemed like wacky cat people. Instead, we just were compassionate people.

After he died, however, I worried I would be viewed as a "crazy cat lady," a term often used to describe a lonely, older or middle-aged woman who lives alone and fills her lack of romance with many cats. I had three cats when he died and still have them. I remember telling fellow volunteers at Reg's memorial service that now I would be viewed as a "crazy cat lady." Now, I can't do hospice and load up my house with cats. Frankly, I think individuals who love and shelter animals in a healthy way (not hoarders) and who consider pets part of the family are wonderful people. But our society often views people who prefer animals to humans as kooky and on the fringes of society. Therefore, I worried I now would be viewed as the stereotypical "crazy cat lady" or nutty animal person. Reg balanced me out. With him gone, I fear that I will just be viewed as peculiar.

Also, he appreciated my flaws, and I could just be myself—flaws and all. For good or bad, I could fully be who I am. For example, one time I was so upset with a friend that I almost lost a longtime friendship. For months, I couldn't let go of whatever had upset me. Reg knew me well enough that he figured out what my problem was and told me in a loving way why I was so upset. After that, I understood why I was being so emotional and was able to forgive my friend. He didn't judge me. He loved me anyway and helped me.

Reg knew if I saw animals dying in a movie or if I heard about animal abuse, I would cry hysterically. He knew about my snake phobia, and he knew if I saw one on the TV, he should tell me to look away. He recognized what would make me angry, even when I would become angry for no logical reason. Now, I feel as if no one knows me well enough to appreciate what will upset me. He appreciated my good and bad qualities. He balanced me out. Now, I feel no one fills the role, and no one truly understands me or knows me fully—and still loves me!

Loss of Friends

Many of the widows and widowers I know, including me, lost friends after our spouses passed away. I must admit I didn't expect that to happen, but it did. Some of it was my fault; I didn't want to be around happy people so I avoided some friends. For example, I had a friend moving to Hawaii and getting married as Reg was dying. She was so happy, and her life was so lucky that it was challenging for me to see her or talk to her. Therefore, I drifted away from that friendship and stopped emailing her or making any attempt to be in contact with her.

As I discussed in another chapter, I lost some friends because we were couples friends. We would go to another couple's house for dinner, and they would come to our house for dinner. I'm no longer part of a couple, so those friends have drifted away. I know my widower friend Laurence also lost many friends when he was no longer part of a couple. He and his wife had been social with other couples. After losing his wife, he lost those friends and frankly, he didn't necessarily want to be around them without his wife.

Not long after our spouses died, I invited Laurence over for dinner. It thrilled him to have somewhere to go and to have someone cook for him. I was glad to have someone to hang out with for dinner. But at the same time, when I purchased the food for a social dinner, I found it upsetting. I felt I should be purchasing food to cook for Reg, not someone else.

I also lost friends because some people just can't handle grief. I didn't try to show up and pretend like I was okay. One friend told me watching me suffer so much and seeing me in so much pain was challenging for her; she said being around me was one of the most grim experiences of her life. Nonetheless, she continued to be around me and stay friends with me. Others, however, could not handle that and chose to exit my life. On numerous occasions, I remember thinking, "Just wait until you have to go through grief. Maybe you'll remember how you treated me."

I know my widow friend Dakota has also lost friends because the friends don't know how to handle grief. Dakota feels hurt by this. She says the friends were kind at the start but as time passed, they stopped calling her or trying to see her. She said her friends don't include her, but that's okay because she would just feel like a third wheel anyway (a common feeling for widows and widowers). She said her friends just went on with their lives and left "little old Dakota" alone and grieving. So in addition to losing her husband, she lost many friends.

Jessica lost friends after her husband died because her friends kept trying to give her advice. They thought she should do things differently or should stop crying in front of her children. Though they had never experienced the loss of a spouse, they felt free to dispatch advice to her. Therefore, she dropped them. Jessica also lost friends because, like me, she could not handle seeing their happy, intact families while hers was so sad. She stopped going to her book club. She stopped participating in events she had once enjoyed. Gina still engages in her social activities. But whenever she's at a party, she looks around at her friends and thinks, "Your husband's going to die soon too."

As I explained in another chapter, Reg's death has left me feeling vulnerable. I was never a fan of rejection, but now it hurts that much more. I don't have my soft place—Reg—to land when I feel rejected. So it's hard for me to put myself out there and ask people to do activities with me. I've tried asking people to attend concerts or plays with me. I've tried to get together for coffee or dinner. But when they say, "No," it hurts me too much. So I mostly avoid asking. My heart hurts too much to risk more hurt. I've had people tell me I should try to make new friends or join new groups. But I just don't have it in me to try to build friendships; sometimes, I don't even have it in me to maintain my existing friendships.

It makes me sad I've lost friends. When Reg was here, it didn't matter that much if I had friends. He was my best friend, and I spent most of my time with him. My mom tells me Reg and I were like a bubble; we existed in our world together and needed no one else. Now he is gone and when I need friends, some have disappeared. Like I said, however, I refuse to pretend as if everything is okay and not be myself. If that means losing friends, then so be it.

I realize that not all grieving people lose friends. Perhaps you can't relate to this chapter. In fact, I hope you can't. But if you've lost friends, don't worry. It's happened to the best of us.

Driving Is Difficult

Many of my widowed friends, including me, found it challenging to drive after losing our spouses. My mom told me that after my sister died, she had a lot of trouble driving. While driving, she was alone and didn't have a role—such as a boss, a mom, or a grandma—to play. When she was being a boss, she was focused, distracted, and in her regular routine. As a boss, there wasn't room for grief (at least in her mind). With my nephew, she didn't show her emotions because she was attempting to help him get through the loss of his mom. She didn't want to cry or do anything that could affect his emotional state even more than it was already affected. Around me, she didn't show emotions because she felt that as the mom, she had to be strong. But in the car, no one could see her; she could let go and just cry.

Therefore, after Reg died, she drove me everywhere for the first couple of weeks. Once I started driving again, I constantly cried and broke down in the car. I'm surprised I didn't wreck my car because I would drive while sobbing. Also, I would shake my head back and forth in denial.

Jessica also struggled with driving. She couldn't have any music playing, and she got lost constantly. She couldn't remember how to drive to places where she had driven routinely for years (even the grocery store). Driving was truly overwhelming to her. My friend Desiree told me she frequently cried in her car. She often felt her husband's presence in the car when she was alone. So the tears would flow. Like my mom after my sister died, Desiree would hold it together in front of her children, but the tears would flow when she was driving.

I realize that women drive as often as their husbands (or maybe even more often). But for whatever reason, my friends' husbands did all the driving when they were together. Reg also drove whenever we went places; I almost never drove until he became paralyzed and could no longer drive. So after losing our spouses, we were forced to do all the driving, which was another shock to the system. My widower friend Laurence, who always drove when he was with his wife, struggled with driving after his wife passed away. He was used to driving, but it still overwhelmed him. In fact, he could no longer have music playing while he drove. He had to have absolute silence.

If you've had trouble driving, please know you're not alone. I don't know what it is about being in a car, but it seems to be more difficult after losing a loved one.

How Can I Be Okay?

While society and friends want me to be okay and "all better," I find that being okay is confusing for me. How can I be okay without Reg? How can I be happy without him? No one tells you that grief and becoming a widow/widower can bring so much guilt and confusion along with sadness and pain. But for me, they have.

A week after Reg passed away, I watched a comedy on TV that we had often watched together. It was a particularly funny episode, and I laughed hard. I remember thinking, "How can I be laughing when Reg is dead?" Ultimately, I decided Reg would want me to laugh. He was always cracking jokes and trying to make me laugh. So, I figured he would be glad to see me laughing. But it felt confusing and wrong to me to laugh, especially so soon after he passed away.

Jessica told me she didn't want people to think this loss is survivable. Had I not lost Reg, I would think that was crazy. But I understand. I also don't want people to think this is survivable. When friends tell me I look good or it's so good to see me laughing or smiling, I want to say, "I'm not okay. Don't be fooled."

I remember going out with my widows group eight months after Reg passed away. One of the widows told me I looked better. I didn't look as ashen and distraught as I had when she first met me. While you would think this comment would make me feel better or glad, it upset me. How could I look better? Did that mean I was learning to live and be content without him?

A year after Reg died, I felt disappointed to see that I was okay seeing happy people on Thanksgiving. I wasn't happy, but I didn't cry seeing cheerful people. That was upsetting to me. How could I be okay?

Similarly, a year after his death, I went to a Christmas party with a group of women I've known for years. I had a nice time. It felt wrong to have a nice time, and I didn't want anyone to think I was okay. I felt that if they thought I was okay, they would forget about Reg, and I don't want people to forget about him.

I'm not the only widow to feel this way. Queen Victoria liked when people told her she had gotten thin, as it affirmed the intensity of her grief. She wanted others to think she was still frail. When people visited her and said she looked better, she got very upset. When *The Times* reported she looked better, she insisted they reverse it.

I remember thinking that surely people would see and understand how much I was grieving by how thin I had become. I almost wore that like a badge of honor. Jessica also became frighteningly thin, much more than me, and also thought it represented or at least showed the world how much she was grieving.

Queen Victoria told her daughter that her misery was now a "necessity." She said, "Yes, I long for my suffering almost—as it is blinded with him!" She declared she would never adjust to "that dreadful, weary, chilling, unnatural life of a widow." Victoria admitted to another daughter that she was "afraid of getting too well—as if it was a crime and that she feared to begin to like riding on her Scotch pony, etc."[x]

If I had not lost my husband, I would think this is crazy. Why would anyone want to keep the grief? But now I understand how Victoria felt. Maybe it's absurd, but it feels confusing, at least to me, to be okay and not grieving. My friend Dakota feels guilty when she has fun; she feels she isn't supposed to have fun. She believes it's not fair she gets to enjoy seeing the grandchildren while her husband doesn't.

My widower friend Laurence had a friend whose wife passed away ten years before our spouses died. Laurence asked him when the pain goes away. His friend said he considered the pain a testament to how much he loved his wife. I feel the same way. So when I have days without pain or heartache, what does that mean? I'm afraid that means some sort of judgment or something negative about my love for Reg. Would it mean I don't love him as much as I claim? Would it mean others would stop thinking about him or missing him?

As I mentioned in an earlier chapter, my widower friend Laurence died. The summer after his death, I had a conversation with Laurence's friend about his death. The friend said he was surprised he was still mourning the death. Then he said, "But I don't want to be over this." I understood what he meant. For me, being "over it"—being over Reg's death—feels as if it would be a loss too.

I saw a TV show recently where a man lost his wife. He asked a minister, who had lost his wife almost 20 years earlier, if the loss gets easier. Specifically, the grieving character said, "Does it get any easier? I mean do you ever stop missing them?" The minister answered, "No, but why would you want to?" Although this was a fictional show, I loved that exchange. That is exactly how I feel!

Pain makes me feel closer to Reg, so it's confusing to me to let it go. Instead, in some ways, I cling to my grief, at least for now. I realize not every widow or widower feels this way though. I suspect most grieving people want to feel okay and to know they can survive this loss.

What Has Helped Me

As I stated in the beginning of this book, this book is not intended to tell you what to do; it's not intended to offer suggestions on how to grieve or get through the loss of your spouse. The point of the book is to let you know you're not alone. Chances are, either I or one of my widow/widower friends has experienced what you're experiencing or felt the way you feel.

As I also explained in an earlier part of this book, it makes me mad when people tell me what to do or try to give me suggestions on how to heal. Therefore, I need to make it clear that I'm not using this chapter to do that. At the same time, I want to give you some suggestions on what helped me and what continues to help me. If you think these fit for you, use them. Otherwise, don't.

I have found other widows/widowers

Being a widow/widower feels extremely lonely. Therefore, I seek out other widows, which probably has helped me more than any other steps I've taken. These widows and widowers understand my pain and don't judge me. As I mentioned in this book's preface, a couple of weeks after Reg passed away, I had lunch with a woman who had worked with Reg. While the two of them worked on a project together, her husband passed away from a brain tumor; this happened almost exactly a year before Reg died.

She and I had never met, but she reached out to me when she heard Reg had died. We had lunch, and she brought me a packet of Kleenex. For the first time, I felt as if someone understood my pain. I asked her how she got through this. She said, "I don't know." Somehow hearing that was so helpful to me. I felt I could breathe for the first time. That night, I actually wanted to eat dinner.

Reg and his sister were not close, but she lost her husband. So I reached out to her after Reg died. She became a lifesaver for me. Every time I told her my pain or communicated the feelings I experienced, she understood and said she had felt the same. I felt less alone. She and I are now good friends, and I'm thankful for that.

As I mentioned before, my friend Laurence lost his wife about a month before I lost my husband. He and I had known each other professionally for years, but we coincidentally were in a group together at a grief workshop right before our first Thanksgiving without our spouses. We decided to get together periodically to try to help each other. I remember the first time we got together, I felt lighter afterward. I didn't necessarily feel happier, but I felt lighter. Someone understood my pain. After that, we became good friends and supported each other quite a lot, especially during the first year.

A little over four months after Reg passed away, I joined a young widows group held by one of Denver's hospice providers. The group contained eight women who were all under 50 years old. All of us had lost our spouses within the previous one and a half years. I appreciated this grief support group because I felt less alone; there was a room full of women who could relate to me. Laurence went to a grief class at the church and felt frustrated because he had lost his wife months earlier, yet someone in the group had lost his grandfather ten years before that. While Laurence had empathy for the man's loss, the distance from death and the relationship were too different from what Laurence was experiencing. However, he still received benefit from attending and participating in the grief exercises.

I was lucky to find a group that was just widows (widowers could come, but none did) with a similar age. I'm still friends with two of the women I met in that group; having them support me and supporting them has been a lifeline and a godsend. Whether the group contains only widows and widowers or a mix of ages and relationships, I believe there is benefit in finding a grief group.

I want to point out that while hanging out with other widows and widowers is helpful, comparing yourself to them is not. I've often struggled with this. For example, Laurence sold his house less than a year after his wife died, which was unfathomable to me. He started dating at the same time. Similarly, four of my widow friends started dating. I cannot even imagine dating yet. But I find I compare myself to them and wonder if there's something wrong with me. I've often felt bad because I perceived others want to move forward faster than me. Should I be dating? Should I be okay?

You may have the opposite experience. You may want to date sooner than other widows/widowers or close that chapter of your life more quickly. So please, if you find other widows/widowers to grieve with and to walk this path with, don't compare yourself. We all move at different speeds, and only we know what is right for us.

I realize you may not have the opportunity to find other widows or widowers, or you may not feel comfortable connecting with strangers. Perhaps you're in a small town, where there aren't groups of grieving people, or perhaps you're just not someone to join a group. That is the biggest reason I wrote this book; I wanted you to have a way to connect—even if just via a book—with another widowed person. But, if you can, I encourage you to interact with other widowed people. In the meantime, I hope this book will at least help you feel connected to, and understood by, other widowed people.

I have seen a grief counselor

My grief counselor, Diane, helped me more than I can ever say. Even though she has not lost her spouse, she works with grieving people every day. She often told me what I was feeling was normal, which was helpful since my friends and family could not understand me. I never felt judged by her, and she never told me I needed to move forward with my life. In fact, she joked that if she even mentioned moving forward, I brought out my claws like a cat and dug in. She also encouraged me to write this book, so I could help other widows and widowers.

If you find a professional to help you, I would suggest they have experience with grief. My widow friend Gina saw a regular therapist, who told her she needed to move on with her life, and it was time for her to be okay. Gina left feeling even worse. I told my grief counselor about this; she said that advice was outrageous and that the therapist didn't understand grief or understand how to work with grieving people.

Similarly, I saw an article written by some therapists who believed that if people grieve their spouse longer than six months, maybe they need medication or behavioral therapy. They said that past six months, the grief was "complicated grief." I felt outraged when I read that. Clearly those therapists have never lost their spouses or anyone that close to them. Otherwise, they would know their theories were ridiculous.

Again, if you can, I recommend finding someone who has experience with grieving people.

I have written a letter to Reg every night

Shortly after Reg passed away, I told my friend how I felt sad that I couldn't tell him about my day anymore. She suggested I write him a letter every night telling him about my day and how I feel. So, I did this almost every night, and it basically became a journaling exercise for me. I had not been someone to journal in my past, which is what many self-help practitioners tell people to do. But for over a year and a half after he passed away, I basically did journal. It allowed me to get my feelings on paper and to tell him about my day. I used these same letters to write this book.

I have spent time with animals

I've always been someone who loves animals. In fact, I'm vegan for that reason. Therefore, animals may make me happier than the average person. But I've found that being around them, especially my cats, has been extremely helpful.

I know I sound like a crazy cat lady, but when my cats sit in my lap or greet me at the door, I feel adored and loved. My cats give me a reason to get up every day and a reason to keep living, especially right after Reg passed away. They make me laugh and smile more than pretty much anything or anyone else. They give me love unconditionally.

Similarly, I love going for a walk in the park and seeing the dogs. Even right after Reg passed away, when the grief was almost unbearable, I would smile when I saw dogs. I especially loved—and still love—when they stop, and I get to pet them and play with them. I truly feel joy seeing animals.

Just the other day, I felt depressed after receiving emails from two different friends who told me about their wonderful vacations with their spouses. I then went to the grocery store, which still can cause sadness since Reg and I used to shop there together. Between the emails and the store, I felt depressed, cranky, sad, and just down. But as I left the store, I saw two dogs waiting for their people in an area cordoned off for dogs. Both were happy dogs who desperately wanted me to pet them, which I did. I felt lighter and happier because of their cuteness and love.

Almost every widow and widower I know feels the same way about their pets. For one thing, for many of them the pets also knew their spouses and went through this loss with them, which bonds them. Animals have a way of bringing joy and unconditional love into their lives.

As I've mentioned throughout the book, I volunteered at an animal shelter for eight years; I saw cats and dogs suffering in the shelter after their person no longer had use for them. So, I won't tell you to get pets if you're not committed to having them for their entire lives. I won't tell you to adopt a pet just to help you feel better if there's a risk you'll relinquish it if/when your life starts feeling happier, or if you meet a new person. But if you're someone who loves animals and is committed, then I encourage you to adopt a pet if you don't already have one. Or if you don't want a pet, find ways to spend time around animals. Maybe go to the dog park or any park where there are dogs.

For some of you, babies might inspire the same love and joy. If that's the case, then I encourage you to spend time with babies or little kids who'll bring you joy, make you laugh and smile, and help with the grieving process.

I have spent time in nature

Sometimes I feel the most at peace when I'm in nature. Thankfully, I live in Colorado, where I can hike frequently. Even immediately after Reg passed away, I felt some degree of tranquility when I went hiking. Because Reg and I often spent our spare time hiking and even spent an entire vacation traveling the national parks to hike, I often feel closest to him when I'm hiking in nature.

Depending on where you live, it may be easy, or it may be impossible to be in nature. But if you have the chance, I encourage you to spend time in the natural world, even if it's just a local park. For me, nature and beautiful scenery have been extremely helpful.

I have stayed connected to Reg

I stay connected to Reg as much as I can. For example, on important days, such as his birthday, my birthday, and our anniversary, I shower with his shampoo, conditioner, and soap. That way, I smell like him and feel connected to him. Doing this brings me some peace.

As I explained in an earlier chapter, I do things such as ride his bike, wear his clothes, and watch the Green Bay Packers to feel and stay linked to him. During my first Thanksgiving without him, I carried Mickey and Minnie Mouse salt-and-pepper shakers everywhere I went. I held them in my hands most of the day, as if somehow that was holding onto Reg. We had purchased these shakers together, so they were an anchor—a connection— for me.

Similarly, I remain connected to his family and friends. For me, I can't imagine just putting him and that life behind me and feeling as if he is completely gone. So, I do what I can to feel connected, which helps me a lot.

Because I believe in life on the other side (see below), I often mentally or even verbally ask Reg to go places with me. For example, if I go to dinner at a restaurant we had enjoyed together, I will say, "Come on Reg. Let's go to dinner." On numerous occasions, I've imagined that he has walked in the park with me.

When I was training for a race, I imagined him running toward me; I picked up my pace because I was so excited to be reunited with him. I imagined it so clearly that I actually felt relieved and happy. Maybe I'm crazy. But it helps me, and that is all that matters.

Queen Victoria also believed the spirit survives death and that Albert was still present in her life. She wore a brooch with Albert's likeness in it. When she went driving in Scotland, sometimes she would open the brooch to show him a view she thought was interesting. Also, she often communicated with him by sitting in front of his bust.

I have honored Reg

I honor Reg whenever I can. For example, I had a one-year commemoration party the weekend after the first anniversary of his passing. I wanted to gather friends and family who knew him and loved him. I had bookmarks made with his photos, his favorite sayings, and some funny things he frequently said. I gave them to each person there and even mailed them to the people out of state who couldn't attend the party.

At my first Christmas without him, I put a small candle in front of each person's spot as a way to remember and honor him. At my second Christmas without him, I set a place for him and put a gold candle and a photo of him (dressed as Santa) on his plate. A Green Bay Packers teddy bear sat in the spot for him. I also asked family members to share their favorite story or memory of him at Christmas Eve dinner.

Keeping the house nice is also a way of honoring him. He built me a beautiful patio in our backyard with lush plants. I make sure it stays weed free and clean to honor him. I also keep up the house so it reflects well on him. It was his house, and I don't want people to think it's ugly. I don't want anyone to think he was a bad provider and didn't take care of the house.

By honoring him, I feel connected to him, and that makes me feel better. Honoring him has helped me in this grief journey.

I have protected myself whenever I can

Whenever possible, I protect myself from feeling sad or being hurt. For example, I stopped going on Facebook. I read an article once that said Facebook has caused many people to become depressed. They see other people's lives and feel inferior or depressed that their lives and their kids aren't as happy or successful. I know even the average person needs to be mindful on social media, let alone widows and widowers.

When I went on Facebook after Reg passed away, I felt bombarded by postings for other people's happy lives. My Facebook feed was full of friends' romantic photos or postings about how wonderful their spouses were. Alternatively, I saw posts from people complaining about their problems. I wanted to tell them to stop complaining; their problems were nothing compared with the loss of a spouse. I quickly realized that Facebook made me feel worse and stopped looking at it.

Gina remained on Facebook but often felt depressed after checking it. She finally took herself off or made it where she only saw the postings from a couple of widows she follows. She now empathically thinks widows and widowers should stay off Facebook or other social media, at least for a while.

While I make sure to protect myself, I also attempt to help myself feel better. For example, I watch TV programs that don't feature romance; I tend to watch more crime shows, where romance is minimized. Not long after Reg passed away, a British TV drama called *Downton Abbey* was popular in the United States. In the show, one of the main characters died in a car crash, and for many episodes, his widow was in deep pain. I'd been a fan of the program even before this happened, but as I watched this widow, I felt comforted. Sure, she was just a fictional character, but I felt someone understood what I was experiencing. Therefore, I went out of my way to watch the show.

Gina became addicted to the TV program *The Walking Dead* after her husband passed away. I've never watched it, but I think it might be gory and certainly has no romance. She said watching the show made her feel better. Like Gina and like me, I encourage you to avoid what makes you feel worse and to pursue what helps you feel better.

I have laughed

When Reg first died, laughing felt inappropriate; I felt guilty when I laughed. As I explained earlier in this book, I watched a comedy on TV within a week of Reg's death. We had watched this program many times, but this time, it was particularly funny. I remember laughing hard and thinking maybe I shouldn't laugh. But Reg had a great sense of humor and cracked jokes daily. Every day he made me chuckle. So, I decided it would please him to see me laughing, and he would want me to laugh.

Almost three months after he died, Reg's sister visited me in Denver. One day, we sat on my couch looking at my wedding photos. His sister hadn't been able to attend our wedding, so she'd never seen the photos. In person, Reg was handsome. However, he was not photogenic. His sister and I laughed hysterically as we viewed some of his unattractive photos. In fact, we giggled so hard we cried. Again, I figured Reg would be happy to see me laughing, even if it was at his expense.

Gina and I hiked quite a bit after our spouses died. During those hikes, we frequently laughed, often about our spouses. We especially laughed when discussing a situation I had one night with my remote control. Reg had linked the televisions in the living room and bedroom. One evening after he died, I woke up and turned on the TV in the bedroom. Out of the blue, the TV switched to a show featuring origami. I was blown away and thought maybe Reg had somehow switched the channel from heaven. I couldn't figure out why he wanted me to watch origami though. Did he think origami would help with grief?

Suddenly, the TV switched to basketball. Reg was a sports fan but didn't watch basketball. I sat there wondering why Reg would want me to watch basketball. Finally, I decided Reg probably wasn't manipulating the TV. I went into the living room and found my cat Taylor sitting on the remote control. Somehow, because the TVs were linked, Taylor had switched the channels as he sat on the remote. Gina said she knew she liked me after hearing that story. We have since cracked up at that story many times.

I recognize that laughter may feel wrong after you've lost a spouse. I also understand that you may not want to laugh, especially when the grief is so heavy. Laughter helped me though; it provided brief moments of respite from the grief.

I have noticed signs from the other side

My mom raised me to believe in the afterlife, so I believe Reg still exists somewhere, just not in a body. I believe that someday, we will be reunited. In the meantime, I've always believed we have the ability to communicate with our loved ones on the other side, and they can send us signs or somehow make their presence known. This belief has been a tremendous help to me. Reg didn't believe in the ability of spirits to communicate after death. In fact, he and I occasionally had disagreements about this. But now he knows better.

One way I believe Reg communicates with me is via songs. For example, I made a video for his memorial service that displayed photos of him while the song "Somewhere Over the Rainbow" played. Most people like this song by Israel Kamakawiwoʻole, but since it was released in 1990, it's rarely played on the radio. After Reg passed away, I heard the song repeatedly on the radio. I choose to believe Reg sent me the song as a sign that he was still with me. As I often tell people, you can't prove to me it's not him, and it comforts me to think it's him; so I choose to believe it's him.

Similarly, two months before Reg passed away, he and I took a vacation in the ski resort town of Breckenridge. An organization called Domus Pacis, which provides respite stays for families and couples dealing with cancer, provided this vacation. After Reg died, the organization created a video to highlight what they do, and they requested interviews from people who had participated in a respite stay. I agreed to do it. As they interviewed me, I sobbed like crazy—full snot included. Five minutes after leaving the interview spot, the song "She Moves in Her Own Way" played on the radio. This song by the Kooks was Reg's ringtone for me on his cell phone. The band released this song in 2006. I hadn't heard this song on the radio in an extremely long time. In fact, I'm not sure I've ever heard it on the radio. Yet, as I drove away from an interview where I sobbed in front of a camera as I discussed how cancer took my husband, the song played on the radio. Some would say this was just a coincidence. I, however, choose to believe Reg played me that song, so I would know he was there and still loves me.

On my second Valentine's Day without Reg, I turned on Pandora, which is an online streaming music service. The first song that played was "Naked" by the BoDeans. That song is the ringtone I had for him on my cell phone. Perhaps it's just a coincidence that "Naked" was the first song that Pandora played on Valentine's Day, a day when I was clearly missing him. But I choose to believe he played it for me. Another time, I went running near the location where we got married. I brought his ashes, so I could scatter some at the wedding sight. When I arrived at the spot, I played my iTunes. I asked that if he were there to please play a song that was obviously from him. The first song that played was "I Can't Help Falling in Love With You" by Elvis. We had danced to that song at our wedding, and he had sung that song to me as we danced at other people's weddings. I choose to believe Reg was there, which made me sob but also comforted me.

I believe Reg also communicates with me in my dreams. I don't think some of the dreams are visitations; rather, I'm just dreaming about him. However, I've had other dreams that felt so incredibly real that I choose to believe they were visitations. For example, just a couple of weeks—or maybe within the first week—after Reg passed away, I had a dream I was walking down the street between the park and our house, which is a street we walked frequently. He rounded the corner and had white light behind him. He was fully healed, and I was blissfully happy to see him. I said, "There you are!" and we hugged. I know with every fiber of my being he was visiting me and showing me that he was no longer paralyzed and no longer had cancer. He was showing me that he is still alive on the spirit level.

Jessica has received communication from her husband via light bulbs. For a while, she thought maybe light bulbs just burned out in her house. But she averaged one light bulb per week for the first six months after her husband passed. She stopped recording them when 101 light bulbs had burned out at the 3.5-year mark of her husband's passing. She could not deny that light bulbs were her husband's way of communicating with her. In fact, on important days, such as her children's birthdays, his birthday, her children's graduations, and more, a light bulb in her house has burned out. When her brother passed away, she didn't know. But the day her brother died, a light bulb burned out. She wondered what her husband was trying to tell her, and the next day she found out her brother had died. Was it a coincidence? Neither of us thinks so; we believe her husband was trying to warn her and comfort her the only way he could.

My friend Tara's husband has also used electricity to communicate with her. Her daughter got married not long after her husband's death, so the two of them visited a bridal shop where her daughter tried on a dress. Her daughter exited the dressing room and asked, "Do you think dad would like this dress?" Just then, the lights in the entire store turned off and then came back on. Sure, maybe it was a coincidence. But they choose to believe her husband was clearly giving his approval.

I could give you many more examples of signs from the other side, but I'll leave it at those. I recognize that believing in signs is a struggle for many people. I understand. It's hard to comprehend, and some religions may discourage this. At the same time, I know the signs have brought smiles and peace to my widowed friends and to me, so I encourage you to notice them if you're comfortable.

I have experienced mediums

If you're unfamiliar with mediums, they are individuals who have the ability to connect with spirits on the other side. They often provide specific validation, so you know with certainty they're speaking with your loved one.

The day before Reg died, I told him I would see a medium after he passed away. I told him I still wanted him to be with me. Two months after he passed away, I saw my first medium. The medium gave me specific information about Reg, so I knew she was truly connecting with him. After that appointment with her, I felt lighter and happier knowing he is in fact still around me and even though his body is gone, he has not left me altogether; he is trying to keep his promise to still take care of me.

Since that time, I've seen quite a few mediums, both one-on-one and in group settings. The first medium I saw in a group setting was Rebecca Rosen, who has been featured on TV and has written best-selling books. My friend had purchased the tickets for eight of us, so there was no way Rebecca Rosen knew anyone's name in the group except the woman who purchased the tickets. The audience contained over 300 individuals, so there was no way she could have researched me or known that my husband had died. My friend's cat, Max, had died after her son accidentally slammed the door on the cat. I never knew this story, but Rebecca asked who in the audience had a cat named Max who got slammed in a door. Rebecca delivered a message to my friend and then asked who in our group had lost a woman to breast cancer. One of my friends had lost her mom, so Rebecca delivered a message to her.

Finally, Rebecca spoke a name that had meaning for Reg and me, which she used to identify that Reg was the spirit with whom she was speaking. She told me he was with his dad. Reg's dad died 35 years before Reg died, and most people didn't even know that about him. There was no way Rebecca could have known that. Rebecca said Reg didn't believe in the other side or mediums when he was alive, which I confirmed. She informed me that he had a whole new appreciation for me now. She knew he died of cancer, and she knew I had Reg's money clip in my pocket.

At a group event with a different medium, I once again got specific validation that the medium could not have known. For example, I set a deadline to complete this very book by May 1. Many of my friends knew I was writing a book, but no one knew I had set a deadline for May 1. I hadn't even told my mom. At the reading, the medium, whose name is Elisa Malangone, said Reg told her May was important for my book. By the way, this medium didn't know I was writing a book until Reg told her at that event. Similarly, I had gone for a walk with my mom just two hours before the event. While walking, my mom and I discussed traveling to Israel. My mom said she would want to travel there, but I said I wouldn't want to travel there given the dangers. At the event, Elisa asked who in the audience had just talked about traveling to Israel. No one except my mom and me knew we had just discussed that! Once again, I was relieved and happy to know Reg is still around and doing his best to stay a part of my life.

At that same event, Elisa asked my widow friend Dakota if she had just purchased new shoes. When Dakota answered that she had purchased a new pair of shoes the previous week, Elisa said Dakota's husband suggested that "for every new pair of shoes, she needed to give up two pairs of shoes." Unbeknownst to Elisa or me, Dakota's daughter had made that exact statement to Dakota when she purchased the shoes. Dakota was elated to know her husband had been there when she bought the shoes and had that discussion with her daughter.

At another event, Elisa told me Reg was saying the "candy was too old." This event took place a few days before Halloween. Earlier that week, I had decided I was just going to use my Halloween candy from the previous year, because I get so few trick-or-treaters and didn't want to buy new candy. That is kind of embarrassing, so I had mentioned this to no one. Yet Elisa said that Reg declared the "candy was too old." I laughed pretty hard. Truth be told, in life Reg would have been horrified that I was thinking of giving year-old candy; so I guess it's no surprise he called me out on it from the other side.

At yet another event, Elisa asked my mom and me what was "up with the bunny." Just two hours before that, I had been at my mom's house, and a rabbit was lounging in her yard. I had only seen rabbits on full alert, but this one was lounging as if he owned the place. I asked my mom if he was dead, because I had never seen a bunny act so casually. Thankfully, he wasn't dead, just relaxing. Then two hours later, Elisa asked us about the bunny.

If you're at all open to the idea, I can tell you most of my widowed friends have felt tremendous comfort being able to connect with their spouses on the other side. Every one of them has had specific validation. In fact, I could write a whole book on the different things mediums have told us. We've all felt happier after our sessions.

Like any profession, there are mediums who are competent and talented at what they do and who are ethical. There are others who are not. If you decide to see a medium, I recommend going to one with a good reputation or who has seen someone you know. Or maybe start with a group event, so you can see if you like the medium without spending a lot of money.

I have stuck to my guns

As I've discussed elsewhere in this book, society wants us to be okay. I know I've often felt pressure to be okay and to move forward with my life. But I've found one of the most helpful things for me is to stick to my guns. If something doesn't feel right to me, I don't do it even if everyone else thinks I should. This was especially true when I received pressure to get rid of Reg's belongings. I know what is right for me, so I ultimately didn't let that pressure get to me. But that took courage and the risk that others would judge me.

Know that you feel the way you do and have a right to feel that way. Friends and family may not understand. That is okay. They haven't walked in your shoes, and even if they have lost their spouse, everyone is different. Do what is best for you. You could be completely opposite of me or exactly like me in this widowhood journey. It doesn't matter. You know what is best for you. Stick to your guns whether people agree with you or judge you.

Of course, I say that with just a little hesitation. If you're feeling suicidal or possibly want to harm yourself, listen to others. Otherwise, know that friends and family care about you and think they're doing the right thing. But only you know yourself and what is best for you.

I have tried to have compassion for myself

This section is similar to the *I have stuck to my guns* section above. On paper, it's easy to think that losing a spouse is just another chapter we have to experience in life. But the truth is, it's difficult and painful. It hurts like nothing I could have imagined.

Sometimes I get frustrated with myself for being lazy, tired, slow to move forward, or any number of things. But when I remember how hard this experience has been and how much it has affected me, I have compassion for myself, which is helpful.

One of my friend has stayed busy

My widow friend Tara requested that I include the idea of staying busy. She said staying busy helped her during the initial stages of her widowhood. She especially enjoyed gardening and watching something grow. My widower friend Brad told me he has a friend who lost her husband ten years before Brad lost his wife. When he asked her how she got through it, she told him she had stayed busy. But, she said by doing that in the initial stages, ten years later she was still dealing with the grief. Therefore, I'm not sure staying busy is all that helpful.

I assumed that if I distracted myself from the grief and tried to pretend it wasn't there, it would cause physical problems for me. My friend Dawn said she never cried and let the grief out, so she believes that led to her rheumatoid arthritis diagnosis. I didn't want that to happen to me, and I figured if I stayed busy, the grief would consume me in my future. Therefore, I didn't use distractions or staying busy as a way to get through the grief. But like I said, Tara thought staying busy helped. Plus, even though this wasn't my experience, I realize it is a common coping technique and certainly an acceptable one. So I've included it for that reason.

Spiritual or religious practices

I didn't engage in many spiritual or religious practices after Reg died. I attended a couple of grief workshops at the church and participated once in a candle lighting ceremony with Laurence. I can distinctly see Laurence standing with his unlit candle, lifting it into the air toward the sky, and lighting it. I could feel the pain resonating off him, and the image still touches me. I never asked him if this spiritual experience assisted him. But we were game for trying anything.

I also started to meditate because I hoped that if I could settle my mind, maybe I could feel Reg or hear him. I lost patience, though, and gave up meditating after a couple of months. Other than those examples, I didn't rely on religious or spiritual practices. I know, however, that these can be helpful for grief.

For example, Dakota says that going to church has been beneficial to her. She attended church services regularly before her husband died, and she has continued after his death. She said her faith has helped her to know that she will see her husband in heaven someday; that faith assists with the grief. She hasn't lost him forever, just until she joins him. Dawn said her husband's death challenged her relationship with God for many years.

288

She has attended church regularly since she was born. But, she couldn't understand how God could allow this to happen. Her husband was in his early 40s when he died, and he was a good man. She felt betrayed by God. However, one day during church service, she felt and saw her husband's presence; she said that at that moment she knew he was in heaven. That brought her comfort. Eventually, she found her way back to God; she has continued to attend church regularly and maintain her faith.

Laurence was involved in his church both before and after his wife's death. In addition to attending church regularly, Laurence also continued his daily meditation practice, which he'd done even before his wife died. He went to France with a church group to see the different cathedrals and experience faith in France, hoping the trip would help heal him. He even attended a weekend grief workshop at a Buddhist retreat center.

A non-widowed friend told me she has turned to yoga when confronting grief. Yoga is a spiritual practice for her, and the yoga studio is a place where she has felt loved and supported.

Time

I hate the phrase, "Time heals all wounds." I don't believe that is true. However, time has helped me in dealing with the pain. I find I don't cry as often as I used to cry. I'm slowly finding my way back to being interested in the things that had interested me in the past, such as standing up for the environment. I've recently started to attend meetings at the state capitol that focus on animal issues. I've also joined hearings on legislative bills related to animals. I even attended a fundraiser for an animal charity.

While I haven't returned to feeling full empathy for others, I do have much more empathy than I had for a long time after Reg passed away. I don't just tune people out like I had wanted to do previously. When I watch the news, I don't feel happy to hear about strangers dying. Sometimes, I even weep when I hear about someone dying because I recognize that the family will now feel deep pain. Recently, there were a couple of airplane crashes that hit the news. Unlike before, I felt sorrow seeing that the passengers had died. It seemed like such a tragic loss. Before, I felt glad I wasn't alone in my pain. Now, I do not.

I can handle being around happy people now, especially at events such as football games and running races. Recently, I looked forward to a trip, which was the first time I've looked forward to anything since Reg died. I now eat healthy food again (though I do miss my junk-food-only times). I even eat kale and blueberries on a daily basis!

I enjoyed Christmas this year. I never thought I would enjoy Christmas again. But this year, I felt sad when it ended and wanted the holiday to continue. I admired the pretty decorations and even listened to the holiday music station on the radio. I still watched *The Christmas Story* and set a place for Reg at Christmas Eve dinner. I can't stand the idea of anyone (such as my brother) wearing Reg's Santa outfit even though my young nephews would be thrilled to see "Santa." I did cry and wish Reg was with me to enjoy Christmas. But, I also enjoyed it.

I now feel gratitude frequently. As I mentioned in an earlier chapter, it made me angry when people told me I still have a lot to be grateful for, and I should focus on gratitude. Even at the start of my grief journey, I had gratitude, especially for my mom. However, it was overshadowed by pain and sorrow. But now, I feel gratitude every day. I'm grateful for my house, which is in a safe neighborhood and is the perfect size for me. It even has a beautiful tree in the front yard that is flowering as I write this. I'm thankful I live in Colorado, where I can hike and be in nature. I'm immensely grateful to my mom, who has been a lifeline to me my whole life. I'm thankful for my friends, especially my friend Meg, who has been extremely supportive during this grieving process. I'm thankful I can pay my bills and have a job that provides me with flexibility. I'm thankful to my cats, who adore me and make me laugh. Sometimes, I feel like my heart will explode with love for them.

So while I hate to admit it, time has helped. I still cry and grieve. I still feel sadness and miss him terribly. I still can't believe he is gone. But the raw grief has subsided, and I laugh often.

The Future

I have no idea what my future holds. I learned with Reg's death that life can change quickly. A happy life can turn into a sad one. I learned that maybe we don't have as much control over our lives as we think. Maybe a sad life can once again turn into a happy one. We will see.

Acknowledgments

Despite everything I've been through in the past few years, I still have a lot to acknowledge and be grateful for. Thank you so much to my mom, Pam Murdock. Mom, I could not have gotten through this experience without you. Thank you for staying on my couch for the first week and driving me everywhere. You never abandoned me, you put your life on hold to help me, and you have walked through this journey with me. Thank you for now being my "date" when I need a date. I couldn't ask for a better mom and friend.

Thank you to Diane Eberle, my grief counselor. Thank you for telling me my feelings were normal, listening to me cry, not flinching when I cussed, encouraging me to write this book, and being one of the first readers. I can't imagine going through this experience without you. You were a lifeline!

Thank you to my friends who have supported me through this experience, and most especially Meg Tilton. Meg, thank you for calling me every couple of days for a year to listen to me cry, let me talk all about Reg, and let me know I was loved. I couldn't ask for a better friend. Autumn Moran, thank you for all the wonderful massages (she is a massage therapist) you gave to Reg multiple times per week to help with his pain; thank you for coming over whenever I needed support after he died. Dave Forrester, my neighbor who has helped me in maintaining my house, thank you for helping me and showing me you care.

Thank you for mowing my lawn, shoveling snow for me, and making me feel safer knowing you are nearby. Kris Seliger, I can't thank you enough. Thank you for listening to me, making me feel normal, and visiting me in Denver during some of the important periods. You were and are invaluable to me. To all my widow and widower friends who have walked this journey with me . . . thank you for letting me share your stories.

To Kathie Beard, Ginger O'Neil, Dianne Armstrong, and Duck and Vince White-Petteruti, thank you for being early readers of my book. To Jenn Hartman, thank you for being my editor. Libby York Stauder, thank you for proofreading it.

Finally, to my loving cats, who miss their daddy as much as I do: Rita, Taylor, and Boo. Thank you for all your love and for giving me a reason to keep going.

Thank you, Reg, for staying in my life although your body is gone. Thank you for loving me and for making me your princess. I miss you tremendously. Until the next time . . .

References

i. Rappaport, Helen. *A Magnificent Obsession: Victoria, Albert, and the Death That Changed the British Monarchy*. New York: St. Martin's Press, 2011, 81.

ii. Ibid., 91.

iii. Ibid., 132–33, 152.

iv. Ibid., 121, 184.

v. Ibid., 103.

vi. Ibid., 126, 129.

vii. Pierce, Andrew. "She can only hope never to live to old age: In her own words, Queen Victoria's unbearable grief after the death of Albert." *Daily Mail*. December 13, 2011. Internet website: http://www.dailymail.co.uk/news/article-2073792/Queen-Victorias-unbearable-grief-death-Prince-Albert.html.

viii. Rappaport, Helen. *A Magnificent Obsession: Victoria, Albert, and the Death That Changed the British Monarchy*. New York: St. Martin's Press, 2011, 102–103.

ix. Ibid., 152–3.

x. Ibid., 158, 170.

Made in the USA
Monee, IL
21 January 2022

89568230R00184